DR. ALVIN BARAFF

MEN TALK

HOW MEN REALLY FEEL ABOUT WOMEN, SEX, RELATIONSHIPS, AND THEMSELVES

A PLUME BOOK

PLUME
Published by the Penguin Group
Penguin Books USA Inc., 375 Hudson Street, New York, New York 10014, U.S.A.
Penguin Books Ltd, 27 Wrights Lane, London W8 5TZ, England
Penguin Books Australia Ltd, Ringwood, Victoria, Australia
Penguin Books Canada Ltd, 10 Alcorn Avenue, Toronto, Ontario, Canada M4V 3B2
Penguin Books (N.Z.) Ltd, 182-190 Wairau Road, Auckland 10, New Zealand

Penguin Books Ltd, Registered Offices: Harmondsworth, Middlesex, England

Published by Plume, an imprint of New American Library, a division of
Penguin Books USA Inc. Previously published in a Dutton edition.

First Plume Printing, August, 1992
10 9 8 7 6 5 4 3 2 1

 REGISTERED TRADEMARK—MARCA REGISTRADA

LIBRARY OF CONGRESS CATALOGING-IN-PUBLICATION DATA
Baraff, Alvin S.
    Men talk : how men really feel about women, sex, relationships,
and themselves / Alvin Baraff.
        p.   cm.
    ISBN 0-452-26830-3
    1. Men—Psychology—Case studies.   2. Masculinity (Psychology)—
Case studies.   3. Men—Attitudes.   4. Group psychotherapy—Case
studies.   I. Title.
BF692.5.B37   1992
155.6'32—dc20   91-39103
                                                     CIP

Printed in the United States of America
Original hardcover design by Steven N. Stathakis

BOOKS ARE AVAILABLE AT QUANTITY DISCOUNTS WHEN USED TO PROMOTE PRODUCTS OR
SERVICES. FOR INFORMATION PLEASE WRITE TO PREMIUM MARKETING DIVISION, PENGUIN
BOOKS USA INC., 375 HUDSON STREET, NEW YORK, NEW YORK 10014.

To
the real Mitch, Paul, Gary,
Ed, Burt, and Sean

and the clients of
MenCenter™
they represent

I know your courage.

The information and cases are factual.
All names, places, and other
identifying material have
been changed to protect
the privacy of the
participants.

//

CONTENTS

ACKNOWLEDGMENTS

More than two years have passed since I began work on *Men Talk*, and many good people have touched me in caring and encouraging ways.

A special acknowledgment goes to *Kevin Hendzel*, translator and writer, who assisted me in completing this final version of *Men Talk*. Kevin had a full appreciation of the importance of my work and knew I was impatient to get this information out to the public; having known me for six years, he is aware of my "mission" at MenCenter. I am convinced that his valuable assistance in writing and editing *Men Talk* has enhanced the quality of this book. Kevin is an extremely responsible and sensitive writer: loyal, willing and capable of producing at a level that I like. Thank you, Mr. Hendzel.

My colleagues at MenCenter, *Richard Mallory Starr*, *Dana L. Moore*, and *Mark Gorkin*, have been very gracious about the necessary delay in our joint projects during the writing of this book. My assistant, *Jayne Keedy*, helped keep MenCenter running, and *Robert F. Williams* extended his faith by including me in his prayers.

A hearty thanks to all of you who have lent an ear, enjoyed an anecdote, and been enthusiastic and excited about the book. It helped me and I appreciate you, including the gang at *Julio's*. I am grateful to my friends: *Joani Powell*, for her love and unique female perspective; *John Truran*, who even enjoyed the first draft; *Lenore Walker*, feminist psychologist, for sharing her writing and media anecdotes; *Mark Crawford*, for his practical assistance and loyalty; and *Doug Abbey*, who saw the original journal as I was writing it and said, " This is it, this is your book!"

Echoing those words were *Carol Randolph*, and *Martha Barnett*, who assisted me in preparing the book proposal. Joining supporters were *Rich Lippman*, author of *Eating In*, for providing technical assistance in editing; and *Audrey Chapman*, who led me to my New York agent.

A special thank-you to *Roslyn Targ*, my literary agent, whose energy connected positively with mine from the beginning. Roz is direct, honest, experienced, and a true original. Her enthusiasm and belief in me and *Men Talk* have never wavered.

My warm thanks to *Arnold Dolin*, Vice-President and Associate Publisher of NAL/Dutton, who is also my editor, for his foresight and courage in recognizing the importance and value of psychotherapy and men's issues. Arnold allowed me to develop my own writing style while constantly pushing me to maintain the highest quality possible.

I was supported every step of the way by special members of the MenCenter Board of Advisors: longtime friend *Jerry Olesh*, who has always believed in me and I hope always will; friend *Richard Morey*, whose advice is always practical and useful; and former colleague *Bonnie R. Strickland*, President-

Emeritus, American Psychological Association, who inspired me to make a visible effort on men's issues.

Supporting family members who maintained curiosity throughout this project are: my daughter, *Ramie Baraff Janis*, who does talk to me and appreciates my determination, along with my son-in-law, *Bruce Janis;* my son, *Todd*, who also talks to me openly about personal issues; my mother, *Betty*, who was ". . . glad that darn book is finished" (she loves me anyway); my father, *Abraham*, who, unfortunately, died before completion of this book, though he was very much alive in my memory as I wrote about fathers and death; and my brother, *Jay*, sister-in-law, *Sandy*, niece, *Laura*, and nephew, *Aaron*, all of whom now know why I was so devoted to writing *Men Talk*.

And finally, thanks to *God*, because I do believe he listens when I talk.

MEN
TALK

INTRODUCTION:

///

UNDERSTANDING MEN

No one understands men. Women don't understand men and men don't understand themselves. Surprisingly few psychologists even understand men, since most men do not seek psychotherapy. In the United States therapy continues to be a woman's domain, with 70 percent of a typical psychologist's practice devoted to women. The gap is even wider when we consider the fact that half the men in that remaining 30 percent are there with their wives or girlfriends. In a typical adult practice, only 15 percent are men who are there for themselves.

Why such a lopsided picture? In our society a man's conditioning strongly discourages him from seeking out therapy. This learning process begins at a very early age and is actually an important part of a man's social and emotional development. Boys and girls are exposed to entirely different sets of teachings and expectations. Girls are taught to honor and understand their emotions. Conversely, boys are encouraged, even forced, to hold in and suppress their emotions. There is hardly a man in America today who didn't grow up hearing such admonitions as "Big boys don't cry!" or "Be a man!" These commands form the young boy's reality. As he matures into adolescence, he learns that when he talks too much about his feelings, he is shunned by the other boys in the group. This is in stark contrast to the reality of young girls, who are encouraged to whisper, gossip, complain, and share secrets. Throughout their young lives, girls place the highest premium on sharing, while boys are expected to place the highest value on competition. Not surprisingly, as boys mature into men they tend to express their feelings through competitive arenas, progressing from "cowboys and Indians" in the early years, through war games and sports in adolescence, and on to business and politics in adulthood.

The result is that a man in our society grows up feeling innately, internally alone. He has learned independence and self-reliance and considers them to reign supreme among his values. He wants to be in control. He cannot imagine ever needing to go for help and rarely considers it an option.

Puberty provides an excellent example of the difference between the sharing, supportive world of the young girl and the isolated, competitive world of the young boy. A mother typically expends a great deal of time and effort instructing and educating her young daughter about the changes occurring in her body. Moreover, when girls discuss their changing bodies among themselves, the atmosphere is one of support, nurturance, and sharing. As every man knows, this is hardly the atmosphere in the locker room. Boys' talk about the sex organs or their development is all wisecracks or exaggerated bragging. In other words, competition. As a result, girls know more about their bodies and what to expect, while boys remain mostly in the dark about their bodies' development. Unfortunately, father-son, or even mother-son, conversations about sexual development remain the exception rather than the norm today.

What a shame! The father-son talk provides an important opportunity for the two to bond. Yet, it's often avoided because both father and son feel so awkward. The father can be reassured that there is no "right way" to discuss sex. But initiating "the talk" is better than no talk at all. Boys also lack a full-time male role model. While girls have a clearer role model in their early years since the mother, *their* role model, is more available and present, the boy's role model, the working father, is still mostly absent. At all levels of society, the mother remains the main influence on the children, both boys and girls, and contributes the bulk of their learning and behavior. The part-time male role model has less of an impact on the young girl, but the boy loses out: He must look to his father for guidance. The young boy learns from this process that being absent is okay. The important element for a father is to be *successful*, to be a good *provider*. This nicely complements the boy's rigorous behavioral training in competition among his peers.

These early years of conditioning produce a man who, when faced with emotional trouble, thinks he should know what to do. If he is strong he shouldn't *need* to ask for help. Though his conclusion is flawed, it's reinforced by society: A young girl in a schoolyard tussle is rescued and protected by either parent; a young boy in the same position is encouraged to "fight it out like a man." In adulthood it is not surprising that women find it acceptable, even sensible, to seek therapy when threatened with an emotional crisis. Yet men generally avoid therapy until they've completely run out of all other options. This means that the typical man begins therapy at a much more advanced stage of emotional or professional crisis. It is in most respects his last resort.

Yet today I have a successful full-time practice that con-

sists of a clientele that is 80 percent male. Clearly the need
exists. In the early 1980s, when I had a "typical" adult practice, I began to pay attention to the neglected concerns and
issues of men in therapy. Actually, it was the women in my
practice who called my attention to the needs of men. I was
hearing a recurring complaint from the women I was seeing
who were completing a successful therapy: "Where are all the
men?" There were no suitable men out there. Simply put, the
men had not kept up with them. The women had been changing for more than twenty years while the men only looked
on.

So I decided to look around and see what was available
in the way of information and support for men in the popular
media and the press. I was surprised to find that magazines,
newspapers, books, and television were flooded with information and support for women on how to dress, have better
sex, advance in business, balance a home and career, and
countless other topics. This bounty of information was giving
these women an adult version of what had been provided to
them as little girls: support, guidance, and the sharing of information. Even more surprising was the virtual absence of
anything approximating this level of information for men. Most
men's magazines were valuable and thorough in providing information for physical endeavors: sports, cars, and outdoor
life. There was a dearth of information for men in the popular
media on relationships, coping, personal growth, families,
stress, sex, or even careers. Until recently there have been a
few exceptions to this, and I've come to appreciate such magazines as *Esquire*, *Men's Health*, and *Men's Fitness* for providing
information on personal growth for men and such authors as
Herb Goldberg and Robert Bly for pioneering efforts in encouraging men to understand themselves. But these are isolated islands in a sea of emptiness.

When I began this new direction in my practice, there
were only a few other therapists who were willing to work

toward establishing a therapy center for men. Good therapists had fairly full schedules with no need to make any drastic change. But again, female and feminist therapists, specializing in therapy with women, were increasing steadily. I felt there was a crying need to address these issues, and I believe *Men Talk* represents an important step in understanding and satisfying this need.

My investigation into men's issues in the early 1980s coincided with a turning point in my career. I had established a successful practice in Georgetown after many years of effort. During the early years of my practice in Washington I developed a specialty in treating alcoholics and drug addicts, in addition to the more typical problems of adults. This was a challenging area for me, and over this period I functioned in many capacities: therapist, consultant, supervisor, and trainer of other therapists. I was also able to draw on my experience as a faculty member years earlier at Emory University, my first professional appointment after receiving my Ph.D. I gained experience in private practice during a three-year tenure in Atlanta. The return to my native Washington was triggered by a typically painful divorce that presented the opportunity and challenge to start anew. The Georgetown practice was enormously satisfying, yet it left me wondering if I was contributing enough to society by helping only a very limited number of people. Even though I was giving free public lectures, I wanted to play a larger role and contribute to this area of men's issues. A great deal of soul-searching and conversations with good friends and respected colleagues followed.

Although there was little concrete support or enthusiasm, I decided to take a risk that could have easily ended in disaster. I decided to establish a center devoted primarily to men's issues and male-female relationships. From a strictly business viewpoint such a move could have been tantamount to professional suicide (a term actually used by one colleague) given

the largely female clientele of virtually all psychologists' practices. But I firmly believed that there were certain elements
of working with men that made this move necessary. Above
all, I needed to make therapy more accessible to men if I
were to attract the kind of men I wanted to reach: resistant,
ambitious, high-achieving, and emotionally blocked men facing relationship crises, emotional frustrations, and feelings of
emptiness, and especially those hopeless men experiencing
the humiliation of impotence. I decided to relocate my practice from Georgetown to the heart of the Washington business
district to eliminate the typical excuses men use to avoid talking to a therapist. I took every measure and went to every
length to accommodate these men: accessibility by subway,
convenient location, flexible hours, sliding fee scales, and both
male and female therapists. Now the decision to actually show
up would become their largest hurdle. I furnished the suite as
a comfortable office environment that has more in common
with a law firm than a doctor's office: It became an inviting,
nonclinical setting. I even went so far as to change my own
style of dress from a more casual look to the more formal suit
and tie, as a way of blending in, knowing it would make it
easier for men to connect and relate to someone more familiar. I intended to make every conceivable effort to connect to
and accommodate these men. I named, and trademarked, my
new practice "MenCenter."

The most surprising outcome of all these efforts wasn't
that the practice flourished (especially after the media took a
strong interest) but rather that I started hearing, for the first
time in twenty years of clinical practice, stories proving that
all the myths one hears about men are absolutely true: Men

do feel they are *not* supposed to cry, they're not supposed to
ask for help, they are supposed to *know* what to do, period.
Perhaps the most gratifying result was how quickly a man was
willing to change once he made the commitment to therapy.
Moreover, in the course of my consultations with colleagues,

it soon became evident that I was hearing about the lives of men who, under any other circumstances, would never have begun therapy at all. I remember being struck by the notion that it just didn't seem fair that this information was not getting out, and that I was the only one destined to hear it. I felt this material needed to be shared, discussed, and explored with other men—and *women*. This was the environment that gave rise to the idea that culminated in *Men Talk*.

I gave much consideration to my selection of the particular men in the group whom you are about to meet. All of them began therapy with me on an individual basis and knew for some time that group therapy would be introduced into their treatment plan. I also maintained treatment with the men in individual sessions while they were in group therapy; they knew they were not being deprived of private time with me. Within the group setting, each man knew and trusted me. I was his special ally. I chose six men for this group who were united by common issues, especially problems in their relationships with women. Yet they also had many of the other issues I commonly encounter in my work with men: anxiety, stress, expressing anger, making decisions, and impotence. Regardless of the differences in education and occupation, all these men have difficulty in expressing feelings (even anger), in communicating, and in creating intimate relationships. My work with men has taught me the value they place on achieving concrete goals in a set period of time, so I chose a six-month commitment for the group as an initial, and extendable, period.

The group-therapy process is unique and affords several advantages that cannot be provided in individual treatment. It allows the therapist to observe how a man interacts with others. It allows the man to connect and open up to other people who share similar problems and concerns. It also provides a rare opportunity for him to learn his effect on others. He will hear direct, honest reactions to his behavior from other group

members: anger, boredom, and lack of interest. He will have
the benefit of their emotional responses, something that is
often denied him in the "real world," where people's first choice
is to walk away or avoid saying anything at all. Each of the
men who takes the risk of opening up in this group will carry
away with him some distinct advantages in life.

The sessions detailed in the following pages and the
men's lives outlined in the dialogue are all real. The biogra-
phies and life stories have been extensively modified and al-
tered to protect identities. The relevant material and
interpretations, however, have been retained in their entirety.
Each session as it reads here is the heart of an actual session,
but it is not intended as a literal transcript. Such a transcript
would fill many volumes and prove exceedingly boring. The
discussion following each session is designed to provide an
encapsulated "interpretation" of the more significant events
that occurred during the session, and to help the reader understand the different levels of communication going on in
the world. I believe the material presented in this book will
prove to be enlightening, informative, entertaining, and above
all, an inspiration for women and men to understand and listen when men talk.

                                              A.S.B.

MEET THE GROUP

///

MITCH, 34, is the spitting image of Kris Kristofferson as a leather-clad biker. Mitch's imposing presence, 6′4″ frame, shaggy red hair, and unkempt beard contradict his shy, sensitive demeanor and his profession as an aerodynamics engineer. He's been divorced for three years and is now in love with **Lynda**, a legal secretary with whom he has trouble communicating. Mitch also has difficulty expressing anger and exhibits anxiety over just about everything.

PAUL, 41, is insensitive and abrasive. He's 6′1″ with thinning hair, clear plastic glasses, and a nasal whine. A Washington patent attorney in the traditional navy-blue pinstripe suit, white Oxford shirt, and striped tie, he's not centerfold material for *American Lawyer*—stomach paunch, bad posture, worn-out suits, and scuffed brown leather briefcase. He looks like an unkempt Willard Scott. Separated from **Sarah**, his wife and homemaker of twenty years, Paul is indecisive about getting a divorce. He exists in a small studio apartment—alone for the first time—which he believes accounts for his disheveled appearance. He is the only member of the group with children—**Betty**, 18, who's in college, and **Abe**, 17, who's living with Sarah.

BURT, 45, is a quiet, reserved army lobbyist and colonel at the Pentagon. Solid and muscular, Burt stands 5′10″ tall and is always neatly groomed, with his clothes pressed and his shoes shined. His penetrating Paul Newman eyes add depth to everything he says. Burt is divorced and lives alone in the same house he lived in with his ex-wife. He currently dates **JoAnn**, a graduate student. Burt was able to solve his original problem with impotence in individual therapy and is using group therapy to help him improve his relationship with JoAnn.

SEAN, 23, looks remarkably like Woody Allen, but lacks the sense of humor. He looks fragile and boyish with a wide-eyed innocence. Sean recently moved east from Arizona to attend medical school at George Washington University. He's a slim 5′9″, with big brown eyes, wire-rimmed glasses, and fine blond hair. Sean always wears faded jeans, sports shirts, and soiled running shoes. He rides his ten-speed bike to group no matter how cold it gets. He's single and lives in a group house in Arlington. Sean is devastated from his broken romance with **Sandi**, a medical student from New York City, who left him.

ED, 36, is Mr. Ivy League. He is tweedy, preppy, and pudgy behind horn-rimmed glasses, a cold, quiet intellectual. Ed is a typical bureaucrat working as a research epidemiologist for the federal government. He is single and has been living for a year with **Ellen**, a teacher. They both grew up in the same northern California suburb but did not know each other. Ed is an adult child of alcoholic parents, trying to solve problems with communication, depression, and low self-esteem. His relationship with Ellen is in turmoil because he can't bring himself to propose marriage.

GARY, 33, is the jokester of the group, cynical and sarcastic, streetwise and insightful. He sees the world through a pair of bad-boy Mickey Rourke eyes. Gary is the only man in the group without a college education, which makes him feel inferior to the others. He is a Washington native and lives alone in a small town house on Capitol Hill, where he's also set up an office for work as an insurance estimator. He's wiry, blond, and neatly groomed, the only son of an abusive and alcoholic father—and a recovering alcoholic himself. Gary is single and feels addicted to sex, which makes his relationship with **Leigh**, a 29-year-old virgin, a painful dilemma for him. Later, Gary starts seeing **Marta**, a foreign housekeeper, for an intensely sexual relationship.

MEN'S FEAR OF
THERAPY

"I don't really want to be here," Mitch mumbles as he stares blankly at the floor, avoiding eye contact of any kind.

An awkward silence falls over the room. The six strangers in my new group therapy session look unsettled. One focuses out the window. Another stares at his shoes. The rest glance furtively around at this room full of unfamiliar faces not sure of what they've gotten themselves into.

"Why?" asks Burt, the eldest member of the group, breaking the silence.

Mitch looks up at me. "I tried to cancel this afternoon. My dad's in town, and I have to get together with him. He never gives me advance notice—just shows up and expects me to drop *everything* for him. Generally I *do* drop everything when my father comes to town," Mitch admits glumly. " That's the way it's always been."

As I listen to Mitch I feel pleased and encouraged that he has actually found his way here after calling two hours earlier to cancel. The call was full of anxiety about group therapy and meeting his father afterward. I strongly encouraged him to come, and he agreed, although he threatened to be late. He wasn't. In fact, he was the first to arrive, bursting suddenly into the room before the session even began.

Mitch has a strong, imposing presence. He's an enormous man, with wild shaggy red hair and broad shoulders encased in a shiny leather jacket. Today, as usual, he thudded across the room in motorcycle boots, carrying a big black helmet tucked under his arm. Yet despite his belligerent air I know from my work with Mitch he is at heart very gentle. He's the shyest of my patients. This is no heavy-leather biker but an aerodynamics engineer who spent the better part of his youth alone in his room, building model airplanes. These apparent contradictions come as little surprise to me now, after decades of working with men.

In fact, all these men, whom I see individually, have their contradictions, too.

If there's such a thing as the "male mystique," this is it: the contradiction between a man's outer appearance and his inner feelings.

There's Paul sitting next to me in a deep black leather chair identical to mine. Paul is an older, louder, narcissistic patient who apparently has no awareness of his own personal abrasiveness. He has recently separated from his wife of twenty years, his first and only love, and is having a terribly difficult time living alone for the first time in his life. He doesn't take much care of his appearance; after all, for twenty years he was dressed and tended to by his wife, and now he's making do alone. He will profit from group therapy.

Opposite Paul, in the center of the light gray sectional, sits Burt, my oldest and perhaps wisest patient. He has a solid, saturnine countenance, and his body is remarkably fit for his forty-five years. He swims long distances every day, partly in an effort to offset the great anxiety and depression that plague him. Burt is a military officer who spends much of his time on Capitol Hill, and he has devoted much of his life to army legal issues. He originally came to me complaining of impotence and stayed for help in establishing assertiveness and self-esteem. Recently, his attention has been focused primarily on his relationship problems with his girlfriend JoAnn.

Almost hiding in Burt's shadow, meanwhile, is Sean, the youngest and most fragile member of our group, a young-looking Woody Allen, delicate, boyish, and perpetually, almost owlishly, wide-eyed. He seems lost and vaguely alarmed. Sean is from Phoenix and his calm Southwestern origins leave him at something of a loss here in the highly focused and competitive world of the East Coast. I happen to think Sean the most privileged man in our group, because as the youngest he'll benefit from the wisdom and experience of the other men, be able to learn from their experiences, and perhaps avoid many of their problems—but he wonders if he really belongs in the room.

Ed, a preppy, slightly pudgy man in his mid-thirties who is confused and troubled by problems with his girlfriend, is seated on the adjacent couch. Ed is an epidemiologist who does mountains of research for the federal government and looks like a bureaucrat from central casting: horn-rimmed glasses, grave countenance, neatly combed hair. He is quiet, reserved, and analytical—a type that is often more difficult to reach in therapy because he tends to intellectualize and speak about issues rather than feelings. As an adult child of alcoholics, he has problems with identity, self-esteem, communication, and commitment; his personal life has also been deeply unhappy. Exposing him to group will draw him out and build up his confidence.

The last to venture into the room for this first session was Gary, the wariest and perhaps most deeply troubled of my patients. For many years a severe alcoholic, Gary missed out on any higher education and as a result is extremely insecure about others' perceptions of his intelligence and social skills. Tonight Gary is neatly dressed in a long-sleeved striped sports shirt and chino slacks—there is a tense air to his tall, thin frame. Gary has Mel Gibson's boyish smile, good looks, and full head of hair. Very much a loner, he has a house of his own in the northeast section of Capitol Hill, where he works alone as an insurance estimator. When I urged him to join us and close the door behind him just ten minutes ago, he entered reluctantly, and seemed genuinely regretful that we must conduct our sessions behind a closed door. After looking around, he seated himself uneasily on the edge of the sectional next to the door, as if to make a quick getaway if things got too rough.

Things can get rough in group therapy. As a matter of course I encourage my patients to face often frightening and troubling problems in the company of vexing strangers. The resulting group process is a special dynamic that will reveal behaviors, fears, tensions, and anxieties that are almost impossible to reach in any other way. It can be frightening, uncomfortable, intimidating.

As Mitch struggles with his feelings of anxiety in our first session, Burt steps in to offer support.

"Are you looking forward to seeing your father?"

"Actually, no," Mitch says with a sad shake of his head of hair. "It's just going to be another drunken scene. My dad drinks, then picks fights, telling me and my sister everything we're not doing right. My sister fights back with him more than I do. The only time I really speak up is when he picks on her."

"So you're the last priority in this situation," I say.

Mitch nods.

Paul jumps in. "Well, as I see it, you're not exercising all your options. Did your old man just pop into town all of a sudden?"

"I knew he was coming, but he never gives us much notice."

"But," Paul continues, "you did know, right? So you could have told him you were going to be busy that night, that you had other plans, or that you could meet to take a walk in the park for an hour but you wouldn't be free for dinner."

Mitch smiles. "I see what you mean. He always catches me off guard when he calls, but maybe I could be a little more prepared for next time . . ."

As Mitch trails off, a silence descends upon the group.

After a time, Paul looks up. "I might as well go next here. My situation is that I'm separated, but the wife and I are kind of dating again. To tell you the truth, I'd like to keep it that way. I've never lived alone in my life, and being in an apartment and just watching TV by myself is for the birds. And after twenty years of marriage, I feel funny trying to 'date' all over again. And there are some pretty scary diseases going around out there, you know. At least I know what's what with my wife."

After a pause, he continues: "Sarah—that's my wife—and I were both just twenty-one when we got married. I've got two kids, teenagers, Betty, who just went away to college, and Abe, who's a junior in high school, and lives with Sarah. She's depressed a lot of the time, and I just decided I'd had enough of it. The separation is something I'm working on getting over, but it sure as hell isn't easy, believe me."

Burt, who is sitting forward on the couch facing Paul and me, nods slowly.

After a silence, I come in. "Well, for what it's worth, Paul, I don't think any man ever gets completely over his first love. Your situation is especially difficult: twenty years of history doesn't just vanish overnight. It's part of your personal history, a part of you, and always will be."

"People are probably telling you to 'get over it,' " Mitch interjects.

"Yeah, I hear that a lot, and it bothers me. I just hate it." Paul grimaces.

"There is something you can do, Paul," I offer. "Try to remember that you *will* work through this. Being here in group is a good start. And know that eventually you *can* have another relationship."

"Not if he's still dating his ex-wife, he won't!" Gary exclaims from his corner by the door.

This gets a nervous laugh from Paul, who tries to shake it off by looking away. Burt and Mitch are smiling, too.

I ask Paul how his son Abe is taking the separation.

"Oh, he's all right. Doing pretty well with it."

"Did you ever ask him?"

"No. But we never talk much about that kind of stuff."

"How about if we role-play it now?" I ask. Role playing, a technique where a group member and I act out roles of other individuals in ways we think they might actually feel, is a common and useful group-therapy technique. "I'll be Abe and you be you," I suggest. Paul nods, and I, as Abe, turn to face Paul on my left, and begin.

"Look, Dad, I'm really pissed at you for leaving me here with Mom. She's your wife, but now you've left and dumped her on me. At least before you left there were two of us not getting along with her! Dealing with Mom by myself is just one more hassle I don't need right now."

Paul seems somewhat perplexed but manages some response. "Look at it this way, son: It won't be for much longer. You're going off to school pretty soon. And I'm sorry, I didn't mean to cause problems for you. Your mom and I just couldn't stay under the same roof any longer. But any time you want to talk about it, I'd be glad to, okay?"

"But Dad," I continue, "I don't see why I should believe that. You weren't really around for me to talk with before, so how will it be any easier when you're not even here? You leave here, you come back home, and then you're gone again. I wish you'd just make up your mind once and for all, so I'd know what I'm dealing with."

This stops Paul, who is struggling for a response.

"Have you had your apartment long?" Gary throws out from his corner seat.

I look past Paul to Gary, catch his gaze, and hold it. I suspect that Gary, like many people in group, has jumped in like this to take the conversation to a safer place for him. I wonder if it is stirring something up inside. "What triggered your question?" I ask.

Gary shrugged lazily. "I guess I connect with Paul's mixed feelings about separating. I'm thirty-three, never been married, and it seems like I should want to. But every time I go out with a woman, I try to find something wrong with her. That way I don't have to decide about marriage. And even if I did get married, what if it just goes nowhere? Then I'd have to decide whether to get a separation, divorce, or whatever. The whole thing's too much!"

"Try to be a bit more specific, Gary."

Gary shifts uneasily and looks around at the rest of the group. "Well, when I broke up with Liz two years ago, I was so . . . God, I don't ever want to go through that again! It was horrible. I felt addicted to her. And she came back to me— just once—to . . . well . . . basically to get laid, and I was practically on my knees begging her to stay after that. I was desperate, totally out of control. That was scary.

"Now whenever I date a woman, I really do think I'm locked in, addicted to her. So I'm with Paul on keeping dating simple—no commitment, no strings attached. I'm just going to let my dick dictate where it wants to be from now on," he states emphatically. "I'm never going to get serious about anybody again."

Gary folds his arms and sits back, looking as though he's confident this problem has been solved.

For a while nobody says anything. Finally Burt looks across to Paul. "So what's your wife—Sarah?—like?"

"Burt," I say, "why not tell us a little about yourself?"

Burt smiles, acknowledging that he's been caught. "Well," he begins, in a careful, detached way, "when I broke up with my wife three years ago, I was devastated. But Rosalind was hiding out and depressed for what seemed like forever. She was always going on and on about how she didn't have her own identity. She was a pretty good writer, but the depression just drove her to distraction. She was a nonwriting writer." He looks up and rolls his eyes. "I really did try to talk, to communicate with her, but I guess I didn't do a very good job. She's the one who finally asked for a divorce. I don't think I would have ever asked for one; I expected that we'd just stay married, you know, through thick or thin. Here I felt it was my duty to stand by her forever, and she walks out on me! *I couldn't believe it.* I should have divorced her myself and saved myself a hell of a lot of grief."

I'm watching Burt carefully. I nod at him to show I understand his pain. I wait for others to come in on this, too.

Suddenly Sean sneezes and startles everyone.

"Maybe that's your opening to tell us something of yourself, Sean," I suggest.

Sean becomes very apprehensive at this suggestion. The youngest of the group, he is clearly intimidated by all that is going on around him. "Well, I guess I don't know what you're all talking about. I'm pretty close to my parents, I talk to them all the time. It feels like they've been married forever."

"So why are you here?" Paul demands from across the room.

"Well, mostly because I just broke up with my girlfriend, Sandi. It's not that we don't care about each other. We're just so different: she's New York, Jewish, Ivy League, top med school. Me, I'm from out West, so I'm a bit more laid back, I take things as they come. I make decent grades and that's good enough for me. I don't even know what I'm going to do with my life yet! I'm in med school but I'm not sure I even want to be a practicing doctor."

Burt, who is crowding Sean a bit on the couch, is interested. "So what's the deal with Sandi?"

"Well, I guess the things that attracted us in the first place, the differences, are what finally tore us apart. I'd still like to get back together, though. Is that too idealistic? Everybody says it is, I hear it all the time. But it's true. I really miss her." As Sean finishes he looks a little deflated. I decide to come in.

"Sean, can you see any similarities between your situation and Paul's?"

Sean shrugs. He doesn't seem at all up to it.

We all sit silently for a while. Rush-hour traffic noises filter up from the downtown Washington streets. As we sit here quietly, it seems the rest of the city is in a hurry to get home.

I turn to Ed. "I'm wondering how you're fitting in with everything that's being said here."

Ed leans forward and pushes up his glasses carefully. We all sense this is uncharted territory for him. "Oh, it's all very interesting," he assures us.

"Could you say more?"

"All right," he continues, looking a little perturbed at me. "It's true, a lot of what you guys are saying makes sense to me. I've been in the same place, too. The longest relationship I ever had lasted three years, and then we sort of went our separate ways. I'm in another one now, but I have all these doubts about whether this is what I really want."

I know there is more to the story than Ed's letting on, but before I can draw him out of his shell, Mitch shifts a motorcycle boot off his knee, and leans forward.

"Well, that's one thing I can say for my relationship with Lynda right now. I like it, I want it, and I don't want to screw it up. In fact, I think I'm going to ask her to marry me. The thing is I just *hate* being alone. I can't stand it. When I was with my ex-wife"—he stops suddenly and breaks into a wide smile—"Whoa . . . I never called her my ex-wife before! Hmmm." Several of the men are grinning back at him as he continues: "She and I just did not communicate. At all, period. So while we were supposedly together in this marriage, I damn sure didn't feel that way. I felt totally alone. I ended up withdrawing even more. And Lynda, the woman I'm living with, says I'm doing the same thing to her, and it scares me. She thinks I need to be in therapy to figure this whole mess out. I'm here because I'm willing to do that, because I sure as hell don't want a repeat of my last breakup." He looks pained. "I don't ever want to go through that again."

I glance at the clock and am surprised to find that we are nearly out of time. I begin to wrap up, emphasizing that I am very impressed and pleased about how they were able to open up as quickly as they have in this first session. Mitch and Burt seem pleased with themselves, too. Ed looks over at Sean and these two appear to be relieved that they made it through. Gary is happy that this first session, the hardest, is over, too. He stands up with a half grin.

I'm as pleased as they are, excited by this group's potential. These men have been unusually active for a new group, and I'm certain they will learn a great deal about themselves, their relationships, and each other as we progress.

INTERPRETATION ———————————

I have discovered that a short personal break after group therapy in the relative isolation of my office is essential to review
what has occurred. I take advantage of this time in many
ways: I review the session in my mind, sort out how the men
are responding and changing, and jot down a few ideas for
review before the next session.

Today I feel optimistic about the progress this group will
make. They are a courageous lot. To enter therapy at all takes
a degree of bravery. For a man to admit to himself that he
has a problem he cannot handle is difficult enough. To acknowledge this helplessness to anyone else, even a skilled
therapist, is even rougher. To confess to strangers, however,
can be frightening. Such is the magnitude of the hurdle faced
by all the group members, and this shared anxiety has already
brought them together. With time this tentative bond will   ≠ GOAL
evolve into mutual respect, trust, and confidence.

This particular group was organized with a specific theme
in mind. Each member has a strong desire to change and
improve his relationship with women. I have seen all six of
these men in individual therapy first; they all know and trust
me. Each feels that I am his special ally. My challenge is to
sustain this feeling and to encourage each man to extend trust
to the others as they all risk revealing themselves in our sessions. All have entered group therapy at my suggestion, on
faith rather than instinct. Group is a more complex form of
therapy than is individual, and through the process each man
will have the opportunity to learn more about how others
respond to him, what feelings and reactions he evokes in those
he is closest to, and how to make meaningful and effective
changes in these relationships.

By beginning this first group session, Mitch was attempting to test out some lessons about anxiety learned from indi-

vidual therapy. At this point he understands that anxiety often represents fear, and that the way to conquer any fear is to go through the feared experience, so he decided to begin the very first session by talking about one of his most difficult topics: his father. This choice pays off for Mitch, as he does feel less anxious and somewhat relieved afterward. Mitch's pattern of handling anxiety has been to withdraw and become silent. What occurred in group was a particularly gratifying breakthrough for Mitch, since as the child of an alcoholic father, his characteristic way of dealing with problems has always been avoidance or denial.

I feel Mitch has taken a risk in presenting his problem with his father to the group and has gained better perspective as a result. However, his response, or lack of a response, to Paul is indicative of another pattern that holds Mitch back: his tendency to grow silent and withdrawn when angry or anxious.

Paul comes in by telling the group that his loneliness is driving him to date his ex-wife, with whom he has been in considerable conflict over the years. Even this unpleasant relationship is preferable to being alone in Paul's eyes. I know from my individual sessions with Paul that the entire dating situation is very difficult and threatening to him. He is also thoroughly confused by his own inability to make a firm decision on the separation and divorce. In fact, Paul's progress toward such a decision is an extremely important element in his recovery and future progress. Nevertheless, Paul's choice to date Sarah is characteristic of what some men do when faced with the loneliness and uncertainty of a separation: they rush back and embrace that which is generally unfulfilling yet familiar.

Burt, on the other hand, represents those men who finally realize that the decision has already been made and clearly understand that either there was a complete lack of ability to resolve problems within the marriage or simply no progress was made in this area, and therefore the odds of future success with the partner appear slim. As a result Burt, like most men, will not attempt to rejuvenate the relationship.

Even at this point we already see that Burt and Paul share certain common experiences in their respective marriages to depressed women. Both men felt hopeless and ultimately helpless to draw their forlorn wives out of their severe depressions. This is not their role; they can't play therapists to their wives. They both withdrew, became emotionally detached, and ultimately fled.

Both Burt and Paul echo the feeling of most men in my practice who are going through separation and divorce: that it is a thoroughly devastating experience and one from which they typically emerge feeling like a failure. It is important to emphasize that this sense of failure plagues men more than most people realize. After all, the majority of divorces nationwide are initiated by women who have taken the time to go through their own painful period before asking for the divorce. The divorce is often "sprung" on the man in the way Burt has related. The man is shocked. Many men are similar to Burt in that they feel a sense of responsibility to keep the relationship afloat and moving forward. When the bond dissolves, the man commonly feels as though this represents his own personal failure as a man.

Clearly, divorce is one of the most traumatic events a man will face during his adult life. Regardless of the circumstances, divorce means not just the loss of a wife but often the loss of children, homes, friends, money, and self-esteem as well. These men experience a terrible, multiple loss.

An important part of my work with divorced and separated men is to assure them that the painful grieving process *does* get done, the pain *does* diminish, and their energy and enthusiasm for establishing new relationships *do* grow. In fact, by the time most men finally come to me, they are depressed and feel nearly hopeless, and these reassurances both have a healing effect and serve to establish the groundwork for a successful therapeutic relationship.

Gary enters the discussion from the corner after recognizing his connection to Paul. This makes it easier for Gary because he feels he now has an ally, in addition to me, who will understand his dilemma. He fears marriage, too—he was so terribly hurt by the breakup of what had been the most intense relationship of his life that he dreads this catastrophe happening all over again. Gary is still carrying around a lot of hurt. He strives to avoid emotional involvement and is simply dating to have sex. Gary's broaching of the intensely personal topic of sex and his choice of the slang term "dick" functions as an "icebreaker" for this group and will in fact enable the other group members to talk about sex more freely and openly. I've discovered that even without such a fast icebreaker, men are quite willing to overcome their general inhibitions about discussing and sharing feelings and anxieties about sex.

When asked to enter the discussion, Sean expresses bewilderment on how there could be so little communication in these men's families. He seems to be especially confused about Paul's relationship with his son. This bewilderment grows out of Sean's view of his own relationship with his family, one that appears to be quite open and supportive, with excellent communication. I do not press Sean on the facts about his family, because he is so uncomfortable in this first session. There's plenty of time ahead.

Ed appears to be "laying low" in this first session, and one cue I pick up immediately is his use of the word "interesting." I find that people who describe something as "interesting" in group are usually avoiding a straightforward admission of how they really feel about what is going on. Ed's superficial comments on his former and current relationships suggest that Ed is being exceedingly cautious and is self-conscious about what he can safely say at this juncture in group.

By contrast, Mitch reacts to Ed's vagueness by offering some strong testimony about his clear feelings for his current girlfriend, Lynda. Mitch's desire to come back into the discussion is further evidence that his initial anxiety about being in the group has diminished and he is now prepared to open up a bit more. Mitch is certainly not alone in his description of a married life that leaves him feeling all alone. He very much wants a successful relationship with Lynda, and his greatest fear is yet another failed marriage. Unfortunately, many men do remarry within a short period of time as a way of avoiding the pain, loneliness, and depression of divorce, and they commonly carry the very same problems, as well as the "bad" feelings, right into the next marriage. It is my responsibility to help Mitch determine whether he is marrying Lynda without having recognized and resolved the problems of his first marriage.

The feelings expressed in this first session are a good indicator of the conventional traumas men suffer when a woman breaks up with them. Loneliness, hurt, depression, anger, desperation, rejection, loss of control: men experience all these feelings, even when the very worst of their relationships dies. They are rarely prepared for the idea of a breakup because they are taught to resist the idea that their feelings are important. Men are commonly driven by the desire to do the "right" thing and therefore are unable to foresee or prepare for the traumas of separation. Additionally, men feel that the grieving process is not what's expected of them. Society demands that men simply stand up, dust themselves off, and get on with life (people saying, "You'll get over it" did disturb Paul). As these men have demonstrated, however, men do grieve, often in profound ways.

This has been an enlightening and revealing first session. As the six men take increasingly greater risks in group by, say, being brutally honest, by confronting one another, or even by allowing themselves to cry, their learning will continue, more of their life experiences will be revealed, and they will find themselves growing in new and unexpected ways.

"GO TO THERAPY, OR GO TO HELL!"

An earlier cancelation has left me with a little extra time before group today, so I am enjoying looking out of the floor-to-ceiling windows onto Farragut Square. These windows and their expansive view are my favorite features of the office. While MenCenter has a handsome conference room, I prefer holding the group sessions in my room; actually, a combination executive office and comfortable living room.

The idea of seeing a therapist is an intimidating notion for most men, so I've carefully created a setting that is familiar, warm, and nonclinical. It's also my preference to be in pleasant surroundings, as so much of my life is spent in the MenCenter suite.

The office has two deep black leather chairs, two light gray sectionals, a side table, a coffee table, and, of course, my desk, which sits at the far end of the room. The artwork suggests individuality, nothing typical of an office. My plants are important: they represent life and growth. There are two palms. One covers an entire corner and the other sits in the window. And a blooming peace lily takes up space on another section of the windowsill.

Since men are traditionally resistant to therapy, and there is the temptation to use time as an excuse, I've purposely chosen to locate MenCenter in the heart of the Washington business district. I've also surrounded myself with colleagues who offer early, late, and weekend appointments and flexible fees, all in an effort to encourage and support men in their commitment to therapy and growth.

Suddenly my buzzer rings and brings me back from these thoughts. This is my assistant letting me know that the group has assembled in the waiting area. We're ready for our second session.

I open the door to Paul's thin frame in a slightly worn business suit. He nods at me and plops into the same leather seat as last week right next to mine. Mitch is close behind Paul, and I am struck, for the first time, how closely Mitch resembles a red-headed Kris Kristofferson. Burt and Ed enter the room together, continuing a conversation from the waiting room, and take the same seats as last week on the couch. In the doorway is Sean, who smiles at me in a sheepish sort of way and takes his spot next to Burt on the couch. Sean seems to be relieved that nobody took his spot. Gary brings up the rear again this week and takes the couch seat nearest the door, which is still available to him. I realize this has some significance, and the others are already honoring his wariness and option to escape.

After everybody settles in, I look around and smile. The tension in the air so evident in last week's session seems to have largely evaporated. Still there is an uneasy silence.

Paul's nasal tone breaks the silence. "So how'd it go with your father last week?" he asks, staring straight at Mitch.

Mitch seems startled by the question but quickly recovers. "Um, thanks for asking. Actually, I got off easy. Didn't have to say too much, Dad did most of the talking. He did have his drinks, and my sister and I just didn't say a whole lot."

"Why did you choose not to talk?" I ask.

"Guess it's the one that comes most easily," he shrugged. "I get real quiet when my dad is drinking, it always seemed to make the most sense." Mitch seems to be increasingly glum with this revelation. "When I was a kid, I'd go off by myself so I wouldn't have to hear him hollering at me or my mom."

"Your dad sounds like a carbon copy of mine," Ed offers from Mitch's right. "You know, I did the very same thing as a kid. I used to hide from them, literally run away when they started yelling at me, but . . ." Ed falters for a moment. "I, uh, sort of have trouble talking about my folks like this."

"Try to go on, Ed," I say.

"Well . . ."

"You don't want to make 'em look like alcoholics, right?" Mitch throws out.

"Yeah, I guess so. I don't mind talking about me or even about me and Ellen in here. But this is different."

"This is why I'm having trouble with this, Al," Mitch says as he looks at me. "When I say these things about my dad, it's like he's some gutter bum alcoholic. He *is* my father, and I really shouldn't be talking about him this way."

"What's your feeling while you're talking?" I ask.

"I feel damn guilty," Mitch responds, staring at the carpet.

Burt leans forward from Mitch's other side. "I always backed away from my father too, because he was a real screamer. It was embarrassing. I even saw a used-car salesman give in once because of the screaming." Burt is talking straight to Mitch. "I just wanted to slink away and die, believe me," he adds with a shake of the head.

"At least you guys *had* fathers!" Paul interjects.

My attention has so shifted to the men on the couch that I am not watching for Paul's reaction. I'm surprised by how suddenly he is shaken.

"Mine died when I was fifteen, and I didn't even know he was sick!" he concludes with a quaver in his voice.

Burt looks at Paul, then at me, then back at Paul. He seems worried that he may have started something.

"Paul, can you tell us a bit more about this?" I ask.

"It was like everything in my family had to be a big secret," he intones. Paul seems to have developed an interest in the armrest, where he's staring, and he's poking at it incessantly. "I only found out my father was sick when I happened to see his car parked outside of the doctor's office one day. So I asked my mom if something was wrong. So she just told me, 'Your father's sick,' but she never said how bad. Little by little I noticed him around more, and then he was just bedridden. One day he died." Paul has stopped picking and falls quiet for a moment. He looks up and almost seems startled that the rest of us are there. "I was so angry about it."

"What were you angry about?" Burt asks. He is looking at Paul and seems concerned.

"I was so angry he left me," Paul replies, as he slides back in his seat. "He just *left* me, stuck me there with my mother and sister."

It dawns on me that this is the same thing that Paul is doing to his own son, Abe. Paul's also been holding in a great deal of pain.

"This is the first time you've ever said that you were angry with your father for dying and leaving you alone," I note.

Paul's eyebrows shoot up for a moment, and then he nods in recognition.

"Take a look at whether holding in all this hurt and anger

might be something that happens a lot in your life, whether it might be a pattern," I suggest.

"Well," Paul reflects. "Yeah . . . I guess in a way I did that with my wife. Sarah would start yelling at me about something, and I'd yell back maybe once, but she'd keep on me, and I just wouldn't answer. That's how I figured it: If I don't answer, she has to stop yelling. God, I hated it. After a while it became automatic: I'd pretend I didn't hear; stare at the TV, and tune her right out."

Ed begins to fidget and seems disturbed by the conversation. "What's going on, Ed?" I ask.

"I'm just thinking that Ellen and I never argue."

"Never?" Gary looks to his left and catches Ed's eye. He is skeptical.

"Never," Ed says emphatically. "When anything comes up, we both get quiet. When Ellen's mad, it's hard to discuss anything at all. Usually she takes a book, goes into the other room, and stays there for an hour or so. The only thing I know to do is leave her alone."

"I want to say something about all this, Ed," I come in. "This is for you, too, Paul, and Mitch." Everyone has perked up a bit. "What is happening here is you are all using behaviors you learned as children. Ed and Mitch run away from their alcoholic parents. Now, this was a good choice as a kid: protecting yourself from the 'big, angry, powerful' adults. Now the scene is different. You're the grown-ups. But you're still using your childhood defenses. Getting quiet, hiding, withdrawing. Paul, you get quiet with Sarah just as you were expected to do when your mother was mad at you."

Paul turns to me swiftly. "Look, I don't like this. Are you calling me a child?"

"No, just the opposite," I counter. "I'm saying you're an adult. And now you don't have to defend yourself with other adults in an immature way. It works better if you stop and confront Sarah. Otherwise you're never going to find out what these conflicts are about." I turn slowly to Ed. "Can you see this too, Ed? Do you understand how difficult it will be for you and Ellen to resolve your problems if you just avoid each other?"

"I understand what you're saying, I really do, but . . ."

"What is the problem between you and Ellen?" Gary asks.

Ed sighs. "Well, the bottom line is that I'm on a fence. I can't make up my mind about whether we should get married. One day Ellen just gave me an ultimatum. Go find out why you can't make up your mind. Either make a commitment or let me move out of here and get on with my life. You know what she said? She said, 'Go to therapy, or go to hell!' "

A ripple of laughter runs through the group.

"How'd you respond?" I ask.

"Oh, I guess I was worried. I didn't want to lose her. And she was dead serious about it. So I came here."

"So how are things now that you're doing this?"

"Well, I can see where Ellen and I are getting closer. But I get frustrated that it's so hard for us to have a decent conversation." Ed starts getting agitated and is toying with his wool sweater. "Like last night we went to see this movie. I wanted to talk about it afterward. But it was like she got real defensive. 'Why do you have to pick it apart? Can't you just enjoy it for what it is?' " he mocks in a falsetto voice. "I told her I wasn't trying to pick it apart. I just wanted to have a conversation about it, maybe understand it a little better!"

"What did Ellen say?" Burt asks.

Ed slaps the armrest. "She wouldn't even discuss it! She said I was being too detailed and analytical, that I should just enjoy the movie. I don't get it. Ellen's not stupid by any means. She's got a master's degree. But I can't talk with her like I used to in my other relationships."

Burt is chuckling and shaking his head. "I have to laugh, Ed. I mean, if you want somebody analytical, JoAnn analyzes anything and everything. No matter what I do or say, she's analyzing it. If I don't say anything, she analyzes that! I can't even be quiet without being analyzed." He pauses. "You wanna trade girlfriends?"

Ed smiles.

Paul looks across at Ed. "You set a date for that wedding yet?"

"Ellen set a deadline last summer, but it passed and nothing happened. Then she set a new deadline for Christmas." He thinks a moment. "It's about nine weeks away. I don't know what to do."

"Draw up a prenuptial agreement," Paul advises. "It's hell going through a divorce and finding out that Sarah might be able to get half of my salary!"

From the looks being flashed around the group, I sense an impatience with Paul. Ed does, too, apparently, and hesitates to answer. I make it clear by my steady gaze that he should continue.

"I'm not really comfortable with that," Ed continues. "It sounds like I don't trust her, like I'm already thinking about a divorce. It's not like I enjoy being undecided, you know." Ed looks around to make sure everybody has heard this. "I feel kind of guilty, because I encouraged her to move in with me, to leave a job and friends in Texas to move here with me. She said to me then that she didn't want to unless there was a possibility of marriage." Ed trails off and goes silent.

"What did you say?" Burt asks.

"That of course it was a possibility. I'd like to buy a house, start a family. But I never made any promises. I guess we also have to worry about the ol' biological clock; she's thirty-two. But if I'm going to get married, I want to be absolutely sure it's the right thing."

Burt has his head cocked toward Ed and has been nodding through this, listening intently.

"What is it, Burt?" I ask.

"Oh . . ." He looks a bit perplexed but then brightens

with recognition. "I identify with Ellen. Isn't that strange? I'm forty-five myself, I worry about what kind of a father I'm going to be at this age." He frowns and looks back at Ed. "I'm not sure JoAnn is really the one for me either."

I notice the clock and decide to wrap things up.

"It's almost time to stop, but I've been wondering why you've been so silent, Sean."

Sean looks up suddenly and catches my eye. "I've just been listening to everyone." He shrugs.

"What's been your reaction?"

"Well, I was thinking you guys are so . . . critical of your girlfriends." He ponders this for a moment. "Are you looking for somebody perfect?"

"I'm not," Burt answers quickly. "In fact, I get the feeling I'm the one who's supposed to be perfect, judging from the way JoAnn is on my case." His gaze shifts to me. "She criticizes me all the time."

"I understand, Burt. Criticism and blame can be so destructive to a relationship. And they can *kill* sex."

"If criticism is constructive, it could be good," Ed offers.

"Ed, when Ellen criticizes you for not talking with her, she's on target. Do you feel good about this?" I ask calmly.

He frowns. "Definitely not."

"Well, see, I don't believe in 'constructive' criticism in a relationship. It's just a cover for old-fashioned criticism. It also manipulates the other person into accepting the criticism without a hassle."

"So there's no such thing as 'constructive' criticism?" Ed asks with surprise.

"Sure," I reply, "and it plays an integral role in a relationship set up for it. For example, between an athlete and a coach, or a director and an actor. Relationships with clearly outlined teacher-student roles. There's no such agreement in a romantic relationship.

Ed seems satisfied with this. He looks around the room

and catches Sean's eye. "I sort of took things away from you right at the end. Did you want to say something else?"

Sean shrugs. "Not really. I just think you need to accept the other person. I know Sandi isn't perfect." After a moment he adds, "But I still love her."

INTERPRETATION

Shared experience is the catalyst bringing the group together. Three of the six have revealed the pain and fright of childhoods spent largely hiding or avoiding their parents. Paul talks about the trauma of the sudden and unexpected death of his father, and how the anger from this event has still not subsided. In fact, this episode and its consequences play a role in Paul's present life. Some of the difficulties these men have in communicating with their women surface during this second session.

It is not unusual that three of the six men—Ed, Mitch, and Gary—all find themselves on the run from adults out of control and hesitate to discuss any aspect of this trauma today. All three men are adult children of alcoholics. One behavioral characteristic of alcoholic and other dysfunctional families is that the child is forbidden to say anything at all negative about the family to anyone outside the immediate family. The alcoholic parents use the defense mechanism of denial, a way of pretending that problems don't exist, and mold the children into using the same denial. The children are then expected to carry on this posture outside the family. This forces the youngster into a state of internal turmoil, because he's told no problem exists, yet he certainly both sees and feels one. The predominant code of keeping secrets within the family has served to isolate these three men. They lost the freedom to interact openly with their friends and neighbors throughout their childhoods, and they were made to feel guilty or ashamed if they let slip with anything that their parents might deem "wrong."

This behavioral dynamic has consequences for the men in their lives today. As I point out to Mitch and Ed in the session, the hostility and craziness of their alcoholic families drove them into withdrawal and isolation from the family simply as a means of protection. From the child's viewpoint, this may be the best protection available. Now, however, they are mature adults who interact with other adults as peers rather than as authority figures. Their continuing reliance on childhood defenses, coping mechanisms, and habits is ineffectual in an adult-adult relationship. Mitch, Gary, and Ed must choose to engage in conflict: this will be an important part of their learning. They'll discover that conflict is a means of resolution that allows a relationship to grow rather than stagnate, regress, or even collapse.

In Paul's relationship with his father, the unexpected death was traumatic, since he was surprised and therefore unprepared for it. Paul had been carrying his anger around before this session but felt too guilty to tell anyone, because he never understood that anger is a natural outlet for grief. Paul's experience is shared by many men in my practice who have not yet learned how to express themselves when they feel angry. These men grew up feeling anger and hostility all around them and were upset and threatened by it. Anger then became "bad." This is why they are so successful at suppressing angry feelings entirely in adulthood. In my work with men I emphasize that minor annoyances, irritations, and disappointments need to be discussed or diffused *right as they happen*. This eliminates the need for intense, angry outbursts that result from long-term suppression of minor (and major) traumas and everyday difficulties that they've concealed or held in rather than diffused immediately by discussion.

Certainly such a behavioral change, like any change, is difficult to make. But the process will be easier for these men by virtue of their presence in the group. The entire group therapy process offers a strong medium for change. Tonight we see that Paul risked discussing a very powerful childhood trauma with men who are relative strangers to him. In fact, this risk to Paul has been reduced tonight by Ed, Burt, and Mitch, since all have spoken disparagingly about their fathers, offering support rather than censure. As a child, Paul learned from his family to expect rejection or anger if he revealed his true feeling about his father's death. Here, however, the men do not respond as critically as Paul anticipated. This now creates a much more fertile environment for honesty and change. The men are just beginning to sense this.

Other consequences of these early learned behaviors are playing themselves out in these men's lives as well. Clearly, Burt and Ed are having problems communicating with the women they love. Ed pleads with Ellen to talk to him about the movie they've seen together. While Ed expounds at length about the virtues and drawbacks of the film, he irritates and alienates Ellen, who is content with a more impressionistic experience. Ed approaches the conversation on an intellectual, "expert" plane and wants to do a thorough analysis. Ellen prefers and operates better on an emotional plane. Thus, as Ellen listens to Ed she becomes increasingly inhibited and intimidated, because she doesn't know what answer Ed is looking for. In this sense Ellen is like Burt, who also is intimidated by JoAnn's probing questions and constant analysis of their relationship. The true irony, however, is that trading girlfriends, as Burt has facetiously suggested, would be disastrous. While JoAnn and Ed certainly operate well on the intellectual plane, they are "experts" at different subjects. Ed focuses on analyzing facts and exploring rationality; JoAnn, on the other hand, examines emotions and beliefs. Burt and Ellen as a couple would be equally troubled, because they would never be able to confront each other and would probably be content to avoid discussing problems in their relationship until they grew to unmanageable proportions.

Ed's dilemma stems from much more than poor communication. His indecision, his confusion, and the resulting guilt about his quasi-commitment to marry Ellen derive from two aspects of his personality. One is that Ed is a perfectionist. He is truly afraid that any specific commitment or decision could be "wrong." Like a perfectionist, Ed procrastinates because he wants to be "right." The other aspect is the residual effects of his own childhood. Ed's parents did not have the kind of marriage that would make him too eager to marry. He wants some assurance that his marriage will be better and more fulfilling than his parents'.

All the men in the group, Ed included, have an excellent chance of achieving their goals. A willingness for self-examination and change through therapy can dramatically increase the odds for a successful relationship or marriage.

///

AVOIDING FEELINGS

"So I figure that if I see Sarah once a week, then I could get my rocks off, and have the rest of the week to do all my other stuff, like get work done, see the kids, that kind of thing," Paul says. "I'd like to date around some, but you've got to worry about safe sex these days, and I hate using rubbers . . ."

"Wait a minute." Gary cuts in. "You mean you want to have sex once a week on schedule?"

"Well, to tell you the truth, Gary"—Paul shifts forward and shakes his head at Gary—"you wouldn't *want* it more than once a week with this woman. Don't get me wrong. I don't hate her or anything, but sex with her just isn't that great. It's something I do to get relief."

We all wait quietly for Paul to go on.

He inhales deeply. "We do it, and I come, but she can't have one anywhere near that soon, so I end up trying all sorts of shit, everything I can think of: oral sex, manual stimulation. It's like I have to work and strain and then *work* even more. By the time she finally has an orgasm, I'm just so happy because now we can *stop!*"

Smiles break out all around, except for Paul, who still looks pained. "I don't think it's my fault, either," he concludes, looking up at Gary.

"What do you mean, Paul?" Mitch asks.

"Well, after I moved out of the house, I went out with this one woman a few times and, my God, that lady would have something like two or three orgasms before I ever even thought about coming! I felt so great about it, like some kind of giant. One other woman"—he pauses for a moment as though he's forgotten her name, and then recovers—"all I had to do was stick my finger in and bingo!"

Gary and Mitch burst out laughing. "Get a patent on that finger, Paul!" Gary throws out. Paul has a huge grin on his face, oblivious to the fact that the men are laughing at him, not with him.

After a pause, Gary recovers and sits up tall in his seat. "I don't have to worry about that these days."

"Oh? . . ."

"Yeah." Suddenly he looks intense. "My girlfriend, Leigh, is—you're not going to believe this—a twenty-nine-year-old virgin!"

Eyebrows shoot up all over the room. Sean seems unfazed. Paul coughs nervously, and we all wait for Gary to continue.

"So you can imagine what it's been like. Sex has become this big issue, a big production because I feel so damn *responsible* now as the guy who is going to take her precious virginity. It's absolutely crazy, and . . ." He pauses. "It's so weird because none of my other girlfriends have been like this. Shit, my last girlfriend just loved sex. It was no big thing. We'd fool around, I'd put it in, she'd come, like two or three times, then I'd come, then we'd order in Chinese and watch the ball game!" Suddenly Paul is very interested.

"Just by fooling around you got her to come three times?" Paul asks with admiration.

"Anyway, I'm not sure I'm completely buying into Leigh's story," Gary continues, ignoring Paul completely. "I'm not sure she's being entirely straight with me." Gary is scratching the side of his long face, and his careful eyes are avoiding the rest of the men. "I mean, maybe she never went all the way before, but she's . . . well, she's too damn good at other things for me to believe that she's totally inexperienced."

"Have you talked to Leigh about any of this?" I ask.

"I tried some, but what's the use? It's just easier not to bother with the sex."

"You *like* that?" Burt asks.

"Ha! You've got to be kidding. Look, guys, I really think I'm just *obsessed* with sex. I've just got to have it. Leigh doesn't understand this. Every day I feel less in love with her because we can't get it on." His eyes shift to the window and stay there. "I think sex is a real problem for me, because I don't put sex and love together. Lots of times when I'm with a woman I don't think about much of anything else." Gary looks back at Burt. "And I never have to love the woman to have good sex. It's just *sex* for me."

"What I want to know," Paul comes in suddenly, "is what's all this emphasis on the 'right amount of foreplay' anyway? I mean, shit, it only takes five minutes, and then, wooosh! and you're in!"

On the couch Burt and Mitch are laughing and slowly shaking their heads. Sean is turning increasingly dark shades of crimson. Gary just glares at Paul.

"Okay, okay!" Paul throws his hands up, "Okay, maybe ten minutes!"

I turn to Paul. "Is that how long you take for foreplay?"

"Uh, well, five minutes or so usually. I don't time it, you know."

The men are still smiling. "I'd say try fifteen minutes, ten minutes minimum," Gary advises, trying to smooth out the situation. He is deliberately polite.

The rest nod in agreement. Paul looks mortified. Sean is sitting on the edge of his seat and still hasn't lost his blush.

"Where are you with this, Sean?" I ask.

"Oh." Sean clears his throat. "Well, I'm still getting used to this kind of talk." He smiles sheepishly and looks around. "Okay. I . . . uh . . . learned a lot from Sandi. I mean, it was nothing for us to spend most of a weekend in bed. And sex was just part of it. Some of our best talks were in bed, just holding each other. Sometimes that would lead into sex. . . . I know that we cared about each other . . . " His words are coming more slowly now. "And she was the first girlfriend I ever really . . . well, loved."

A long silence. I catch his eye. "Sean?"

"Oh, I was . . . thinking about Sandi." He looks across at Paul and sits up a bit. "And I'm also wondering about you. Do you ever, like, do anything spontaneous when you have sex, like what I just described?"

Paul shakes his head.

"What?" Sean asks with disbelief. He is getting angry, too. "Look, Paul, I mean do you ever have sex just on the spur of the moment?"

Paul looks directly into his eyes. "I got blown by a chick I met at Baskin-Robbins once," he says defiantly.

Sean rolls his eyes, and Gary breaks into a big smile: "Don't tell me: flavor of the month, right?" This gets a big laugh all around, with the exception of Paul, who appears not to have heard it.

"So, Sean," Gary looks across the room, "when was your most spontaneous moment?"

"Oh." Sean slowly smiles. "It was with Sandi. In New

York. We were in this highrise building. We got on the elevator and I pushed the button for the top floor, and she just, well, she just *looked* at me, and I understood instantly. We started hugging and kissing and then her hand went up the panel and pushed the "Stop" button and before I knew it we were getting it on right there in the elevator. All it took was one look."

Everyone sits in silence with this for a while.

"Ed, where are you on what we've been discussing?" I ask. I've noticed that Ed has been listening intently but has yet to say anything. He seems to be hiding in Gary's shadow.

"Oh, I've been listening and really relating to what you two were saying about sex," he offers, nodding to Gary and Paul. "Mostly I'm wondering what it is about the way society views sex that puts this expectation on the man to bring a woman to orgasm?"

"That's a legitimate question, Ed," I say. "But I'm wondering, on a less intellectual level, what you yourself are feeling about it."

"Well," Ed responds, "I guess I'm having sort of the same problem with Ellen. After I have an orgasm, I am totally wasted, just out of it, but it feels like there's this job I've got to finish. I was also thinking about this old relationship I used to have, where we had lots of sex, but it was all . . . well, it was all pretty mechanical." He looks over at Paul. "I was relating to you in this sense because you do seem pretty mechanical about it."

Paul sits straight up. "Now, wait a minute! I don't want you to think that I'm just a *machine* or something. I mean, I'll mess around some, do some petting, and—"

"Paul," I interrupt, "could you just listen for a minute?"

"But they're talking like it's the only way I ever—"

"Paul," I say, "can you listen to what they're saying? From the way you describe your sex life, they're getting the impression that it's very mechanical: They're just responding to what you're telling them. It's important that you learn that this is the effect you have on them and on others. Try just listening to their responses."

"Okay." He looks skeptical.

"Well, I didn't have much of a sex problem in my first marriage in the early years," Mitch says softly. This is the first we've heard from Mitch today. He has been quiet, but intensely interested. "By the time we got divorced, there was no sex and no communication at all. Sex was only part of it."

"You know, you're right," Ed says, "it really is a matter of communication. Like with Ellen now. She's just trying to force me into marrying her, and she's using sex as a weapon. It's her way of forcing me."

"Wait, I thought you said it was communication," Gary objects.

"Yeah, it is. She's so moody she spends all her time all by herself reading in the bedroom and then she dismisses me by saying she's just not in the mood. But she does say," he pauses for effect, "that if we get married she'd want sex more!"

Gary groans.

"Then I think about Paul's situation with his wife, and I know why he doesn't want to stay with her," Ed continues.

"I stayed with *my* wife too long, that's for sure," Burt observes.

"I agree," Mitch interjects. "I don't think Paul should stick with Sarah just for the convenience of it, either."

Burt nods and looks at Paul. "Look, twenty years of bad sex is too much already." He halts and seems to have another thought. "You don't have to ask our permission to leave her, you know."

Paul nods carefully and shifts his weight in the chair. "You're right. But God, the guilt. You have no idea . . . "

"Well, I'm listening."

"The thing is: It wasn't always bad with Sarah. Sex was all right when we were first married and getting along pretty well. But then she got depressed, went on medication for it, and it was never good anymore after that." Paul begins to run his hand through his hair. "I was just thinking. Maybe the depression was just her way of leaving me. In some ways we were separated long before I moved out."

Burt smiles. "Paul, remember what I told you about my wife? She just up and divorced me one day. And she was depressed *all* the time. I didn't know what to do about it. Seemed like nothing I did could make her happy. But I'll tell you, her decision to divorce me was the best thing in the world for her. Once she stopped blaming me and took control of her life, she got back on her feet." He adds after a pause: "That's the truth."

"Yeah," Paul says. He seems less than enthusiastic.

Sean isn't finished with Paul yet and has seemed distracted through this whole exchange. "I'm just wondering, Paul, did you and your wife ever hug or just, well, cuddle?"

"Nope." Paul's voice has developed a hard edge. "Never did much of that. And to tell you the truth, one of the nice things about being separated is being able to sleep alone. I mean it. Sarah was always all over me when I tried to sleep. She was always sort of inching closer to me all night long, so I finally bought a king-sized bed so I could get some sleep."

"I'm the same way, you know," Gary offers. He appears to be talking to everybody, not just Paul, now. "I don't like cuddling that much, and I know I tend to jerk in my sleep. If a woman moves over during the night, I practically jump right out of bed!"

This seems to surprise everybody, especially Sean. "Oh God, I loved snuggling with Sandi," Sean exclaims. "That was really one of the best parts."

"You know—" Ed begins, but I hold up a hand.

"Sean?"

Sean is starting to tremble and sink back into the couch. He is on the verge of tears.

"What's going on, Sean?" I say softly.

Sean begins to breathe in short, shallow breaths and is fighting for control. Tears begin streaming down his cheeks as he rests his head back against the couch. He is staring at the ceiling.

We all stay quiet and watch Sean carefully.

Finally, I come in. "Your feelings are okay, Sean, stay with them."

Sean shuts his eyes tight and begins to shake his head. "I . . . I lost my best friend," he whispers. He seems incredulous that he's never realized this before. "Sandi was my best friend. And now she's gone. We'd made all these plans . . ." his voice trails off.

Gary reaches for the tissue box and hands it over to Sean.

As we allow Sean some more time, I realize the session is almost up. I feel it is important to offer some encouragement and support before allowing the session to end.

"Sean," I begin, "what you are going through is similar to grieving the death of a loved one. It's normal, healthy really"— I look around the group—"to let out these deep feelings of loss and hurt." I pause and allow him to absorb this.

"Okay?" I ask.

Sean nods.

"This will continue to hurt for a while, Sean. It just means that you're human. Those feelings are okay. If you can hang in, and keep letting them out, you'll be able to deal with this and get through it."

Sean looks at me. He appears relieved.

INTERPRETATION ────────────

This session reveals the very different approaches of the men to sex, relationships, commitment, and expectations. It is readily apparent that Paul is the most mechanical in his approach to sex. Some of Gary's resentment and anxiety surrounding his lack of a sexual relationship with his girlfriend also surface. Sean seems almost baffled by Paul and Gary as he relates the tenderness and love of his former relationship with a twinge of idealism. Perhaps the most valuable aspect of this session is how clearly we see the lines drawn between men who seek to establish relationships with feelings, commitment, and attachment and those who struggle to avoid them.

From the very outset it is clear that Paul's view of sex is essentially a mechanical one. We hear that sex with his wife is just to "get his rocks off" and is done "just to get relief." For Paul, the purpose of sex is solely to have an orgasm. Much of Paul's view is due to lack of sexual experience and lack of emotional and physical affection in his early years with his mother and father. Sarah was his one and only sexual partner prior to the separation, and this relationship itself was fraught with early sexual difficulties. In fact, early in their marriage Paul and Sarah were both so unprepared for a sexual relationship that the marriage was not consummated for three months.

Clearly Paul's difficulties in his relationship with women go far beyond his lack of appreciation for foreplay. In large measure, Paul has become focused almost exclusively on his own needs to the exclusion of others'. Paul is effectively "stuck" here and has difficulty appreciating the other emotions evident in the group session. When Gary frets about the health of his relationship, Paul alone is intrigued solely by Gary's sexual prowess. Through the whole session Sean senses that Paul has no appreciation for his pain, and he continues to quiz

Paul about cuddling in an attempt to uncover and identify with any common feelings of vulnerability or pain. Paul insists that he never did much cuddling and in fact is glad to have a bed to himself now. This isolation even shows up in the group, as Paul's lack of empathy for Gary's anxiety, Sean's loss, or Ed's marriage proposal dilemma has served to separate Paul from the group. This isolation comes to the surface when Paul vigorously objects to the idea that in sex he is just a machine. He is hurt that the men don't understand him, but even more important he is beginning to feel increasingly secluded from the group because of his own lack of a sense of sharing with group members. Paul wants to belong.

Gary wants to belong, too, and so we are hearing, for the first time, about a very difficult area for Gary: his anxiety and confusion about what to do in his relationship with Leigh. Her virginity has become a severe burden for him and an obstacle for them both. Gary is both resentful ("I feel so damn responsible") and concerned ("as the guy who's going to take her precious virginity") and obviously confused about the direction things will take. It is encouraging that Gary feels comfortable enough to bring this up: it is a positive sign of his growing trust of the other men.

Sean finds all the talk of sex and intimacy to be a bit unsettling. He does, however, make a good adjustment and goes on to share with the rest of the group a lot of the tenderness and caring he felt for Sandi. It is important that the other men hear this from Sean because it so dominates Sean's outlook in the group. He is still suffering from a difficult loss: the pain and rejection of his first love. As the youngest member of the group, Sean retains some measure of youthful idealism: he believes he came from an ideal family, and he tends to think in ideal terms. The loss of Sandi had a shattering effect not only on Sean's emotional state but also on his entire idealistic view. The men now see this: As the conversation shifts to cuddling, the softer, warmer feelings touch Sean's

sadness and reveal the extent of his loss and his hurt at being
jilted. Sean is able to release these feelings in a very healthy
way by crying.

The very different reactions of Paul and Sean to cuddling, closeness, and bed-sharing highlight a central and important difference between Paul and Gary, on the one hand,
and Sean, Burt, and Mitch, on the other. Both Paul and Gary
want to be left alone when they are asleep, or are near sleep,
a time when we are all quite vulnerable. They are also the
two men who have a great deal of difficulty with feelings,
especially negative feelings, and seem to be content to have
sex without emotion or commitment. In fact, both Paul and
Gary seek relationships that are devoid of feelings because
they are less demanding and less threatening. Sean, Burt, and
Mitch, on the other hand, relish the warmth of their partners
and do not fear the vulnerability of this position. These are
the men who have learned from the positive experiences of
their early marriages (Burt and Mitch) or relationship (Sean)
and are content to seek out and reinforce these feelings. All
six men find themselves struggling with issues of commitment
and attachment to women as they explore these relationships.

SESSION 4

//

SEX: LEARNING THE WOMAN'S SIDE

"Paul called in sick today," I announce as soon as everyone has settled in. "He says he caught a flu, so he won't be here today."

After a moment Ed looks over at me. "You know, I think we may have beat up on him too much last week." The others smile with recognition.

"Really, I know I was a little pissed at him," Sean offers. Burt and Mitch exchange an uncomfortable look. It occurs to me that as irritating as Paul can be to the group, he does fire everybody up and keeps things going. We miss him today.

"Anything else?" I ask Sean. He shakes his head and looks out the window.

"Well, I know how I feel," Burt says suddenly. "Frustrated! I've been going with JoAnn for nearly a year. She's real expressive, always says what's on her mind, right then and there." He looks around to Mitch and then to me. "And lately, it seems like she's always criticizing me."

"About what in particular?" I ask.

"Oh, communication, sex, you name it." He and Mitch exchange a smile. "I feel like I'm doing better at sharing my feelings, but I still get tongue-tied when she jumps on my case."

"How's that?" Gary asks with a frown. He looks as if he's worried he may have missed something.

Burt looks over his crossed legs at Gary. "Well, one reason it's hard to come right back with answers is that a lot of times she's griping about our sex life." He coughs nervously but quickly shakes it off. "Once, before I met JoAnn, I had a problem with impotence. But after some work with Al," he nods at me, "I managed to get over that, and for a long time the sex with JoAnn was just great." He smiles.

"So what's the problem?" Gary persists.

"Once JoAnn got pregnant, and got an abortion. I think it may have been because she felt it was too early in our relationship." Suddenly Burt looks pained. He uncrosses his legs and leans forward. "The whole thing was, God, it was emotionally grueling. I really want to be a father, you know, and I'm already forty-five." He shakes his head and spreads his hands open as though he's pleading with Gary. "I wonder, maybe I'm already too old to be a good father!"

We all wait quietly for Burt to go on.

"So here's the deal. JoAnn is thinking about marriage and a baby." Slowly he begins to shake his head again. He is examining the pattern in the rug. "But she's not sure. She wants to get her career going, she's finishing up her M.A. now, before having kids." He looks up and catches Gary's eye. "The problem is, when she gets hesitant, I start questioning the relationship. Then she gets scared I really want a child more than I want her."

"Is she right?" Ed asks quietly.

"Well, sometimes, like now, when she's criticizing me all the time, I think maybe she's right, that I do want a child more than I want our relationship. And I have to decide that pretty soon, because the lease on her place is running out, and we're talking about her moving in with me."

Gary appears surprised, and after a time he looks away.

Ed nods. "I can understand that constant criticism. It seems that no matter what I say or do lately, Ellen always gives me hell for, well, for being the way I am. Then she stomps off and buries her nose in a book."

A shadow of pain crosses Mitch's face.

"Mitch?" I ask.

"I'm listening," he says reluctantly. "Listening, but not liking it," he says. Mitch's large frame seems to have shrunk a bit. "It reminds me of my own marriage." He pauses. "For six years my wife always told me that she didn't need orgasms to enjoy sex. And you know, at first I'd ask her if she had one just to check it out, and finally she told me to quit bothering her about it. So I did! I believed her." Mitch looks surprised about this now. "So one day," he turns and looks directly at Burt, "we're fighting about something, and all of a sudden she starts bitching about our sex life and how I'm so selfish. I couldn't believe it! So I just stopped trying." He throws his hands up in resignation. "Just stopped completely."

"Did she ever bring up the subject again, Mitch?" I ask.

"No. And it was downhill from there. We never had sex again. That was it. Six months later we were divorced."

Suddenly the room feels very heavy. It's already dark outside in the November evening, and the mood in the room begins to reflect it.

"You know," Burt interjects, trying to brighten up the mood, "it's not easy to talk things out at a time like that, Mitch. I mean, lately JoAnn complains that I always come too soon. She likes lots of foreplay, which is fine with me, but by the time I get inside her, I've been excited for quite a while, and it's hard for me to hold back."

"Have you tried anything, any methods, to hold back?" Ed asks.

"JoAnn was talking about this 'pinch method': stopping and pinching the tip of your penis to keep yourself from coming." Burt seems pretty skeptical about it.

"I'd say the best thing is to keep things simple, Burt," I say. "The last thing you need is anxiety about some new technique. If it seems like work, something you have to stop and think about, you're going to resent having sex." After a moment I add, "How about if you just stopped the friction for a little while?"

Burt's face is blank.

"You don't have to withdraw," I continue, "just rest a little. I bet she'd be glad to wait."

Burt nods slowly. "But remember, now that we use rubbers, I have to think about practical stuff, like making sure we haven't run out of the damn things, getting the packet open, putting the stupid thing on . . ."

"That makes sense," I agree. "How about using the condoms to your advantage?"

"Are you kidding?"

"Not at all," I respond. "Maybe using the condom could be a part of foreplay. For example, why should it be *your* job to put the rubber on? JoAnn could play with it, flirt with it, use it on you like a feather."

Burt is staring at me like he's yet to hear anything he can use.

"Look, Burt," I continue, "right now you're thinking of the rubber as something that's in the way, but just imagine if it's rolled onto you slowly, sensually, teasingly. . . . A condom doesn't have to be just a tool for . . . uh, your tool."

This gets a smile out of Burt. "Well, I never thought

about it. It does seem like a lot more fun than we're having now, anyway."

This is so important I decide to involve everyone.

"Burt, how about a role-play?"

He nods.

"I'll play JoAnn, and you be you." I pause for a minute, then begin again as JoAnn: "Listen, Burt, I hate to bring this up again, but you keep leaving me so unsatisfied and frustrated. You have the orgasm, you hop out of bed, go to the bathroom, and get rid of the rubber—and I'm lying here waiting, wishing you'd never gotten out of bed to begin with! I want us to work this out so that we can both be satisfied."

"JoAnn," he responds, "you know I want that, too. Don't I always get back in bed and hold you and help you have an orgasm? You're good at making yourself come, which is fine with me. I guess I thought it was okay with you, too."

"Sure, it's okay sometimes, just not every time. If I'm making too much of an issue of it, tell me. But I do want you to hear my side."

"To be honest, JoAnn, lots of times 'telling your side' feels more like putting me down, and then I don't know what to say."

"Well, I don't have all the answers, either. But sometimes I wonder if you come so fast because you're somehow mad at me."

"I don't think I'm mad at you, JoAnn. It's just that sometimes it does seem like you're about to come, your breathing changes, you move differently. So I go ahead, and you don't come! Then I try to keep going, but it's hard as hell to continue, and I don't think I'm any different from most men. But after all that foreplay—"

"Burt, you make it sound like you're just doing the foreplay as some kind of favor to me!"

Burt gives me a hopeless look, but the other men are smiling. They've all heard this at some time in their lives.

I turn to Mitch. "Next?" He shrugs and nods.

I begin as Mitch's first wife, Janet: "You just don't care about me, Mitch. You're so selfish. You have your precious orgasm and that's the end of it. I don't even get a chance to get worked up!"

"Well, Janet," Mitch answers with his hands stretched wide open, "you always told me you didn't *care* if you had one or not!"

"My God! If you're so into yourself that you can't see that I—Oh great, now I look like the bitch. Just don't bother me about it anymore! Just drop it!"

Mitch stops the role-play. "That's all there was, Al. We never talked about it again, never had sex again." He looks away. "I couldn't have gotten it up anyway."

"Mitch, remember that the most common factor in impotence is anger, so this is perfectly normal."

"I know." He still looks a little chagrined.

I turn to Ed. "Ed?"

"Al?" He laughs nervously.

"Your turn. You be you. I'll be Ellen. Ed, you always avoid making love with me whenever you're mad. If I say anything negative at all, you won't come near me."

"I don't think that's true at all, Ellen."

"Well, that's how it feels, so why would any woman try to be open with you the way you want her to?"

"But I still don't get why you won't open up to me!"

"Maybe because it scares me. Maybe because if I let myself be vulnerable, you might leave."

"Well, I'm scared, too, Ellen. I worry that if we don't open up to each other now, we'll have a big blowup later. I think you hold in all your feelings, especially when you're mad, and that sometime after we're married, you'll sneak up and clobber me with all of it! So how do I get you to share feelings with me now?"

"Guarantee me that if I do open up, you won't leave me."

"How am I supposed to do that, Ellen?"

"Marry me!" I answer triumphantly. The men all laugh knowingly. Ed turns scarlet. He has taken it seriously, as it was meant.

I look over at Gary, who is on the edge of his seat. He is eager to go next, so we begin with me as his girlfriend, Leigh.

"I gave myself to you, Gary! I thought you'd understand what it meant for me to let you be the *first.*"

Gary answers almost sleepily, as though he's already been through this discussion a hundred times. "So why did you? You're almost thirty, for God's sake! It's not like I forced you! Hey, you don't want to have sex anymore? No problem! We won't have sex!"

"Just like a man!" I say, falsetto.

Gary breaks out of the role-play. "You got her pegged, Al. That's exactly what she'd say."

"Okay, Gary," I say, "how about her side? Tell me what you think she really wanted to hear from *you.*"

"Oh boy, okay," Gary says, uncrossing his legs. "Uh . . . how about, 'Oh Leigh, you're the most wonderful lay I ever had. I sure do appreciate that you saved yourself just for me and I just can't *tell* you how privileged I feel.' "

The others are snickering, but Gary's on a roll: "And . . . uh, let's see . . . 'Oh, thank you, thank you, thank you. Let me get down on my knees and tell you how I never thought somebody would save herself for twenty-nine *long* years and then decide that I'm the special one who gets it. If I'd only known, I would have made it really special. I would have sent out for flowers, maybe a little brass band. Oh, please *do* forgive me.'

"That what you mean, Al?" Gary asks, grinning. He's almost out of breath.

"Well, is that really what you think she wanted to hear?"

"Yeah, it is, come to think of it. Maybe a *little* less exaggerated," Gary answers. He's gaining his composure again, and he's slid back on the couch. "But you know, the thing is that I *didn't* feel all that. So what do I do? Go ahead and say all this stuff because she wants to hear it?" He looks around the room. "What are we supposed to be doing in this group, anyway—trying to be open and honest or learning lines to use on women?"

"We're here for honesty," I say. "You've still got to be you. But you'll have an advantage if you understand more about how she feels, regardless of how you choose to react to it."

Gary acknowledges this with a shrug. There are several other nods from the men on the couch.

I look over at Sean in his corner of the sectional, and he returns my gaze. "Ready to give it a shot?"

"Sure."

I begin again, this time as Sandi, his former girlfriend: "Sean, I've learned a lot of nice things with you about sex. But now I hesitate to have anything to do with you, because you're always grasping at every little hint that I might want to be your lover again. I need time to think. I have to consider my career and, well, lots of other things."

"Well, Sandi, at least that's more honest than you've been in a long time."

"You're right. I do wish it could have ended a little more nicely between us."

"But Sandi, if you'd be more up front with me like this, maybe we could still work things out."

"Maybe, Sean. I just need time to think about it, okay?"

"That's fair enough."

We end the role-play here. "Any reactions?" I ask in general, looking around.

"Aside from the fact that you deserve an Academy Award for Best Actress?" Gary quips.

I smile and wait.

"Well, I got a lot out of it," Gary picks up again. "I know that's how Leigh thinks—and I just now realized I can't handle it. I'm going to have to end it with her."

"That's your only choice?"

Gary seems mildly surprised. "I think so."

"What about the possibility of talking with her about how each of you feels about all that 'special stuff'?" I ask. "Maybe by having a talk like that, she'll understand better how your feelings about sex differ from hers." I pause. "You might have a chance to expand the relationship rather than run from it," I add.

"I don't know. I can see what she's saying." He shakes his head, looks disgusted. "Seems I should have learned all this relationship stuff in high school, like everybody else."

Ed looks over at me. "My reaction is that I kept hoping you were going to give me some advice on how to get Ellen to open up. I still haven't figured out how."

"Well, role playing is not really about giving advice," I point out as I look around at the other men. "Something did occur to me as we were doing the role-play, Ed: Are *you* really sharing your feelings with her? It might be a good idea for you to consider setting the tone by volunteering more of your own feelings—and I don't mean talking about intellectual things."

Ed nods slowly. He appears to be giving this some careful consideration.

I notice we only have a few moments left, so I try to wrap things up with Ed.

"This kind of problem isn't one you want to try solving after marriage," I tell him. "You need to learn to start communicating now—it's the only way you'll find out if she's really the woman you want to marry."

"I understand."

INTERPRETATION

The multiple role playing in tonight's lively session has high-lighted many of the difficult areas in these men's relationships and lives. As is often the case in role playing, it has been especially useful in helping the men understand their partners' positions, both how and why they feel the way they do. Several different elements of these relationships surfaced during the role playing: criticism and the damage it does to relationships; the confusion, poor communication, and resulting misunderstanding in sex and lovemaking; and the anger, frustration, and pain of failed relationships and marriages.

Tonight's session actually began on a slightly different note, however: Paul's absence. After his experience in the group last week (where Paul felt not only isolated but misunderstood as well), it is likely that the explanation for his absence goes beyond his illness. It has been my experience that there is a strong psychosomatic aspect to many illnesses, particularly those that are easily contracted: colds, flu, and the like. Paul's experience in childhood, where such misunderstanding or anger was punished by isolation because he had been "bad," could have laid the groundwork for feeling sick: here was something that would serve to isolate and protect him from the group. It is indeed regretful that Paul missed the session: he would have benefitted handsomely from it.

In fact, the real issues in this session surfaced as soon as Burt started with his one-word description of his mood: "Frustrated!" Clearly Burt and JoAnn are locked into a difficult position. Burt feels threatened and confused by what he feels is criticism from JoAnn, while JoAnn herself is frustrated and unsatisfied with some of Burt's sexual practices: bounding out of bed soon after his orgasm and occasional premature ejaculation. What really drives this dilemma is the dynamic of their encounters: JoAnn raises an issue by criticizing something Burt has done; Burt in turn takes this as an attack and immediately goes on the defensive. There is little doubt that the relaxed and comfortable mood needed for sensuality and sexuality vanishes here. The culprit in this case is criticism. I have come to believe that there simply is no such thing as constructive criticism in such cases. In most cases such phrases as "You're not satisfying me," "You only care about yourself," or "You're not good enough" immediately drive the partner to a defensive position. It is much more useful and constructive to use similar phrases to refer back to oneself: "I'm not feeling loved," "I'm frustrated," or "I feel neglected" not only are less threatening statements but they open the door to frank and open discussion as well. Not coincidentally, these are the phrases I've chosen for the women in my role playing. As we have seen, they have had the effect of prompting more open and honest dialogue.

One result of this dialogue is that Burt and JoAnn reveal a lack of understanding of what annoys or upsets the other. Burt does what he and many men feel is the natural thing after orgasm: get the condom off before he loses his erection and it falls off. It hasn't occurred to him that he needs to tell JoAnn this. Likewise, JoAnn has never let Burt know that this little excursion away from the bed leaves her feeling alone and abandoned. Unfortunately, such objections rarely surface until a whole multitude of minor complaints have accumulated and crossed some magic threshold, at which point a whole cascade of grievances spill out at once: "You have an orgasm too fast," "I can't stand it when you get out of bed like that," "I don't like not being able to continue" all come out at a staccato pace, and often leave the man, especially Burt, at a loss for words. It is important that such concerns be aired as soon as possible and not be left to accumulate and fester. This way they can be dealt with immediately and the two people can head off painful confrontations.

An excellent example of failed communications is demonstrated in the role-play with Mitch. Like most men, Mitch wants to bring his partner to orgasm. I know from my work with Mitch that he has asked Janet how he could help her to have an orgasm, and Janet replied that she could enjoy sex without an orgasm. What doesn't surface until later is that Janet took Mitch's question as pressure for her to have an orgasm, and her reply is designed to simply take away this pressure. Mitch proceeds with his own satisfaction believing that Janet really doesn't need an orgasm, and the stage is set for the confrontation we observe in the role-play. A more straightforward reply by Janet in this case could have resulted in a different outcome: experimentation, mutual support, and encouragement.

Of all the men in the group, Gary probably has the best idea of what a woman wants in bed. Yet Gary's problem is an entirely different one. Gary is avoiding a strong connection to Leigh because he fears commitment and above all wants to keep from encouraging her in any way. In fact, Gary fears the feelings associated with commitment because he equates such feelings with addiction. Gary's way of keeping the emotions down is to use humor and stay light about the subject both in the role-play and in the relationship. At one point he even suggests that the solution is to break off the relationship. I immediately encourage Gary to consider options other than escaping or running away from Leigh, as they are likely to serve him better in the long run.

A lot of work in therapy is about considering other options. The realization that these options exist often grows directly from the kind of honest and straightforward dialogue we have had in tonight's role playing.

///

WHEN MEN CRY

"When do you ever get over breaking up?" Sean asks in a slightly quavering voice.

In his worn jeans and tennis shoes, Sean looks the part of a typical student. Tonight he is sitting back on the couch, staring up at nothing in particular. His young, round face looks troubled. The other men are watching him carefully. Nobody speaks.

"There is no definite time period, Sean," I come in finally. I look around at the others, quite aware that each has a similar story of rejection and pain from some time in his life. "Anybody here have a similar experience?"

"Well, how long were you going together?" Paul asks with sort of a shrug.

Sean looks up at him warily. "A little over a year . . . uh, a year and two months," he says softly.

"What?" Paul exclaims. "A year and two months! Man, that's nothing. Try getting over a twenty-year marriage!"

"Hey, she was my first love!" Sean throws back, glaring straight at Paul. Burt and Gary exchange a smile and shake their heads, clearly in response to Paul's comment. Sean sits up suddenly. "And maybe . . . maybe we had more love in our twelve . . . uh, fourteen months than you had in your twenty-year marriage!"

Sean appears to be gaining some energy from this exchange. He's become a bit wide-eyed and his pale complexion is gaining some color.

"I've had a couple of letters from her, too, you know." Suddenly Sean frowns and seems temporarily lost. "They don't say much, though."

"Is there anything about wanting to get together again?" Burt asks from Sean's right elbow.

Sean shakes his head slowly. The energy has drained out of him by now.

"What do you want them to say, Sean?" I ask.

"I . . ." Sean stops abruptly and looks away. He is fighting tears but is determined to answer. "I want them to say that we'll get . . . get back together again." These last words break his resistance, and he begins to sob quietly.

A lot of uncomfortable glances are exchanged around the room. Sean waves his hand in my general direction: "Go on to someone else."

Now most of the men are sitting quite still as though they want to respect Sean's pain. Gary, however, looks as though he's about to climb the wall.

"Where are you, Gary?"

"What?" He's startled by the question.

I take a moment to shift my look in his direction. "How does seeing Sean's pain, his raw emotion, make you feel?"

"Awful!" Gary shudders. Something in Gary's tone makes this entirely believable. "I know how shitty I felt when I got dumped a couple of years ago." He takes a deep breath. "It was very bad news. Remember, I told you guys about her. She was my 'addiction.' God, I was down on my knees with my arms around her legs and I just wouldn't let her go!" He ponders this for a long moment, and then looks up at Sean. "It's worse being dumped. Being the 'dumpee.'"

Paul is nodding his head vigorously.

"Actually, I let myself cry," he says straight to Sean. "It helped."

Sean cracks a weak smile but looks away.

"You know"—Gary brightens suddenly—"there's this lady that lives above me, and sometimes she gets into a snarling round with her boyfriend, and afterward I can hear her crying and moaning for half the damn night. *Nobody* hurts like *this* lady, let me tell you!" He looks around, but nobody says anything. "Well, I think, Oh my God, at least I don't feel as bad as she feels!" He slides back on the couch, seemingly satisfied with this explanation.

Ed is frowning at Gary as though he has no idea why he got off on this story in the first place. He looks at me for an instant and then down at his right foot, which is crossed over his left leg, Ed's perpetual pose. "Okay," he begins. "*My* biggest breakup"—he stops and looks at Sean—"it wasn't my first love, was about three years ago." Ed is speaking in a very matter-of-fact voice, almost like a reporter. "As far as I was concerned, this was *it*, *the* relationship. I was just sure we were going to get married. One night, right out of the blue, she dumped my ass. I was stunned." Ed looks to his right, where Gary is staring at him, listening intently. "I remember, I just felt . . . numb."

"So you're a 'dumpee,' too. Did you cry about it?" Gary asks.

"I don't really cry about anything," Ed replies. This appears to surprise even him. "I do have dreams about crying, though. I dreamed I cried for my father once. It was a powerful dream: bitter, horrible sorrow."

Burt has cocked his head and looks puzzled. Ed sees him and realizes probably some explanation is called for.

"For most of my life my father, my parents, were in politics." He begins. "They were always away from the house. You know, going to parties, receptions, functions, and being seen. Of course they were both drinking like crazy the whole time, and one day it all just came crashing down: my father lost his job, his career, his whole life, really."

"How would your father feel if you were to cry?" I ask, trying to bring Ed back to his emotions.

Ed looks at me for a moment and then grows quiet. He is thinking. "He wouldn't take me seriously. Actually . . . you know, he'd walk away."

"Why do you think you were crying in the dream?"

"I'm not really sure if it was for myself or my father, his career, the fact that we were never close, whatever. I couldn't say."

"Ed, your deep sadness *is* coming out in your dreams," I point out. "This is how you are dealing with it. Your dreams are very powerful. I would encourage you to let yourself cry when you're feeling it."

Ed nods.

"Ed, let me ask you something," Mitch interjects. This is the first we've heard from Mitch today. "When you broke up"—he looks hesitant for a moment—"uh . . . when the woman broke up with you, did you ever talk about the reasons why, about what went wrong?"

"Nope. I just remember going home after that date in a daze." He looks Mitch straight in the eye. "I never spoke to her again."

"I want to say something," Sean injects. He is leaning forward now and is running his hands through his blond hair. "I really feel . . . dumb. Crying here. Before I came to group," he coughs, "really, it's been all week, I've been debating with myself: Should I bring all this mess up or just let it go?"

"What was your debate?" I ask. "Say it out loud."

"Okay." Sean pushes his hair away from his forehead, and I see that his swollen eyes have vanished. He has brightened considerably. "On the one side it was like—how would it sound to talk about the breakup? I mean, everybody here has been married six years, twenty years, or whatever; they've got all this experience." He clears his throat and continues. "But then, on the other side, I realized that I really do need to say something and the stuff in my life is important, too."

"Any reactions?" I look around at the men.

"Actually, I'm glad you did say something, Sean," Burt offers. "I sit here next to you every session, and you always look so preoccupied or . . . distracted, or whatever." He smiles. "Now I know what's been going on."

"Yeah, well, I don't think anybody ever gets over a love completely," Gary shrugs. "I know I think about Liz every day of my life."

Burt catches my eye and smiles. We had been discussing this very issue in individual therapy just yesterday.

"In therapy we imply that you get over it," I now say, "but I'm not so sure, personally. I think you always carry some love for the person you gave your heart to. Still," I add, "it's important to detach our feelings from one love relationship so we can focus that energy on others."

Burt nods, and Mitch smiles at me. He is leaning back on the couch with his arms spread wide.

"So," Paul says, looking at Sean, "do you go to pieces over other things, too?"

Sean looks at me then back at Paul. "Not at all," he assures him. "In fact, I've never fallen apart about anything else at all!"

"Do you cry, Paul?" I ask.

"Nope. Never do."

"What do you do when you're upset, then?"

"I get depressed." Paul is looking at me a bit defiantly.

"The two can go together, you know."

Paul doesn't say anything for several seconds. "My parents never showed any emotion about anything at all." He scratches his face and looks over at Sean. "I went out with a woman for two years in college. After we split, I couldn't do anything. I didn't date anyone for seven months. I just didn't have the energy. Then Sarah came along and I married her right out of college."

"So how are things with Sarah, Paul?" This is Gary, who's been carefully following Paul's relationship with his wife.

"I'm still seeing her—once or twice a week, remember?" Paul replies, looking over at Gary. "But she's the one who wants the sex."

Gary breaks into a broad grin. "So you're *servicing* her, huh?"

The whole couch breaks out laughing at this. Even Paul chuckles.

"Paul, you seem a bit out of it today," I say after things have settled down.

"Just been a bit down. My flu."

"Hey, Paul, if you were home with Sarah, would she be fixing you chicken soup?" Gary is grinning at Paul all over again.

"Are you kidding? She hates it when I'm sick. She pretty much ignores me."

"You know, your flu made you miss a great session last week," Burt points out. In the role-plays, Al played every girlfriend we ever had and didn't have to change his dress once!"

"I sort of like the one he had on," Gary cracks with a smile.

INTERPRETATION ————————

In tonight's session, the pain and uncertainty of Sean's situation with Sandi laid the groundwork for the other men—specifically Gary, Ed, and Paul—to discuss two issues that are especially powerful for men: loss of love and control, on the one hand, and the ability (or willingness) to cry, on the other.

Sean, too, finds himself struggling with a powerful and profound loss in his broken relationship with Sandi. For the first time Sean finds the courage to speak up and start the group, as he is driven by the pain of this loss and a desire for support from the other men. In many respects, this group is foreign and detached to Sean; late in the session he describes how he feels here: a younger man with little of the experience or wisdom of the older group members. But nonetheless Sean still finds the strength not only to start the session but also to face Paul down when confronted. In this he is eager to defend the intensity of his love for Sandi. As his first relationship, this was the most powerful love experience of Sean's life. The intensity of love, like that of any emotion, depends on the individual, and Sean's ability to love grew from the love of his parents. In fact, Sean did come from a very physical family where a lot of touching and contact was the norm, so this more evident affection, an element missing in the families of the other men, allows Sean to express outwardly the warmer feelings, sadness and hurt, in crying. Sean is alone among the group members in his ability to cry in such a situation. It is much more of a struggle for the others.

The strongest resistance in this area is from Paul. In fact, Paul, unlike the other men, is unwilling even to extend an element of understanding or empathy to Sean—he dismisses the entire episode ("Man, that's nothing") by comparing it with his own dilemma ("try getting over a twenty-year marriage!"). Later in the session we learn that Paul never cries at all but just gets depressed or withdrawn. This is a natural result of Paul's family setting in childhood, where emotion was simply not expressed: no crying and virtually no displayed emotion of any kind.

The two men also have difficulty connecting on any empathic level: Paul dismisses Sean's pain as a minor nuisance, while Sean himself has little appreciation for the magnitude of Paul's own loss, which extends far beyond just the loss of love and really constitutes the loss of an entire identity: husband, father, provider, and family man. Yet unlike Sean, Paul is extremely hesitant to express these feelings in any way that will make him vulnerable or will involve crying. So although the two men certainly have shared experiences of pain and loss, their different modes of expression prevent them from connecting on any meaningful, supportive level.

Gary, however, has been hurt badly before, and he has found crying, though not in therapy sessions, to be a healing release. The important difference between Gary and Paul here is that Gary is willing to admit to the group that he has felt rejected, unwanted, and unworthy as the "dumpee." This admission is a way of connecting to Sean and providing some support, and a difficult admission for a man to make. Traditionally, men want to see themselves in control. When a woman initiates a breakup, this puts the man in a powerless, vulnerable position. In fact, Gary's story reveals just how far this feeling of helplessness and desperation can go: he found himself begging her not to leave him.

Ed also relates how he was stunned by a woman who dumped him several years ago. The suddenness of the announcement, the fact that it was unexpected, seemed to surprise Ed more than the rejection. He does not react by crying or hurting but rather by abandoning the entire issue: he never speaks to the woman again. This was his way of coping, but it was not a healthy solution. With this choice Ed never learned why the relationship failed—even though in the session Mitch thought it important enough to make a special effort to ask about it—nor was he able to learn how to avoid some of the same problems in his future relationships. Perhaps most important, Ed's refusal to experience the pain means that he carries a lot of hurt and sadness around with him. The fear of this happening again is part of Ed's difficulty in committing to Ellen. Yet he *does* have strong feelings, which come out in the dreams. We see these strong emotions in the dreams where he cries bitterly over his father and his early life with him. The fear of this happening again is part of Ed's difficulty in committing to Ellen.

Dreams are a potent medium for the subconscious mind and reveal a great deal about our inner selves and lives. I consider dreams to be valuable sources of material for work in therapy, and generally I will spend a great deal of time with patients in dream analysis and discussion. I have also found that the material in dreams is virtually always about the dreamer. In Ed's dream the pain is coming from inside: Ed was crying for himself and his loss of his relationship with his father and a yearning for a close, strong bond to him.

The repression of crying among men is common. All men learn at a very early age that crying due to pain, fear, or emotional trauma is not the thing to do. As young boys we all want to be "grown up," so we begin to suppress the urge to cry and continue to suppress it well into adulthood. Paul and Ed do so today, as we have seen in the session. Gary, Mitch, and Burt all defend crying as healthy and have cried at various times in their adult lives, yet they would not cry in a group session. Sean has cried in our session tonight and in doing so demonstrated the dilemma a man faces: Sean is very worried about looking "dumb" for crying, even though it is his natural response. It is gratifying that by the end of tonight's session the positive aspects of crying have become apparent: Sean is not only visibly relieved and alert, he is also more responsive and engaging in the group discussions.

MARRIAGE, COMMITMENT, AND REMARRIAGE

"I had a good weekend for a change," Paul announces to no one in particular. Paul is encased in one of his conservative blue suits that has gone a bit shiny with time. He appears satisfied with this announcement and looks around the group, but nobody responds.

"Yeah?" Gary says finally.

"Uh-huh." Paul looks vaguely relieved. "I went out with Sarah on Saturday and I had a date with this woman from the office, Annette, on Sunday night." Paul is beaming.

Burt meanwhile has leaned forward and is pulling nervously at his pants leg. I notice that Burt has on a bright blue and yellow wool sweater tonight, unusually colorful for Burt. Something Paul has said has got him going.

"Look, Paul, I don't want you to take this the wrong way, but . . . well, when are you going to make up your mind?"

"You think this is easy?" Paul is looking right at Burt.

"Look, I *know* it's not easy, I just wonder when you're going to move past it all." Burt has his hands spread wide open as though he's pleading with Paul.

"It's *not* easy," Paul continues as though Burt had said nothing. "Just being around Sarah for any time gives me the willies. But I can't bring myself to actually divorce her." Paul stops abruptly and looks over Burt and out the windows. "You know, I kind of like what we've got now: I get to see her on weekends, and I'm still free to do what I want the rest of the time." He looks back at Burt and smiles. "She wanted to know where I was on Sunday."

"So where is this going?" Burt asks. He is growing a bit impatient with Paul.

"Look, I've already stated my position to her. She knows it. Let *her* file for divorce." He shrugs. "Save me all the guilt."

Mitch is shaking his head. "No way. You'll still feel guilty."

Silence.

"Look, what's the deal with sex," Gary interjects, breaking the silence. "Didn't you two agree to just sleep with each other?"

Paul nods. "Yet Sarah must know that if an act of God lands another woman in my bed, I'm going to sleep with her."

Burt looks away and shakes his head. He probably suspects, as the others do, that it will be an act of Paul that lands a woman in his bed.

"Do you *like* sleeping with Sarah?" Gary asks with a grimace. He wants to stay with Paul on this, although his tone reveals he already knows the answer.

"Not really. It's for her, after all."

Gary nods. "Leigh and I ended up having sex again Saturday night." He shuffles forward on the couch and suddenly grows very intense. He looks over in Paul's direction. "I *don't* want to sleep with this woman! I don't even like lying next to a woman in bed. I can't get to sleep with her right there in my face!" He has both hands open wide about a half inch from his face. "I'm not used to it and . . . it really pisses me off!" Gary is flushed a bit, and now both of his hands are clenched into fists.

"What happens when you do sleep with a woman?" I ask.

"I wake up every time she touches me," he mumbles. "You know, I used to think I was royally fucked-up because of this, but not anymore. I've just sort of accepted it." He shrugs. "The other women do, too."

"Huh?" Burt asks with a frown.

"Well, I should say my *last* girlfriend did. I didn't mind sleeping with her, actually." Gary has calmed down considerably and is actually smiling a bit. "But then, she was sort of small."

"What did *she* say about it," Burt asks, "your not liking to sleep with women, I mean."

"She said she understood. She also broke up with me, so who knows?"

"Yeah, well it bothers me, too, Gary," Ed says with a nod, "especially when it's hot and you get all sweaty." Ed is leaning back on the couch with his body angled roughly in Gary's direction. "One thing about Ellen: During the night she sort of inches over towards me, and at some point I have to wake her up and ask her to move over or she's going to push me right out of bed and out onto the floor!" A wide grin spreads across his face.

"So how *are* things with Ellen?" Mitch asks. "Get her that ring yet?"

Ed smiles. "We had a really nice dinner last night. It was her birthday."

"So what did you get her, Ed?" Mitch and Ed are just grinning at each other now.

"Actually, I bought her some hand-carved jewelry boxes she admired from a trip we took awhile ago."

I shudder with the vision of Ellen excitedly opening the

first small jewelry box in anticipation of a ring and finding it empty.

"Did she like them?" Mitch asks.

"She loved them." Pause. "She wants to move out of my apartment."

Nobody says anything.

"Because of the boxes?" I venture.

"I don't think so."

"How do you feel about her moving?" I ask.

"Well, it *does* bother me," Ed responds as he scratches behind his ear for what seems like an eternity. He looks at me. "I'm not as upset this time, compared to the first time— that is, when I first came in to therapy."

"I don't understand this. What's the problem?" Paul demands.

"Look, Paul, I'm just not sure I want to get married. I can't make a connection to Ellen. She won't talk to me." He's shaking his head. He looks like a young professor disappointed in a student. "I can't discuss anything, art, literature, that sort of stuff, with her at all—"

"Wait a minute," Paul interjects, uncrossing his legs and leaning forward. "You know what I want to do? I just want to reach over there and take you by the shoulders and just shake you silly! Make up your mind! What's the big deal, anyway? You two get along, you have good sex. Marry her already!"

"Were you listening to me at all, Paul?"

"Yeah, sure, you can't talk to her? Okay. Cheat on her by going to some Mensa meetings or something. You like her except for a couple of things, right? I don't like a damn thing about Sarah; well, I *care* about her, that sort of thing but . . ." Paul pauses. "I never really *liked* her." He gestures in Ed's general direction. "At least you *like* Ellen."

"Sure, I like Ellen. I think the two of us have different ideas about relationships, though, Paul," Ed responds, a little cautiously. He looks as if he's afraid to set Paul off again.

"Yeah, okay. But here's another question for you: Do you *know* what you really want from marriage?"

Ed frowns. "I do think about it a lot, in case you couldn't tell."

"No, no, I understand. That's not what I mean. It's just that I think marriages work out if people really believe in the institution of marriage." Paul shifts his weight in his chair and seems lost in thought for a brief moment. "Look at me," he continues. "I got into a marriage without even thinking about any of the stuff you're agonizing over, and even though I'm separated now—and I see Sarah every week—I felt more secure five years ago in a bad marriage than I feel right now!"

"Paul, Ed can't marry Ellen and just expect her to change," Burt protests.

"So marry her the way she is."

"No way," Burt responds. "It would never work."

Ed is watching this exchange go on like a Ping-Pong game.

"Can you say more, Burt?" I prompt.

"Sure," he says, smiling weakly at me. "I just don't think people change much unless there's some big event, like a major catastrophe, that's all."

"So you don't think people can change in ways other than through traumatic events?"

"No, people change, develop, grow, what have you, slowly as well. I just think it starts off with some disaster."

"I think that is true in most cases," I reply. "Usually it takes some crisis to force people to take a look at their lives." I am thinking about Burt's struggle with impotence. "Certainly both you and JoAnn have grown over the past several months at your own pace. You've been doing quite well at it."

Burt nods.

"I may have a crisis of my own at Thanksgiving," Ed says wearily.

Burt looks over at Ed, and we all wait for him to continue.

"The thing is, Ellen wanted to be engaged by Thanksgiving. Then we planned to get together with my folks for Christmas." He looks up at us and shakes his head. "I have a whole calendar of deadlines with this woman."

Burt takes this comment as addressed to him.

"Ed, it might be a good idea if Ellen knew you were trying this hard. Just tell her you are working on this problem of, well . . ." He struggles for a word ". . . hesitation."

"We have talked about it some."

"Yeah, well, this time talk about it after the holidays, okay? There are enough emotions to deal with this time of year without getting into all that, don't you think?"

"That's for sure. I'll keep that in mind." Ed smiles back at Burt but then scans the room nervously.

"What's going on, Ed?" I ask.

"Well, I'm a little worried. I sort of took the whole session today."

"I really wouldn't be too concerned about it," Paul says. "I don't know about you, but *I* certainly got something out of it."

"Such as . . . ?"

"I had no idea people gave so much time and effort just to the idea of getting married. I just jumped into it myself, didn't give it much thought, you know." Paul reflects on this a moment and then adds: "I never knew people went into marriage thinking about the possibility of divorce."

Mitch suddenly looks surprised. "This from the man who pushes prenuptial agreements?"

"Hey, Sarah is going to get half of everything I own. I can't afford dates as it is!"

"You know, I wanted to ask you about that," Sean pipes up from his corner in Burt's shadow. "What do you do . . .

no, well, um, how do you actually go about meeting . . . women?"

"I've tried a few things, but it's still real hard for me." Paul rustles uncomfortably in his chair. "There are dances, parties, that sort of thing advertised for singles in the Weekend section of the *Washington Post*. I've gone to a couple of those." He brightens a bit. "I think I'm going to answer a personal ad from *Washingtonian* magazine."

"What's the difficult part about it, Paul?" I ask.

"Have you tried being single after a twenty-year marriage?" Paul asks incredulously. He then looks away from me, clears his throat, and frowns. "The real hard part is this: I'm at a party and I go up to a woman who looks pleasant enough, and ask her to dance, and she just looks me straight in the eye and says *No.* "

"Yeah, well, I'm not having much better luck than you are, Paul," Sean says. "You know, people think things are just so easy on campus, that it's just a picnic picking up all these available women. But it just isn't true! At least for me it isn't." He shrugs.

Sean seems lost in thought. We only have a few minutes left in the session when Mitch looks over at Paul. "Paul, if you were getting married today, would you insist on a prenuptial agreement?"

"Yep, sure would. You should, too."

"No way would I do it," Gary objects. "Marriage is a big thing. If you're going to go through with it, you might as well go for the pie in the sky." Ed is nodding his assent. "I don't go for prenuptial agreements, contractual marriages, that sort of thing."

"Contractual marriages . . . ?" Sean looks bewildered.

"Sean," Ed explains with an impish smile, "a contractual marriage would be where you are up at the altar and the minister asks you, 'Do you take this woman to be your lawful wedded wife?' and you say, 'I do . . . for five years.' "

INTERPRETATION ─────────

One strong and recurrent theme in these group sessions has been the men's struggle with issues of commitment, attachment, devotion, and separation with the women in their lives. Tonight's group discussion has revolved around the two opposite poles of this struggle: Paul's attempt to come to terms with the end of his twenty-year marriage and Ed's inner debate over beginning a marriage of his own. Even Sean and Paul, who have found little common ground in group so far, attempt to make a connection on this issue: their shared contempt for dating and fear of rejection.

Of all the men in the group, Paul certainly has the most ground to cover in overcoming the problems related to the collapse of his marriage. For his entire married life Paul let Sarah define his role in the marriage and yielded to Sarah's decisions on virtually every aspect of their married life. Like Paul's mother, Sarah had the power. Now Paul finds himself in a separation with no guidance on how to behave. On the one hand, he finds himself clinging to Sarah as a means of reducing his separation anxiety and loneliness, a common response of recently divorced men. On the other hand, Paul is desperately pulling away from Sarah. In this session alone we learn that Paul doesn't "like a damn thing about Sarah" and that she just gives him "the willies." In fact, Paul's central dilemma now is that Sarah isn't around to tell him what to do. What Paul is looking for in our sessions, although certainly not consciously, is for someone to give him permission to divorce Sarah and to assure him that nobody will be mad at him if he does. Such a guarantee would also relieve Paul of any guilt. Yet it is exceedingly difficult for Paul to actually make this decision by himself.

Ed, meanwhile, is finding it difficult to make a firm decision to marry Ellen. The issues surrounding this relationship are much more complex, however, as there really are two independent modes of thought and action going on here. For her part Ellen repeatedly tries to pin Ed down to a specific date—a deadline, in effect—and these dates come and go without even an engagement ring. What these deadlines do succeed in doing is upsetting Ed: He withdraws from Ellen and broods over whether he should actually marry someone like this. It would be more useful for Ed to confront Ellen and assure her that he *is* working on it (as Burt encourages Ed to do in the session) and that her continuing deadlines are doing nothing but making him angry. Some of this anger was spilling out in his choice of gifts. Ed's empty jewelry box was a bit too close to the "real thing" to be entirely innocent. This gift was an unconscious expression of his anger. Yet in response Ellen does not get openly angry as she should: She expresses her anger in an indirect way and once again tries to get even with Ed by threatening to move out, hoping to scare him into a commitment. Here Ellen drew attention to what was *not* included in the box, rather than to the gift itself. Their reluctance to confront each other openly has contributed to this situation where they are simply "stuck." In this respect, Burt's advice to Ed to approach Ellen with an honest, straightforward explanation is right on target.

One aspect of Ed's difficulty with commitment is reflected in his brief exchange with Gary. Both men are exceedingly uncomfortable sleeping in the same bed with a woman. In a previous session Paul, too, claimed that sleeping alone was a major benefit of separation. In this session Gary gets very agitated when he discusses having a woman "right in his face." Not coincidentally, these are the three men who are most reluctant to let women into their inner lives. The reason they are so disturbed and threatened by such a sleeping arrangement is that they feel vulnerable when sleeping. We are *all* vulnerable when we are near sleep. It is difficult for Ed, Gary, or Paul to defend himself, keep a woman at bay, or run a mental "censor" when he shares a bed with a woman. Simply put, the men feel safer sleeping alone.

When sharing a bed was last discussed, Sean was shocked to learn that some of the other men preferred a bed to themselves. Sean continues to have a very rough time adjusting to Sandi's absence, both from his bed and his life. In tonight's session, Sean recognizes, to his credit, that he and Paul do share some problems and anxieties as the two men who have suddenly found themselves thrust into the dating world all over again. Dating is all the more difficult for these two men, as the relationships they are ending were with their first loves. In fact, neither Sean nor Paul was ever very comfortable with dating. Paul avoided going out altogether for a full seven months because he was rejected by a girlfriend. He later met, and married, Sarah. Sean is beginning to feel pressured by his friends into finding somebody new, and he's uncomfortable with these expectations ("People just think things are so easy on campus, picking up all these available women"). Both men want to avoid possible rejection because it is hard to deal with. I've found that most of the men in my practice who are "suddenly single" are intimidated by this fear. It is difficult for many men to make the transition from the security of a committed relationship to uncertainty and rejection in a new dating situation. For his part, Paul has found a few new avenues for social interaction, and this intrigues Sean, who has yet to really test the waters. Sean's reluctance lies in his silent hope that Sandi will eventually want him back.

SESSION 7

//

RESISTING CHANGE

"You know, Ed, I think I know how you feel," Mitch begins. Tonight his large frame is pitched forward on the couch, and he is speaking softly in careful phrases. "Last week Lynda gave me an ultimatum." Mitch's shaggy red head turns to Ed and he smiles slightly at this word. "She wants to be married by next summer." His gaze slowly moves to the floor.

Ed eyes me for a minute then looks back at Mitch. "Any reason for a deadline in the summer?"

Mitch nods. He is still examining the floor. "We planned to take a trip to Europe, and she thinks she wants to be married by then." His voice has trailed off to almost a whisper.

Ed and Burt exchange glances. We all wait.

"Mitch . . ." Ed says, but he stops himself abruptly and looks momentarily confused. "I thought you *liked* Lynda."

Mitch's head does another bob up and down, and he

takes a deep breath. "It's just I don't know if I'm in favor of
. . . if I want . . . this marriage."

"Oh." Ed says nothing more. He seems to be digesting
this when Paul begins to shuffle nervously.

"I don't understand this," Paul declares finally, peering
right at Mitch. "Why won't you marry her?"

"It's not that I *won't* marry her, I'm just having trouble
with the idea of getting married." He frowns and begins to
pull nervously at his own fingers. "The whole idea of a fancy
church wedding is just really . . . well, I really don't want it,
and Lynda does."

"You were married before, right?" Burt asks from Mitch's
left.

"Yeah, for six years."

Burt ponders this for a moment. "Well, Mitch, I understand why you want to ditch the church wedding idea. At
least I think I do." Burt watches for some response from
Mitch, but Mitch is just waiting patiently.

"Okay," Burt says, "a formal church wedding with the
same friends, family, ceremony. They might think you're getting pretty good at this!"

"Yeah, plus it's an incredible hassle."

"Mitch," I say, "what else is there?" I've been watching
Mitch carefully. His quiet, smooth voice and downcast mood
tonight are very much unlike Mitch. "The cold feet you are
having must be related to more than just a church wedding."

"Yeah, that's true. I'll tell you what," Mitch says, sitting
straight up. "I liked Janet, too! Six years of marriage, everything sailing along fine, and then we hit the skids. I don't even
want to *think* about it."

"Could you say more, Mitch?" I ask.

"God, do you know what it was like that last year? Five
years of happiness and one year of hell. I was so unbelievably
. . . *lonely*, I thought I was going to crack up." Mitch is examining the wall behind Paul and me. "I've just been thinking

about all the things that went wrong. All those things *I* did wrong." Mitch pauses briefly, then looks down from the wall at me. "It could happen all over again this time, you know. I was sure I'd be happy with Janet forever when we first started out."

"Have you discussed any of this with Lynda?"

He shakes his head. "Not yet. The odd thing is, we are communicating better than we have before, but I still haven't said a thing to her about any of this."

We all sit quietly with our thoughts for a while.

"Have you two considered some other arrangement, like living together first?" Burt offers finally.

"Well, yeah, I have, but Lynda would never go for it, and neither would her family, particularly her father." Mitch smiles. "We're talking a very traditional family here. And Lynda has never been married before, so this is all a big deal for her." Mitch shrugs, but he is slightly flushed now and appears to be a bit more self-conscious.

Paul catches his eye. "You know, the way you've been talking today, the way you look—it's sort of what happens to me when I'm depressed, or weak, or low on energy."

Mitch reflects on this. "It's not that, really, Paul. I'm . . . just a little uncomfortable in here today, talking like this." He lets out a breath. "And nervous, too, I suppose."

"What is it you're afraid of, Mitch?" I ask.

"It's just hard to do this in front of a group of men." He anxiously scans the other faces. "I don't know if you all will really understand me . . . or you might think, or say, something about me that might really hurt . . . something negative, you know."

I nod at Mitch. "Speaking in front of people is really one of the hardest things to do, especially in here." I think it's important to give Mitch some encouragement, and he's been very open with the group today. "There aren't many of us who want to hear negative things about ourselves, Mitch. It seems like a normal concern."

Mitch smiles appreciatively but says nothing further.

Silence.

"I had dinner with Sarah last night," Paul says glumly. He is leaning hard on his right elbow in the chair and seems more disheveled tonight. "I had to see her last night because she refused to see me over the weekend."

Gary frowns. "Weren't you supposed to see her *only* on the weekends?"

"That was our agreement, but all sorts of things have changed in the last couple of weeks. Two of Sarah's girlfriends are mad at her and they have her convinced that *I'm* using *her* for sex, if you can believe that." Paul is shaking his head sadly. "Plus, her mother told her the same thing, so now it's gospel truth!"

"So did you sleep with her or not?" Gary asks.

"Wait! I've been trying to avoid it, remember? Last night after dinner she announced, 'No more sex,' which was just fine with me. I'd be happy to have a brother-sister relationship, actually. So after we've settled all this, I'm happy as pie, and we're driving home, and now *Sarah* decides that 'hands-off' rule is a big turn-on, now *she* wants it!" Gary and Ed exchange smiles. "She came on to me so strong that I got right out of the car and walked off a ways. That stopped her cold."

"So you *didn't* have sex with her?" Gary wants an answer.

"Hell no, I didn't. *She's* using *me* for sex, remember? Not only that, I just felt terrible at dinner anyway. She spent the entire evening just blasting me for ruining the marriage, not giving her enough money, for leaving Abe alone at home with her, just about everything you can imagine." Paul is looking bitter. "So I didn't feel real sensuous."

Mitch looks over in Paul's direction. "What do you want from Sarah, Paul?"

"I want her to say that she likes the separation and wants to be independent. I don't want to be around her." He looks out the window. "The fact is, I'm happier alone than with her."

For a moment we are quiet.

Finally Gary starts to shake his head in recognition. "I know what you mean, Paul." He looks around at the others. "Did any of you see that article on bachelors in America in the *New York Times Magazine?*"

There are a few nods.

"I thought a lot of the bachelors in the article have some of the same problems we discuss in here," he continues, "like the reluctance to commit to a woman." He looks at me. "A lot of the men have just decided to live alone or get a dog. Some have just dropped out of the dating scene altogether." I get the feeling Gary is just reporting the article to me; I'm one of the men who hasn't seen it.

"How does this apply to you, Gary?" I ask.

He eyes me warily. "It makes me feel better about not being married, or living with someone, if that's what you mean." He smiles. "And I'm getting a hell of a lot more work done!"

"Will that be your whole life?"

He shrugs. "I don't know right now. It's just that I don't like the idea of a woman in my apartment. And there just aren't a whole lot of women around worth marrying, as far as I'm concerned." Gary folds his arms and sits back at this comment, confident that it is the last word on the subject.

Burt, however, doesn't leave this alone. "That might be okay for the next ten or twenty years, Gary, but what then? I don't think people want to live and die alone, do you?"

"Look, I don't know. But I'll tell you this: I'd have broken up with Leigh by now if I didn't think it'd disqualify me from group."

Burt frowns. "What in the world are you talking about?"

A flash of anger crosses Gary's face. "All we ever talk

about in here is our relationships with women! I figure if I
haven't got one, I don't belong in this special club anymore.
So I'm sticking it out with Leigh."

"That's the *only* reason you're still seeing her?" Mitch asks
with astonishment.

"Yeah. And I'll tell you what else. This group is breaking
into two halves. Me and Paul know how demanding women
are. We know they'll just suffocate you if you let 'em." Gary's
gaze shifts to Ed and Mitch in the center of the couch. "You
two let yourselves be so damn manipulated by women, it's
unbelievable! This is the way I see it: Me and Paul are the
men. Ed and Mitch are just totally pussy-whipped."

"So where does that leave Sean and Burt?" Ed asks
calmly. He has no reaction to being called "pussy-whipped."

"Well, I don't think Burt knows what he wants, but he's
still trying to figure it out. Sean, well . . ." He shakes his head
sadly. "Sean doesn't even know how much of a sucker he is.
Sandi's got him." He cocks his head slightly in Sean's direction. "Sean, look, Sandi's probably not exactly sitting on her
hands in Chicago, know what I mean?"

Sean looks away. Ed and Mitch exchange glances, but
nobody says anything to Gary. Everyone is trying to absorb
this outburst.

I decide to explore this further.

"Gary, try to relate your feelings about women to your
family experiences."

Gary shrugs. "I came from a family of women, really. I
was the youngest—I had three older sisters. Most of the time
my poor mom was trying to defend herself against my father,
who was totally out of control!" Gary rubs his mouth slowly
and looks around. "I was a pretty normal kid."

"I'm wondering, Gary," Mitch says in careful tones, "do
you think it's possible that you got a little spoiled by all this
attention from the women in your family? Did you know what
they wanted?"

"Sure. I did all the things boys normally do around the house. I took out the trash, washed the cars, raked the leaves, that sort of thing." He returns Mitch's steady gaze. "I don't think I'm much different from other men on this, you know. I think I know what women want."

Before Mitch can respond, Sean clears his throat and looks at me expectantly.

"I have something I need to talk about." He looks flushed and tense. "Look, I hate to butt in like this, but I have to tell you I won't be here next week. I'm flying home to Phoenix and I have a layover in Chicago. Sandi and I are going to meet for a few hours at O'Hare."

I see Gary roll his eyes.

"So are you looking forward to it?" Burt asks.

"Not yet. I'm too nervous—I just don't know what to expect." Sean is breathing slower and more deliberately. We all wait for him to continue.

"I don't even know what we'll talk about, to be honest."

"Are you going to ask if she's seeing anybody?" Gary asks with a hint of sarcasm.

Sean grimaces. "I dread the answer. But maybe it would do me some good to hear it."

"You know what I think you should do?" Paul exclaims with a smile.

"No, what?"

"Sneak up behind her and reach around and grab her tits!"

Sean looks stunned. Ed's face is buried in his hands.

"Okay, okay," Paul concedes. He looks disappointed in these two. "Try the Paul test instead."

"I'll bite." Sean looks less than enthusiastic. "What's the Paul test?"

"If she touches you, she's interested. If not: forget it."

Sean opens his mouth, but nothing comes out. Burt takes

this as an opportunity to move things away from where Paul is taking them.

"Sean, look. It probably is a good idea to find out where Sandi is. It will be better for you in the long run. Frankly, the way I see it, if this thing with Sandi isn't going to work out, you've got to get your heart and soul out of it."

"I'm trying, believe me."

INTERPRETATION

Change and the role it plays in these men's lives is beginning to take center stage at this point in the evolution of the group. Mitch finds himself resisting an enormous change urged on him by Lynda. Paul is still reluctantly accepting the changes in his relationship with Sarah. Gary confronts all the men with an accusation that the group itself has changed. Sean, too, has to deal with his changed relationship with Sandi face to face for the first time since the breakup.

Tonight Mitch's resistance to the idea of marriage was ignited by Lynda's ultimatum: Ed was quite accurate in his observation that until tonight's session, Mitch had spoken glowingly of his relationship with Lynda. Mitch is upset because he feels Lynda is forcing something on him. He resists the idea of being told what to do, even though the ultimatum applies to an event over a year away that once appealed to him. Certainly many other aspects of the marriage are unsettling and strange for Mitch: Lynda's desire for a formal church wedding and her reluctance to agree to a live-in arrangement. Added to this is the reality that Mitch prefers the status quo. He hates change, and marriage is an enormous one. So Lynda and her ultimatum represent a lot of new experiences for Mitch; so many, in fact, that they stir up his fear of failing in a second marriage. But Mitch's decision to be in group means that he is committed to change. We know as early as the first session that Mitch claimed he entered therapy because he "didn't want to lose Lynda." Mitch simply doesn't want to be forced into a decision.

Tonight Paul feels cornered, too: He is confused, bewildered, and angry with the unpredictable changes in Sarah's behavior. The pressure on Sarah to end the sexual relationship with Paul came from her "support network": her friends and parents. In fact, their insistence put Sarah in a bind: She felt obligated to follow their advice to avoid losing their support. Once Paul has agreed, happily, to Sarah's demand, she reverses her position and urges Paul to have sex with her. It is encouraging that at this point Paul demonstrates some of the progress he has made by being able to refuse to have sex on demand and have more respect for what he feels. This represents a significant step for a man who did everything his wife wanted throughout their twenty-year marriage.

Sex on demand is a dilemma for Paul, as it is for many men. Men commonly feel that they should be able to have sex on demand, and that it is their obligation to provide it: They expect themselves to be ready whenever the woman wants sex. Traditionally it has been considered "unmanly" for a guy to say no. In this respect, Paul has been admirably insistent that Sarah respect his wish to maintain the "brother-sister" relationship.

Gary has been very forthright in tonight's group as well. As the talk of the men's relationships with women continues throughout our sessions, Gary feels increasingly isolated from the other men, because his relationship with Leigh is not going well at all. Gary *does* want to be an integral part of the group and wants to feel connected. His decision to confront the men is based on his view that the men either give in to women (and are therefore "pussy-whipped") or are bewildered and stuck in their relationships. His only real connection is to

Paul, the only other man who says no to a woman. Gary is taking a lot of risks in this confrontation: He calls the men names and takes the chance that he may generate anger and rejection. In fact, Gary is doing the group a favor: Not only has he broken the ice to encourage discussion of new topics, he has also made an opening (by his own example) for the men to confront one another. This will have a positive effect on their efforts to make stronger connections both here in group and in their life outside.

//

THE MAN'S BIOLOGICAL CLOCK

"So, how'd it go at the airport?" Ed asks with a hint of a smile. Ed seems more relaxed tonight—he's almost buried in the couch—yet he's eager to find out how things have worked out for Sean.

"Well . . . okay, I guess," Sean replies, looking quickly over at me. He appears to be surprised by the attention.

"So what happened, Sean?" Gary asks impatiently.

"It was pretty good, actually, considering our planes got rescheduled and I had to hike halfway across O'Hare to find her." Sean pauses and smiles with the memory. "She was standing there and I walked up and tapped her on the shoulder. She was so surprised to see me! She gave me a huge hug and . . . she kissed me, too." Sean's voice has gone soft now. His gaze shifts to some blank spot on the wall behind Gary.

"What kind of kiss?" Paul demands. "Sister? Mother? Lover?"

"Huh?" Sean looks startled, then seems to remember the Paul test. "Oh . . . it was good—not real passionate, but it made me feel a whole lot better." He grins back at Paul, who shrugs and looks over at Gary. Gary has the beginnings of a smirk on the corner of his mouth. He looks as though he's about to say something, but he clears his throat instead and looks at the floor.

Sean shrugs. "We only had five minutes, you know. We talked about seeing each other at Christmas—same place— the airport. I'm thinking of going to New York in January, too."

Gary catches my eye, and he looks impatient, but it's Ed who speaks. "What does Sandi think about it?"

"We haven't made plans yet," Sean answers quickly. "I just can't deal with asking her right now. I've got too much going on in the lab and about three weeks before exams—"

"Look," Paul interjects suddenly, "when are you going to make up your mind about this?"

Sean stops abruptly, shocked at the interruption, but Paul is on a roll.

"Can't you see how wishy-washy you're being? Not only that—you're boring me to tears!"

Down the couch, Ed's jaw suddenly hardens, and he glares at Paul, who is looking defiant. Gary is mildly amused.

"Thank you for the encouragement, Paul," Sean replies dryly.

"You know, Paul," Burt says calmly, looking directly in his eyes, "I don't know why you're so impatient with Sean, anyway. It's taken him, what—four weeks?—to open up like this in here, then you just shut him down with all this 'wishy-washy' stuff." Burt is shaking his head. "Not real supportive, in my book."

Sean senses an opening and jumps in.

"I don't see that I'm any more wishy-washy than you are with Sarah, Paul! When are you going to make up your mind on Sarah? You ever going to divorce that woman?"

"Some comparison. I was married to her for twenty years!"

Sean rolls his eyes. "Here we go again."

"It's not some adolescent romance," Paul adds as an afterthought.

Burt and Ed start to chuckle at Paul's notion that it was an "adolescent romance," but Mitch is shaking his head slowly in disgust.

"Mitch?" I ask.

Mitch's gaze meets Paul's. "I'd be really pissed if you ever put me down like that. Reminds me of what my father used to do." He leans forward on the couch and suddenly seems much bigger. "I wouldn't stand for it."

Paul's eyebrows rise in mild surprise. "I didn't mean it as a put-down."

Mitch looks skeptical.

"Paul, does Sean remind you of Abe right now?" I ask.

I notice that Sean is momentarily confused, but he seems to then remember that Abe is Paul's son.

Paul nods. "Yeah, he sort of just goes on pointlessly, too."

"So you get impatient with Abe like this?"

"Actually, I guess I do." This is enough to slow Paul down. He pauses for a while to examine one of the ferns in the corner. "Come to think of it, Abe *is* pretty talkative at first, but after about twenty minutes or so, he quiets down. You know, he doesn't say anything at all. I have to start asking him questions or the conversation would just die." Paul grows silent at this and looks around expectantly.

The room is quiet.

"In fact," Paul comes alive again, "I remember the other day I was taking Abe and Betty to the mall, and out of nowhere Abe interrupts this conversation I'm having with Betty and tells me to quit yelling at her. I really didn't know I was yelling at her in the first place!"

"Why *were* you yelling at her, Paul?" Burt asks.

"Oh, I don't know. Some stupid thing she did."

This cracks up half the men on the couch, but Paul looks momentarily bewildered.

"Look, Paul," Burt offers with a wry smile, "you can't expect Abe to talk to you for more than that twenty minutes if you're constantly down on him."

Paul pauses, then leans over toward me. "Do you think I'm down on Abe all the time?"

Before I can answer, Sean interjects: "I do."

Paul and Sean exchange looks, but neither speaks.

"I think you're treating Sean like you treat your own kids," I reply to Paul. I've decided to answer a slightly different question from the one Paul asked. "You treat your kids as though what they say is unimportant. You treat Sean as though what he feels, his relationship with Sandi, is unimportant."

"Oh." Paul looks at me momentarily, then peers at the floor. He seems to be willing to give this some consideration, so the group falls silent once again.

Finally Ed smiles, and sits forward. "Good news," he announces. "Ellen gave me a stay of execution."

"So that's why you look so relaxed today," Gary says, nudging him in the arm.

"Yeah, it's true. We talked things over and decided there are a few problems we really have to work on before we could ever be serious about marriage." He shrugs. "I felt a whole lot better."

"How does Ellen feel about it?" Burt asks.

"Actually, I think she was relieved, too. Things were a whole lot lighter between us the whole weekend."

Burt nods, but Gary is frowning.

"I don't understand why there was the pressure in the

first place," he says. It's not clear if this is a question or a statement. Ed treats it as a question.

"Ellen talks a lot about the fact that she has only a limited number of eggs left, and each month, there's one more gone, so she's running out of time."

He looks at Gary expectantly, but Gary is silent.

"I'll tell you," he sighs, continuing, "I'm sure glad we worked this out. I dread the idea of losing her, having to date all over again . . . being alone."

"You're really lucky, you know," Paul says, gesturing in Ed's direction. "You're a man who's having his cake and eating it too. Two years of living with a woman, good sex, a relationship—and you don't have to get married."

"We're still discussing it."

"I know. I'm just jealous of you. I'd sure like that kind of deal."

"You're jealous? Paul, I've never heard you talk like that before," Ed says with a faint smile.

"I know. I'm trying to be more understanding." Paul looks uncomfortable. "I don't want everybody to think I'm an asshole."

"Who called you an asshole?" I ask.

"Well, nobody did. You guys . . . I just get the feeling you think I'm really insensitive."

I look around at the men. "Reactions?"

"Yeah, I have a reaction," Sean says suddenly. "Fuck *you*, Paul, I'm twenty-three years old and no adolescent."

Gary, Ed, and Burt are dumfounded. They look from Sean to Paul and back to Sean.

Sean is flushed, but he's not through with Paul yet. "Sandi meant as much to me as Sarah did to you." He looks over at me. "I guess I *do* think he's insensitive!"

The men share a laugh that breaks the tension.

"Okay"—Paul holds up his hands—"I know. But it's true—you *do* remind me of my son, and he *is* an adolescent."

"Okay, Paul, but I'm not. Don't think I'm just going to sit here and take this kind of treatment."

"What kind of treatment? You want me to be softer? I don't want to sit here and try to figure out how to say something more politely, you know. I just want to be myself! I'm tired of being attacked."

"Who do you feel is attacking you?" I ask.

"Burt," he responds. "Every time I get into something with Sean, he jumps in on his side."

I know we won't resolve all these issues tonight, but I hope Burt can at least give Paul something to take with him before the end of the session. I look in Burt's direction, but he's already sitting forward, ready to go.

"I don't intend to attack you, Paul," Burt says, "it's just that I think Sean deserves the time in here. You have plenty, you know. Also,"—he spreads his hands wide in Paul's direction—"I thought *you* got something out of that exchange: Now that you know more about how your children see you, maybe you have an idea of what to do about it."

Paul is frowning, but he looks at Burt and slowly nods.

INTERPRETATION

This was the first major confrontation between group members. At eight weeks into the group process, the men have not only learned the value of open, honest exchanges, but they have also begun to reap some benefits from the resulting confrontations. This interaction is a valuable component in group therapy, because it allows each member to learn his effect on others and also to apply this learning after practicing in the safety of the group.

Tonight's confrontation between Sean and Paul was set

up by Sean's report on the events with Sandi in the Chicago airport. Sean paints a rosy picture of what was actually a very brief encounter with Sandi in a crowded public place. In the process, Sean reveals his idealistic view of the relationship and his unwillingness to act on either Gary's or Burt's suggestions and encouragement to move beyond this point. Paul grows impatient with Sean because he is waiting for any facts that would indicate the situation has changed. When none are forthcoming, he jumps in with a demand for facts ("When are you going to make up your mind about this?"). We soon learn that Paul treats Sean much like he does his son Abe. Tonight it's almost as though Paul is quizzing his own son by demanding that he get to the point, while Sean/Abe clams up as soon as he feels Paul's critical attitude.

In fact, Sean does not engage Paul until Burt intervenes. Then Sean accuses Paul of being wishy-washy, too, while Paul once again dismisses Sean's "adolescent" relationship. At this point, the other men, particularly Mitch, are becoming agitated at Paul's condescending attitude toward Sean. In truth, Paul's impatience with Sean mirrors his impatience with his son, Abe. Paul's very limited range of emotions and responses to his children resulted from a severely emotionally deprived childhood. He has lacked empathy, patience, and curiosity in his relationship with both Abe and Betty, which is the same treatment Paul received from his parents. Much of Paul's "hardness" is merely a cover for a frightened man who wants to be liked by others.

Paul exposes some of his vulnerability by admitting that he fears the men think he's an "asshole." Paul chooses this term, even though it's never been voiced here. Paul feels attacked by Burt anytime he gets into a confrontation with Sean. Paul's right, in one sense—Burt's clearly responding to Sean in the same way as Paul: as a father. Burt wants to be a father more than anybody in the group. He senses Paul's harsh attitude toward Sean, so he naturally comes to Sean's rescue as the "good father" he wants to be, something he missed with his own father. Burt had a highly judgmental, critical father, and his strongest desire is to avoid this when he's a father. Sean is the beneficiary of Burt's fatherly kindness in group.

Although Sean's blunt rebuke of Paul seems caustic, it was important for Paul to hear it. It is likely he would shrug off a confrontation of any less intensity. This one has captured his attention. If Paul chooses to follow these suggestions, this encounter could prove to be a valuable catalyst for improving his interaction and connection with his own children.

SESSION 9

//

VIOLENCE: A MAN'S SHAME

"I don't know what to do about Betty," Paul begins with a slow shake of his head. "She'll be home for the holidays. I've got to take her for three whole weeks." He is rubbing his forehead so intensely I'm suddenly worried he'll leave a bruise.

The room grows quiet. Mitch coughs into a cupped hand but says nothing. We wait for Paul to continue.

"She could do anything, you know, she's got the run of my apartment. Last time she stayed with me she ran up ninety bucks in long-distance calls on my number!" Paul pounds his armrest for emphasis. "I made her pay for those and I'll be damned if I'm going to pay this time either!"

Gary is eyeing Paul cautiously; he's not sure it's safe to come in with a question right now.

"Paul," Gary says finally, "why is she staying with you if you don't want her?"

"It's not that I don't *want* her, I'm just afraid I can't *handle* her." He shrugs. "She's a teenager. She just does whatever she wants." Paul looks right at Gary. "What if I have to go on a business trip?"

"So?"

"So she'll have a couple dozen teenagers over in my apartment in ten seconds flat. What a joy. Plus the place just reeks of smokes when she's around."

"You could just tell her not to smoke in the apartment," Mitch suggests with a shrug.

"I've tried that. It works for about three days, and then she just blazes up in front of me."

The door pops open suddenly, and Burt walks in. He shuffles a bit as he crosses the room and sits in the center of the couch. Paul's eyes follow Burt's progress to his seat. Burt looks up at him apologetically and motions for him to keep going.

"But I do have the last word on what goes on in the apartment," Paul continues. "If she gets totally out of control, I'm still bigger than she is, so I'm sure I can handle it."

"You're *bigger* than she is?" Gary asks.

Paul nods.

"What are you going to do, pound her into submission?"

"Uh . . . well, no. It's just that she's gotten so big she intimidates Sarah, and I'm not letting her do that to me."

I notice Burt is looking terribly uncomfortable during this. He's rubbing his chest slowly and frowns every time Paul speaks. I catch his eye, but he looks away quickly.

Gary is nodding. "I remember one time in my life when I got that way: violent with a woman, I mean. It only happened once. I was living with this woman right after I turned eighteen. I came home drunk one night, and we got into a terrible, violent fight. At one point I just hauled off and smacked her halfway across the room." He's shaking his head in disgust. "It was awful." He looks up at Paul. "I think there's some basic character defect in me that comes out when I'm drunk. I've been sober for six years, and I've *never* had the urge to do that since."

Paul nods slowly. "I've had to get physical with Sarah. Not hit her, but one time I had to restrain her after she—*she*, mind you—attacked *me*. She wanted to scratch my eyes out! I had to pin her down and wrap her in the bed sheet just to hold her down!"

"Look, I'm not feeling well, you guys," Burt says abruptly. He's slightly flushed, and his right hand continues to massage his upper chest.

"It started at work this morning, this pain in my chest, and up here." He motions to his shoulder. "I don't know, maybe it's the way I have to hold the fiddle during practice."

"What's the feeling, Burt?" I ask.

"I'm a little worried. I've been thinking about my father. He died of a heart attack."

We are silent for a moment.

"I know what that's like," Paul says. "My father died of a heart attack, too." He shifts to face Burt a bit more directly across the glass table. "Last year I had a pain right there"—he indicates his upper chest—"and I went to a walk-in clinic for an EKG. I'm glad I did; it was an incredible relief to know that I was okay."

Burt nods and looks over at me. "Maybe I should head over to G.W. Hospital and get checked out."

"I think it's a good idea," Paul states emphatically.

"Are you scared?" I ask.

"A little."

"Burt, you're free to go, if you want to, but I think you will feel better if you talk about your feelings. Was any of the discussion bothering you?"

Burt shakes his head.

"Then I think he should play it safe. Get a doctor's opinion," Sean interjects. He is worried about Burt.

"I don't know what to do," Burt says.

I sense the eyes focused on Burt and me. I don't want to push Burt out the door and alarm him, yet I don't feel comfortable forcing him to stay in the group.

"It's your choice, Burt," I say.

"I'd better go," he says, rising slowly. He retraces his route back around the table. I meet him halfway and walk him to the door.

"Please call me later and let me know how you are feeling," I say.

He nods and closes the door behind him.

There is a stillness in the room as the men exchange nervous glances.

"Do you think he should have gone?" Gary asks.

"It probably was a good idea," I respond. "He needs the physical check first, then we can talk at our next session." I pause and smile at Gary. "It wouldn't make sense to keep Burt talking if he's really having a heart attack."

Gary laughs and looks over at Ed, who is grinning broadly. Sean and Mitch both look relieved; Mitch's arm is now draped across the back of the couch. The tension in the room has mostly lifted. Everyone seems glad Burt is getting checked out.

I decide to take the conversation back to where we were before Burt's problem.

"So, Gary," I say, shifting my weight in his general direction, "was there any violence in your family when you were young?"

Gary shrugs. "Not really. No smashed heads, no broken bones." He pauses. "I had a few run-ins with my dad, though. He could be a real macho asshole." Gary is shaking his head and gazing out the windows. "He'd butt up against me with his chest and give me the old 'I dare you to hit me' routine. What a jerk."

"So did he actually *hit* you?" Paul asks.

Gary eyes Paul for a moment and then nods.

"Once when I was sixteen, I was six feet tall by then, I was doing the dishes, minding my own business, when he came up from me on my blind side and slapped me hard across the face with the back of his hand." Gary stops and looks over at me. "I told him right there that if he ever hit me again, I was going to hit him back. He knew I meant it."

"Did you ever do it?" Mitch asks. He is sitting forward on the couch, and his leg is bobbing up and down nervously.

"Nope, but I came close." He stops momentarily to reflect. "There was one time at the dinner table." He looks over at me and smiles slyly. "I guess I wasn't practicing my Emily Post manners, so he took his dinner fork and slammed it down through my right hand. Damned near pinned it to the table."

Sean is staring wide-eyed at Gary in disbelief. "He actually *did* that to you?"

"Sure." He holds out his hand to reveal several small dots by his right thumb.

Paul is shaking his head. "Never had any of that with my parents. They were real passive, quiet, reserved."

Mitch clears his throat and manages to stop his bobbing leg. "Well, I've had my share of problems with the old man, but he's never actually whacked me." He looks over at Gary. "Usually he just screams at me until I've had enough and I just clam up."

Gary nods.

"What are you feeling as you're telling this, Gary?" I ask.

"Well, I don't feel very good about it." He eyes me warily, "It wasn't a happy time. It's hard to go over it all again. I guess I'm sorta . . . well, embarrassed."

"Embarrassed suggests shame." I pause. "What are you ashamed of?"

"Maybe I'm the one who goofed. I feel ashamed at blaming my father for something that wasn't his fault. I probably could have avoided the whole thing by avoiding *him*. I could have moved out."

Mitch is nodding, but Paul leans toward Gary on his left.

"So why didn't you?" Paul asks.

"Well, I tried, when I was sixteen. But . . ." he lets out a long sigh and stops.

"But . . . ?" Paul prompts.

"But my mother threatened to commit suicide if I did," Gary says emphatically, peering straight into Paul's face.

Ed shakes his head in disbelief. Paul breaks away from Gary's gaze and looks at me a little sheepishly.

"So you stayed?" Mitch asks.

Gary nods. "I had to, for Chrissake. For another two years."

"Gary," I say, "you are carrying around a lot of guilt, about *not* being responsible enough."

Gary shrugs. "Probably true."

"You were being burdened, Gary. You parents had a responsibility to help you grow up," I continue. "Instead you were threatened and abused. It doesn't have to be broken bones, a swollen face, or black eyes, you know. Your father drew blood with a sharp fork—that's abuse. Your mother made you responsible for her life—that's abuse."

Gary looks at me and nods. "My old man always ragged on me, too—he was always putting me down. He could really make me feel like shit."

"It's hard to grow up believing those put-downs," I say.

"Yeah, well, it was no picnic. It makes me feel for kids, teenagers trying to figure out their lives on their own." He's got Paul in his intense gaze now.

Paul stares back but remains silent.

"I think you're being narrow-minded about Betty," Gary says at last. "She's just a teenager with a lot of energy, Paul. Try going to a bar in Georgetown and check out how much energy is floating around in there."

"I know. I just don't know how to handle it," Paul says a bit defensively.

"Paul, why not consider some alternatives with Betty," I offer. "You could call her to talk and let her know you're feeling anxious about her visit."

Paul shakes his head. "I'm not sure how I'd even approach it."

"Well, a good start would be appreciating that this visit is an adjustment for both of you—she's probably just as anxious as you are. You'll both feel better talking ahead of time."

"Okay." He nods, looking over at Gary. "I'll think it over."

Gary looks pleased with this outcome. He looks at me, then at Paul, and smiles.

INTERPRETATION

Paul's anxiety over Betty's visit in tonight's session has focused attention on the struggle many men face to be successful, loving, and empathic fathers. Having endured a difficult, emotionally deprived childhood, Paul finds fatherhood trying, demanding, and ultimately vexing. His efforts to connect with his daughter falter, and communication between them becomes even more difficult. Paul's own childhood experiences were limited, so his range of understanding of his daughter is equally limited. Gary helps Paul to see the narrow-mindedness of his approach, and in doing so he reveals in some detail the sad events of his own abuse at the hands of his tyrannical father. In fact, tonight's session becomes a forum for discussing violence (Gary's adolescence) and dominance (Paul's physical struggles with his wife). This conversation becomes so threatening to Burt, whose childhood fears were of his father screaming out of control, that it magnifies his physical discomfort. His fear of the rising pain in his chest drives him to seek medical attention. His discomfort grows as the discussion becomes more graphic and threatening.

This discussion is launched by Paul's view of Betty as a "problem." Paul's anxiety toward Betty is natural, since Paul himself was treated like a perpetual problem by his anxious mother. Her children were problems that she needed to control. In fact, on many occasions in his early life Paul was confined to his room, locked in the clothes closet, or placed on the toilet for several hours at a stretch just to relieve his mother of having to deal with him. As an adult, Paul entered a very traditional marriage in which his wife was responsible for the children and in which he adopted the same notion that his children were simply potential problems. Now that Paul is separated, he is having to deal with his children, for the first time in his life, on a one-to-one basis. Rather than considering the possibility that he and Betty may both be anxious about the visit, Paul views the entire situation as threatening: one he must control. Gary and I both help Paul see that Betty is probably equally uneasy and upset at having to stay with Paul at all. It is important for Paul to think of Betty as his daughter: a young woman who is troubled and confused by the separation, and one who needs his guidance and assurance that he won't desert her, too.

Gary's questions to Paul lead to some powerful revelations about Gary's own adolescent life. Tonight for the first time he reveals some of the physical and emotional abuse of his adolescence, although he never recognized this as abuse before. During his early childhood Gary was his father's favorite, and his father was proud of him. As Gary moved into adolescence, his need to establish independence and individuality was perceived as a threat to his father: His father simply did not recognize Gary's need to grow. The abuse and arguments started on this issue, and Gary grew increasingly unhappy and confused by these attacks because he had no idea what caused his father's severe anger. Gary, like his parents and sister, turned to alcohol as an escape from this treatment. In so doing, Gary was incorporating his father's abuse and dislike of him by now abusing himself with alcohol. When Gary got his father to quit hitting him, he started hitting himself. In tonight's session, I urge Gary to recognize that he was indeed abused. Once he is able to confront this reality, other feelings surface: embarrassment and shame over his father's behavior, and guilt from the belief that he was responsible by not successfully avoiding his father. The latter is another example of Gary beating up on himself—of blaming himself for his parents' insensitivity.

As tonight's discussion focuses on rising levels of parental tension and even physical violence, Burt, who fears violence in any form, becomes increasingly agitated and upset. This topic hits Burt from two directions: It is his worst childhood memory—escaping from his screaming father—and it also touches on his special concern: What kind of a father will he be? Will he repeat his own father's mistakes? In this session, these two worries drive his anxiety way over the threshold. Burt was not having a heart attack—he was having an anxiety attack. It was my decision to give Burt the choice of how to deal with this attack, hoping that he would stay and confront the emotional, yet willing to accept his need to attend to the physical. He chose to leave, thereby avoiding the talk of violence that so intimidated and unsettled him. He will have to confront his fear later.

//

IMPOTENCE: A MAN'S HUMILIATION

Burt is toying nervously with his wool pants. Several minutes have passed since I closed the door, and nobody has said a word. All eyes are focused on Burt. He is growing increasingly self-conscious as the silence continues.

"Okay, Burt, I'll bite. How are you?" Ed asks from behind his horn-rimmed glasses. Tonight I am struck by how strongly Ed resembles a young, ambitious scientist. Only the lab coat is missing.

"Oh." Burt looks up, startled. "I'm okay." He shrugs. "Well, my heart is okay." He smiles weakly.

"Burt," I ask, "do you remember what we were talking about last week when you left?"

Burt nods. "Sure." He gestures in Gary's direction. "You were telling us about what happened with your girlfriend: the time you hit her when you were drunk."

110

Gary nods back at Burt but says nothing.

Burt looks back at me expectantly.

"What were you feeling then?"

"I was worried about my heart!"

". . . and your feeling?"

"I guess . . . anxious."

"And what feeling do you connect with violence, Burt?"

"Fear. I was afraid." Burt pauses a moment. "And definitely *more* anxious." He smiles. A lot of the tension has gone out of Burt's shoulders; he's a bit more relaxed.

I wait for him to go on.

"Well, you got me going, too," he says, looking back at Gary. "I do remember getting very uptight. But I'm okay tonight." His gaze drifts back to me. "We can talk about something else now."

"Let's stay here for a minute, Burt," I say. "What else is making you nervous?"

He eyes me for a minute then leans slightly forward.

"Okay. I'm worried about this." He taps the ear with the hearing aid. "I've got a sixty percent hearing loss in this ear and I'm going to have an operation on it this week."

Ed winces. I notice Paul nodding with assurance.

"I think I have a hearing loss, too," he says. "Half the time I can't hear Abe even when he's in the same room." He shrugs. "Must be getting old."

Burt frowns. "Getting older really worries me, you know. I feel myself slowing down." He is examining his broad hands from behind. "Cuts, little things. They're taking a lot longer to heal."

"How involved is the operation?" I ask.

He shakes his head. "It's minor surgery. It'll take about an hour and a half. Still . . ." He pauses and looks right at me. "I don't want to go under the knife."

"I can understand that," I say, nodding slowly. I pause for a moment. "You know, it's really a normal feeling. Being scared. The way I see it, minor surgery is when it's surgery on someone else!"

Burt seems relieved at this, then nods.

"I'd hate to have somebody cutting up *my* ears," Ed says with a shudder.

Burt's eyes shift to Ed then back to me. "Well, maybe that's why I'm so uptight lately. Plus the house is in ruins. Everything is unbelievably hectic." He begins to rub the back of his neck. "JoAnn is moving in and she's redoing things all over the house. Plus the workmen have been in and out all week."

Gary coughs and looks past Burt out the window.

"So what did I miss out of your life from last week?" Burt asks, trying to divert Gary's attention from the window.

"A lot." Gary's gaze shifts down from the window to meet Burt's.

"So . . . ?"

"So that's what you get for having a heart attack, or anxiety attack."

"And you're not going to tell me."

"That's right. You miss things. You've got to be here to play."

Gary is not going to budge. He is engrossed in examining the carpet. Finally he looks up at me.

"You know, the thing is, I don't even know why *I'm* here. When we first started this group, I thought we'd be talking about relationships. My relationship hasn't changed that much, and I'm getting bored with this damned issue. I want to talk about something else."

"Reactions?" I ask, looking around the room.

Burt is rubbing his mouth slowly. I sense he is still a little disturbed by Gary's last response to him.

"Well, I know I'm excited after some sessions and not so turned-on by others," Burt says with a shrug. "The beginning sessions in here were a lot more spontaneous, I think. It seems people are holding back a lot more now." He says this straight to Gary.

"Hey—I talked more than anyone last week!"

"I think *you're* holding back more now," Ed interjects, looking to Burt on his left.

"What?"

"I don't think you've said much in group, at least compared to the rest of us." Ed has skidded forward on the couch to face Burt more directly. "In fact, when you got all upset last week, I thought you were getting ready to drop out of the group!"

"Oh . . . well, I never really thought about that. I *like* group. I like being able to talk to you guys without having to worry about what people will say."

"Yeah, this is the only place you can really do it, you know," Paul says. "I can get away with saying things in here without having to face any of you at dinner or in a meeting." Paul rolls his eyes.

"What's your reaction about group so far, Ed?" I ask.

"Well, it makes sense to me on two levels."

Suddenly I have this vision of Ed donning a white lab coat and getting ready for a lecture.

"On one level we can work together on a common problem as a group. On another level it's valuable to have a bunch of men together, because, well, let's face it, men rarely open up like this, so . . . maybe it will help us all on the outside." Ed looks surprised that he ended with this statement.

"You're right," I say. "Everything you learn in here is absolutely applicable outside. Still what are the *feelings* that go with that thought, Ed?"

He smiles. "It's helped me. It's true. I can speak up a lot more now when before I'd just stay quiet. I can see it at work. I'm talking to more people and they're coming to me a lot more for my opinions." He pauses to examine the glass table.

"Now that I think about it, I actually can talk about Ellen more, too."

Silence.

"Well, I can't figure out if I'm moving forward or what," Paul says finally. "Now that I'm ready to buy a condo, I just don't know if it's the right move. Maybe I should buy a house instead. I don't even know if I'll get the loan." Paul is shaking his head slowly, then abruptly stiffens. "What if Sarah finds out and tries to take half of it?"

"I wouldn't worry about that," Mitch says suddenly.

"Oh?"

"Paul, I really think all this is a smoke screen for deciding about Sarah. You've got to do something about that, make a commitment to change, go through with the divorce, something, I don't know."

Paul nods. "I just got so used to it. I *liked* being married. But I'm not getting involved with any other women now."

"It might be a little soon for you," Burt says across his folded legs. He shrugs. "I don't know, Paul, you still seem so, well, so *angry* with women still."

Mitch nods in agreement.

Burt uncrosses his legs and leans forward. "I know that after my marriage to Rosalind went poof! I was angry at women for almost two whole years. I stayed away from women. Actually, I couldn't get it up anymore, so I just gave up on dating." He lets out a long, slow breath. "After I met JoAnn, I had to deal with this impotence problem. It's what got me into therapy originally. Once we talked it out, I was amazed at how fast it went away. Anyway it took me almost two years to get into therapy because I was so pissed at women."

Mitch lets a small smile of recognition spread across his face. "You *talked* yourself out of impotence?"

Burt shifts uneasily. "Well. talking to JoAnn, and not trying to have sex if I was mad at her. She was a big help. It never happened to you?"

"Yeah, I had a rough bout with impotence, too. I felt so humiliated. I only survived thanks to my friends."

"You had the same friends after the divorce?" Paul asks. He's incredulous.

"They were *my* friends from before the marriage. Janet never really liked any of my biker friends."

Paul nods. "It seems all our friends are gravitating to Sarah, not me."

"That sounds familiar," Burt says with a wry smile. "I had to start all over after Rosalind."

"Yeah, well I'm miserable," Paul says from the bottom of his chair.

"Look, Paul," Burt says with a surge of energy, "why not buy the condo and fix it up? You'll realize you have a life of your own, something away from Sarah."

Paul's chin barely raises off his chest. "I don't know."

"Well, it's certainly worked for me. Ever since JoAnn decided to move in, she's been redecorating my house like a crazed weasel."

Finally Paul smiles.

"I'd hate to have a woman running around my house screwing things up," Gary says, shaking his head.

"Yeah, but you don't understand," Burt says, a grin slowly spreading across his face. "JoAnn is on a search-and-destroy mission. She's going to track down and obliterate anything that ever belonged to Rosalind. She's throwing out all sorts of my old stuff left over from the marriage. Every time I go upstairs I have to duck all the projectiles headed out the door!" Burt slides back on the couch. "Actually, it's about time. I'd let the house go, really, and I feel terrific about her redecorating."

I come in with an English accent: "As Professor Higgins would say, when a woman comes into your life, your serenity is gone. She'll redo your whole place, top to bottom." I grin and drop the accent. "I don't remember the exact words."

Paul looks blank, but Burt smiles in recognition. Gary leans over at Paul. "It's *My Fair Lady*, Rex Harrison's line, right, Al?"

I smile.

"Yeah, it's great," Burt continues, "but there is a down side to it all. Now that JoAnn has moved in, she has a real presence. She's on me all the time about what I'm thinking or feeling."

"Ugh," Gary grunts, as his hand runs down the full length of his face. "How can you stand having a woman all over you like that?"

"Well, like I said, it's the tough part. But I'm willing to do, to learn, whatever it takes. I figure communication is what I need to work on. I couldn't make it work in my first marriage, and I'll do *anything* to avoid that living hell, let me tell you."

"How is it different for you now?" I ask.

Burt pauses. "What we do is sit down and talk at least once a day about everything, about what's going on. We've also agreed to separate rooms and some private time apart."

Paul snorts. "Man, I thought you two were just living together! What's the big deal? You sound like Sarah's lawyers splitting up property, *my* property."

"I think it's worth the effort at compromise, communication, Paul," Burt replies. "You of all people should know the cost of screwing up a relationship."

"Yeah, that's for damned sure. But I'd never agree to separate bedrooms."

"We don't have separate bedrooms. Just separate rooms, separate space."

Paul shakes his head but remains silent.

"I'd say that a relationship that allows for some privacy sounds pretty good," I suggest.

Burt smiles, but now Gary is shaking his head.

"I don't understand this. What's the point of living to-gether—is it like some practice run for marriage?"

Mitch and Burt exchange smiles, and I realize that Gary is the only man in the group tonight who doesn't want to live with a woman.

"Ellen thinks it is," Ed says. "I'm a little less sure."

"Yeah, well, if I lived with a woman, I sure wouldn't get married. It just doesn't make sense to go that far."

"Have you thought about living with Leigh?" I ask.

He shrugs and looks past Burt and out the windows. "I don't know. Sometimes I think about it, but . . . well, I sort of hope I will meet someone better." He lets out a long sigh. "That's what I'm holding out for."

INTERPRETATION

As the men relate the more intense emotions of anger, re-sentment, and anxiety, each member of the group is faced with having to respond to these emotions. In tonight's session Burt recognizes that his attack of the previous week was an anxiety attack, and even goes so far as to recognize Gary's angry, violent story as the source of his fear. In that case, rather than confront his anxiety Burt ran from it, much as he attempts to run from the anxiety of his ear surgery ("We can talk about something else now"). Like many men, Burt ex-presses anxiety in a physical way, even though the cause of the anxiety (Gary's frightening story) was in no way physical. Certainly Burt's upcoming surgery is a cause for anxiety. But in our session the topic of surgery simply opened the door for

Burt to express some of his other anxieties: aging, his previous anger at women, and his present feeling of being overwhelmed by JoAnn. Burt's task in therapy will be to confront the fear underlying his anxieties by going through the feared experience. He has been successful in this area before: Burt's relationship with JoAnn grew and prospered after he confronted, and experienced, the anger, severe anxiety, and humiliation of impotence. Tonight we learn that he is confronting his feelings of uneasiness with JoAnn by making an intense effort ("I'll do whatever it takes") at communication and compromise. In this way, Burt is making progress. Yet in therapy progress rarely follows a straight, direct path: In the space of one week Burt has gone from fleeing the anxiety generated by Gary's story to proudly announcing his commitment to facing the anxiety of living with JoAnn.

Paul is very confused about whether he is making progress in therapy at all. In fact, Paul's marital situation has changed little since he first entered the group, and he continues to deny himself the opportunity to stand completely on his own. Paul is lonely and "miserable" because he's put himself in a bind: he's not married, not divorced, and not single. This situation has not changed in the last few months because he continues to lack the confidence in himself to break with Sarah. On the other hand, Paul has had some very positive results from therapy so far: His interaction with people at work is improving because of what he has learned from being in group. He has also had, for the first time in his life, limited success with women, even though he is not involved with anyone now. Paul feels much more confident and happy when recounting these aspects of his life. Yet there is much ground for him to cover. As Burt pointed out in the session, Paul is still very angry and apprehensive with women, and these feelings are standing in the way of any new meaningful relationship. Paul feels damaged by women. This is a difficult problem for him since his anger toward women, which has existed

since childhood, continued through his marriage with no outlet. He has only recently begun to release some of this anger
in therapy. As this process of release continues, Paul will find
that a lot of his current feeling of tension around women will
fade.

Gary, too, feels tense and uncomfortable as Burt re-
counts the living arrangements he has agreed to with JoAnn.
Gary's response to Burt's story of new intimacy is to draw the
line ("I'd hate to have a woman running around my house
screwing things up"), maintain control, or withdraw ("How can
you stand having a woman all over you like that?"). Clearly,
at this point in his life Gary is feeling threatened by closeness
and intimacy. In fact, he is afraid of being committed, what
he thinks of as being "trapped." This is an especially frightening outcome for Gary, because he has been trapped by
women repeatedly in his life, with the most disastrous consequences. He was trapped for two years in his family by his
mother's threats of suicide if he left, only to fall into an addicted relationship with another woman where he felt equally
trapped. At this point Gary sees relationships as being too
binding, threatening, and ominous.

One consequence of growth and development in therapy
is that the men begin to question not only their progress but
also the value of the process itself. As high achievers these
men are very goal-oriented and practical: They tend to think
that a certain number of sessions will result in a "cure." This
is especially true of Ed, who is very fact-oriented ("It makes
sense to me on two levels"). While Burt is more effective than
Ed on the emotional level, he still tends to withdraw and
conceal his own emotions unless confronted or questioned by
me in group and by JoAnn at home. Ed's statement that he
thought Burt was about to drop out of the group last week
indicates how far removed Burt appears to Ed. Yet when
questioned, Burt acknowledges the security and safety of the
group and is committed to staying with it. Paul seems much

more comfortable with the group members than with people in the outside world: this is the only place he feels a sense of belonging. Gary, too, is feeling very connected to these men. His desire to speak about other issues indicates that he is feeling secure enough with them to move on to other areas. While Mitch does not say directly what he thinks of the group, we do learn the value he places on his male friendships ("I only survived thanks to my friends"), and his comments in tonight's session to Paul are right on target. He's now mentioned a humiliating experience, his bout with impotence. That's extremely difficult for a man to discuss. So, as the man most reluctant to be in group, Mitch has made fine progress.

SESSION 11

//

YEARNING FOR MISSED FATHERS

"How are you doing, Mitch?"

Mitch smiles weakly back at me and runs a hand slowly through his hair. Tonight he is soaked through, his black leather riding outfit offering little protection from the driving snowstorm. He coughs roughly and sits forward. Mitch is much bigger than any of the other men—he's an imposing presence even when he's drenched.

"I'm okay . . . doing better, really," he mumbles haltingly. He catches Gary's frown out of the corner of his eye and realizes the men need to hear what has happened in his life this week.

He takes a deep breath. "Okay . . . my, uh, my father died last week."

"What?!" Gary exclaims. Paul is startled, too. He's sitting bolt upright in his chair with his eyes fixed solidly on Mitch.

For a moment nobody says a word. Ed is the first to come out with a complete sentence.

"I didn't even know he was sick."

"Well, he wasn't sick, really, it was a sudden, massive heart attack." He pauses to wipe more water from the tangled hair matted on his forehead. "I just got back from the funeral today. It was down in Alabama, and I really didn't think I was going to make it back."

A calm silence descends. The sloshy sounds of rush-hour traffic rise from the street—they are the only sounds in the room.

"How've you been doing?" Ed asks softly.

"It's been rough, let me tell you," Mitch says, almost in a whisper. "We all drove down to Alabama for the funeral: Lynda, my sister, and I. We got stuck in southern Virginia for damn near three days, so I couldn't even be there to make the funeral arrangements." He's shaking his head in disgust. "I called Steve, a friend of mine, from our hotel, and thank God he handled all the details, the arrangements you have to make, you know."

Paul is shaking his head in sympathy. Gary is still stunned and hasn't said a word.

"How'd the funeral go?" Burt asks from Mitch's left.

"Huh?"

Mitch's still at the funeral.

"The funeral. How was it?"

"It went fine, actually." He pauses to examine the glass table. "I was really surprised by all of my father's friends there. I didn't even know half of them." He looks at Burt, who is leaning toward him to catch the words in his whispers. "They had so many really nice things to say about him." He shakes his head. "Things I really never knew anything about."

"Such as . . . ?" I ask.

He sighs. "They were all big buddies. I think two of the guys were in the war with him. He'd helped a few of the locals out when things got rough down there. One guy said he was the most decent, honorable man he had ever known."

Burt is still leaning in his direction. "What do *you* remember about him?"

"I remember him being drunk, that's what I remember," Mitch mutters miserably. "That, and the fact that he was so goddamned pushy and demanding, and . . . well, overbearing. I was just scared to death of the man when I was a kid." He looks up at me. "I really wish I could remember him like his friends did."

Silence.

"Where are you, Mitch?"

"Pissed. I feel cheated. I'm his son. Why didn't he show *me* his good side? . . . Just doesn't seem fair."

"You're on target, Mitch," I say.

"My father died of a heart attack, too," Burt says. He looks over at me for a moment, then back at Mitch. "I remember being real shaky around that time, even though he was pretty far up there, seventy-four, when he died."

"My father was only fifty-five. Can you believe it?" Mitch says as though he's still trying to convince himself. "I figured he'd live to seventy-five at least. I was even trying to work things out with him, you know?"

Gary and I exchange glances.

"Were you still talking to him when he died?" Gary asks.

"Well, yeah, he was in town a few months back. But that's not what I mean. Two weeks ago I sat down and wrote out this letter to him. It took a while just to get up the courage to do *that*."

"What did the letter say?" I ask.

Mitch is rubbing his mouth nervously. He looks down.

"I didn't really know how to put it. In the letter. I guess the most important thing was—that I . . . well, I told him . . . I wanted him to know I . . . accepted him. As a man and as a father. I also said . . . wrote that I loved him."

Mitch's voice has gotten shaky and he won't look at anybody now. He's staring straight down between his legs at the carpet.

Before I can ask Mitch what he is feeling right now, Gary jumps in.

"Did he ever see the letter?" Gary asks.

Mitch shakes his head. "No, but I did. I found it on his dresser when I was down there. It came in that day's mail."

Silence.

After a time, Paul sighs. "All this talk of death just makes everything else so . . . I don't know, insignificant." He shrugs. "My old man died of a heart attack at forty-nine, so I feel like I have this legacy—will I be next? Will I die of a heart attack in eight years when I hit forty-nine?" Paul shudders suddenly and looks down at his shoe.

"Well, Mitch, I tried the same thing with my father," Gary says, scratching the back of his neck. His head is cocked away from Mitch and the rest of the men and is facing roughly toward the ceiling. His gaze shifts to Mitch for an instant, then moves slowly down to the glass table. "I really wanted to patch things up with him," Gary continues. "He's a pretty hard guy to approach, and God knows we had one hell of a history. So we did actually talk a bit. But as things went on I got really pissed at him. He just wouldn't say anything. I'd kid him a bit, toss him a magazine, ask him what movie he wanted to watch, and he'd just *stare* at me." Gary pauses. When he begins again his voice is more slow and deliberate. "One day my mom calls me and I come to find out he has some nerve disease that rendered him speechless. He couldn't talk. At all."

Mitch is nodding.

"It's sad, really," Gary continues. "He's pretty much given in to the situation and spends all his time watching television. And this is a man who just *loved* to read, and hated TV."

"Were you ever able to connect with him?" Sean asks

from his corner. He's been so quiet we are all a bit surprised by his voice.

Gary shakes his head. "No, but I bought him a brand new television set for Christmas. He seems to like it a lot."

Sean smiles and nods.

Silence again. A lot of heavy emotions in the group tonight. These silences are becoming more frequent.

"I wonder where the rest of you are right now," I say, looking around at the others.

Paul coughs and smiles a thin grin. "I had a great time at the River Club last Sunday. Went to this singles dinner where you change seats with each course and that's how you meet everybody. Driving home I realized I had a lot of fun." He slows to brush off his pant leg, then looks over to me. "It's too bad Sarah can't be out enjoying herself."

"Does that bother you?" I ask.

Paul nods. "It's a shame we never could have fun together. In a relationship for twenty years and no fun. But we *were* close, that's for sure. There were days I could predict her every move . . . finish her sentences for her." He pauses. "I was so close to Sarah, it was almost overwhelming. Suffocating." He looks at me. "There were days I was sure it would kill me."

"Yeah, every woman does that to me!" Gary says with a smirk.

"How do you feel about it now?" I ask Paul.

"I'm one hell of a lot freer now. I'm more alive. Last session helped me. You were right, Burt. I've been stuck." He smiles. "I'm doing things I've never done before in my life."

"You do seem to be getting over Sarah—slowly, but, hell, it's progress." Gary smiles.

Paul shakes his head slowly. "Not enough. It's going to be a long time before I trust a woman again. That's it." His gaze drifts slowly over to Gary. "They're vultures, you know."

"Do you really think that, Paul?" Sean asks. He is totally mystified.

"You bet. For the first time I realize I may be alone for the rest of my life."

Sean shakes his head sadly.

"Paul, you are trying to change now. You're doing the work," I point out. "Your views of women will certainly change, too."

"Yeah, well I'll never be like Burt over there." He eyes Sean, too, but says nothing to him.

Burt smiles. "Do you *want* to be like me, Paul?"

"No way. You're always so *cozy* with JoAnn, trying so hard to get along."

"Sure I am. The fact is, we're getting very serious." Burt glances briefly at me. "We're even in couples therapy together now."

Paul rolls his eyes.

"How's that going?" Ed asks. This is something Ed has been considering, too.

"It's tough. After our session yesterday JoAnn wanted to talk and talk about what went on, but I just wanted to leave it alone and enjoy the drive home." He folds his arms slowly. "She always pushes me like that."

"She's a very expressive woman, Burt," I say, smiling.

"She sure is. And I'm trying to deal with it, be more responsive, that sort of thing. My latest method is this: If she wants me to drop everything to talk to her, I tell her I'll be with her as soon as I finish whatever I'm doing."

Gary frowns. "So? Is that the solution?"

"Yeah. I used to just keep silent and continue working. I think she felt totally ignored." He shrugs. "I wasn't ignoring her, of course. I just didn't want to talk right then."

"Sometimes I really worry about you, you know," Paul says suddenly.

Burt looks surprised. "What do you mean, Paul?"

"I just get this feeling JoAnn wants to capture you. I'm very suspicious of her—of her motives." He looks at me and shrugs. "Maybe I'm just negative on women, I don't know."

I look over at Burt. "How do you feel about Paul wanting to protect you?"

"Well, I'm shocked. It's not something I would have expected from Paul, that's for sure. But it's a nice thought."

"Yeah, well, the woman's got you in her web, look out," Paul warns.

I smile. "Burt, you're surprised because it seems that you and Paul have such different views on things, especially women." I pause for a brief moment. "But consider this: If you met Paul when you were married to Rosalind, who was depressed all the time, at the same time Paul was married to Sarah, who was also depressed, you two might have hit it off right away."

Burt nods. "I don't doubt that. I was a different person back then."

"Yeah, well I'll be around to keep an eye on you now," Paul says with a hint of a grin.

"Do you really think she's trying to trap me?"

"I wouldn't put anything past her, past any woman who wants something."

"Really?" Ed asks, interrupting this exchange. "Okay, Paul, Ellen wants a baby. At least I'm beginning to hear a lot about it lately. So what's she going to do to me to get it?"

"Watch the diaphragm. Check for pinholes."

"You've *got* to be kidding!"

"It's no joke," Burt observes. "JoAnn was born that way."

"What?" Ed exclaims. "Look, I can't believe Ellen would ever try to trick me into marrying her."

"Believe it. It happens *all* the time," Paul concludes, with a shake of the head.

"JoAnn's father didn't want more children," Burt continues. "So her mother tricked him. And she tells it as a joke in front of him."

"She appears to be very narcissistic," I say.

"Definitely," Burt agrees. "She only thinks of herself. JoAnn had a hard time with her and with her father, because he could never stand up to her."

I smile. "Sounds like she was queen for a day, all the time."

INTERPRETATION

Tonight's session began on a very sad note. The death of Mitch's father set the tone for the gloomy mood this evening, yet it also stimulated discussion of topics that are traditionally very difficult for men to face: aging, illness, and death. Moreover, it once again focused attention on a powerful issue for all of these men: their relationships with their fathers.

I can't emphasize enough the importance of the father-son relationship in these men's lives. All the men, on one level or another, have been struggling to deal with the pain and loneliness of childhoods in which their fathers were often viewed as a remote, unfeeling, dictatorial enforcer. Mitch's confusion at the funeral over others' fond memories of his father is characteristic of men who have to bury their fathers after a stormy relationship. Like Mitch, many men ask themselves, "Why didn't *I* ever see the good side of my father?" In fact, Mitch's father saw himself as the breadwinner of the family, the one whose role it was to maintain order and to discipline the children. So what Mitch observed was the side his father chose to show him. What he recalls is the discipline, the criticism, the alcoholism, and the fights. He remembers a father with exceedingly high expectations of him. This relationship has survived into the present day. Mitch has continued to make every effort to please his father. In therapy, Mitch has been learning how much of his anxiety and withdrawal in his adult life are directly related to his early interactions with his father. When he decided to write the letter, Mitch was at the point where he felt it was time to quit waiting. It was time to establish a dialogue. He wanted his father to know he didn't blame him for all of his troubles and he loved him. This was a significant step for Mitch. He went from avoiding the father, dreading him, to a place where he wanted to approach him and connect with him. He had been moving from anger toward acceptance and, ultimately, forgiveness.

Many of the men in my practice mirror Mitch's experience: They yearn for a close, warm relationship with their fathers, a relationship that has long eluded them. Not surprisingly, even though these men are not close to their fathers, they do see them as role models and sense at an innate level that they will follow in their footsteps. Often this is taken quite literally: Paul fears he will die of heart failure at forty-nine like his father; Burt worries that chest pains signal his own heart attack is just around the corner.

Three men in the group—Mitch, Burt, and Gary—all have worked to the point where they feel comfortable attempting such a reconnection to their fathers. Sadly, Mitch's attempt came too late. Gary initially had some success before the onset of his father's illness. His willingness to keep trying is reflected in his gift of a big television set. He wants his father to be happy even if there is now very little chance they will ever connect in a meaningful way. Before his father's death, Burt was able to reestablish a good relationship with his father, whom he remembers fearing as a child because of all the yelling and screaming, ironically related to the pain and sadness prompted by Burt's divorce from Rosaland. It was during this period that Burt's father came to his assistance and they were able to interact. Yet even in this relationship, Burt felt his father never really understood him.

In my work with men I feel it is important to stress that the purpose of therapy is not to blame. The purpose of the therapeutic process, especially in the case of difficult father-son relationships, is to understand and experience the anger, pain, and frustration, and eventually to move beyond it to acceptance and, finally, forgiveness. It is also important to recognize that the parents, as human beings, have limits. I assure these men that their work in therapy will not only help them deal with their own anger and pain but will also help them to be better fathers. These men have a chance to change their own personal history. The past has already happened; therapy is designed to influence the present and the future.

COURAGE AND CONFRONTATION

After the men have settled in, I close the door. Burt looks over at me and smiles. Ed coughs and shifts to face me; Gary and Paul have just finished a conversation begun in the waiting room. They are now ready to start.

"Before we begin, I have an announcement," I say. "Sean has dropped out of the group. I spoke with him on the phone today, and encouraged him to come in tonight to discuss it, but he refused. He said he feels that he just doesn't fit in."

At first nobody says a word. I notice Ed throws Paul a hostile look, but he is silent. Gary nods slowly as though he has anticipated this.

"What do you expect?" Paul says finally. "He's such a lightweight. I knew he couldn't handle it."

Ed sighs and looks over at Gary, who is shaking his head.

Gary catches my eye and shrugs. "I never really expected him to come back last session, to tell you the truth."

Burt nods his assent.

Paul turns to me. "Didn't *you* see this coming?"

"Not this way," I reply. "I thought Sean would have made it tonight. That he would have at least talked out *why* he wants to leave. It would be better for him, and for us, if he did."

Meanwhile Mitch's black boot is tapping at a rapid pace. He's remained silent so far, but his eyes have been shifting nervously among the men during this exchange.

"Mitch?" I ask.

"Is . . . it okay if I just start now?"

I nod.

He lets out a quiet sigh. "Last night I had this dream that really upset me. I really don't know what to make of it."

"What was the feeling during the dream?" I ask.

He shrugs and slowly runs a hand across his brow. "I don't remember a single detail. I just remember waking up in the middle of the night, all nervous, breathing real heavy. I just lay there for a while. I was pretty soaked." He smiles a little sheepishly. "I couldn't get back to sleep."

"It sounds like an anxiety dream, Mitch, about a conflict going on inside you. What do you think the conflict is about, Mitch?" I ask. I'm hoping for some material about the dream itself.

Mitch answers without hesitation, "Lynda."

Paul has been listening intently to Mitch's story, and now he's growing annoyed. "What *about* Lynda?"

"I think its about my decision to propose to Lynda. I've been getting really anxious about it lately." Mitch looks to Burt, who is sitting on his left. "I'm mostly worried about another marriage ending in divorce, you know?"

Burt nods. "So did you propose?"

"Well, not yet. I told Lynda I wanted to wait until Friday,

wait until I had a chance to talk it over with Al. So she just blew up and said 'forget it! I don't want to go out Friday at all!' "

I smile. "You know, Mitch, it's a rare woman who likes being told that her boyfriend wants to talk over a marriage proposal with his therapist first!"

"No kidding," Burt says emphatically. "If I told JoAnn I wouldn't propose without talking it over with Al, I'd hate to be around for the explosion!"

Mitch shrugs. "Sure, whatever. But the whole mess has got me spinning around inside."

"Look," Paul says, leaning over on his left elbow to face Mitch directly. "I don't want to throw cold water on all this, but there's something here that's bothering me. Your father just died. I know what that's like . . . how hard it is to go through a loss like that." Paul pauses to examine his forearm. He's taking time to chose his words carefully. "So is it possible that this thing about marrying Lynda is so you won't lose her? If you marry her, you won't lose another person close to you?"

Mitch nods, a little surprised at Paul's insight. "Well, it's a possibility. Actually, I've thought of that."

"Well?"

"I really don't know the answer, Paul."

"How about living together first, as a sort of dry run," Burt suggests. His comment is for Mitch, but he's grinning across the table at Gary.

Mitch hasn't seen this. "I couldn't do that, really. She's real traditional, remember?"

"Real *traditional?*" Paul asks, amazed. "You're sleeping with her, aren't you?"

"Well, of course."

"Some tradition!"

"I just want an old-fashioned proposal, that's all, Paul. It's nicer, she'd appreciate it more. It's a lot more romantic."

"Mitch, I've got a question," Ed says, leaning forward to

see around Burt. "Did Lynda really mean it when she said she wouldn't marry you unless you got into therapy?"

"Yeah, she was dead serious. It really scared me at the time."

"I see Lynda's position now as a compliment to you," I interject.

Mitch is staring right at me with a blank look on his face.

"She wouldn't marry you before, Mitch. And she obviously *does* want to marry you now. So she must be seeing some positive changes in you."

He shrugs and then slowly begins to nod. "That may be. We are communicating a lot more now, but a lot of it is just opinion—'Did you like that movie? What do you want to do tonight?'—that sort of thing."

"Do you ever discuss feelings?" I ask.

Mitch shakes his head. "I can't talk to her about what I'm feeling right now. I don't know how she'd react."

"You're right, Mitch," I reply. "You don't know how she'll react. Her reactions are hers and are not under your control. That may be why Lynda is angry—another reason why she canceled out on you Friday. She senses that you're still holding back."

"I *am* holding back."

"I know. You need to discuss this kind of thing with Lynda."

"Now or when I'm married to her?" He smiles.

"Are you that committed to proposing this Friday?"

He nods.

"In that case, I would at least caution you to take your time in making a life decision, especially when you're changing as much as you are," I say. "Take a little time to consider making a life decision when you are changing so much. Also, we know that you *are* still going through the grieving process over your father's death, whether you're aware of it or not."

Burt comes in before Mitch can answer.

"A proposal isn't the same thing as marriage, you know."
I smile at Burt. This is a good point.

"That's certainly true. But my advice still stands. Especially the part about talking to Lynda about your anxieties."

Mitch is listening carefully, and he nods. This is a lot for him to take in at once.

Silence.

"How about some advice for me?" Gary asks.

"About what?"

Gary collects himself and sits forward on the couch. "I'm in a complete state of confusion with Leigh. We've broken up twice, and she keeps coming back, wanting to get back together."

"Don't you want to?" Ed asks.

"Not really. The truth is, the longer I date someone, the more it becomes like a habit to me. Eventually I have to try and *break* the habit." He stops and begins to slowly rub his open palms together. "The longer I stay with Leigh the harder it will be to break the habit. I don't want to become addicted to Leigh."

"Do you love Leigh?" Paul asks.

Gary flashes a sudden, angry look at Paul and says nothing.

Paul looks over at me and raises his eyebrows.

"For what it's worth, I don't think you sound addicted to Leigh," Burt offers with a shrug.

"What do you mean by being 'addicted,' Gary?" I ask. I'm pushing Gary in a sensitive area.

For a long moment Gary says nothing. When he finally speaks, his voice is tight and angry.

"I don't want to be overwhelmed. Out of control."

"I can understand that."

Gary is sitting quietly, angry and pensive.

"Addictions *can* take over your life," I say finally. "Ordinarily, for something to qualify as an addiction, you have to give it priority over the necessities of living."

"Man, you are full of advice today!" Paul says in exasperation.

"It sounds as though you're mad at me, Paul."

"No, I'd just rather get feedback from the rest of the group than sit here and listen to your advice!"

"What's with you today, Paul?" Ed demands.

"I'm really getting disappointed in this group, that's all. I'm not happy about the kind of feedback I'm getting." His gaze drifts to me for a moment, but he quickly looks away. "I've started looking around at support groups to see what's out there. I want everyone to interact in here more and not just nag at me all the time."

"That's funny, I get the feeling you nag at us, Paul," Mitch says dryly. "What do you want from us?"

"I want more support."

"Paul, we *have* been helping you with all kinds of things," Ed says quickly, "your divorce, your relationship with Sarah, new women in your life—"

"Don't forget about Betty," Mitch interjects.

Ed nods. "That's true."

Gary clears his throat and leans forward. He looks ready to join the conversation again.

"I understand a little bit of where Paul is on this," he begins slowly. "Sometimes I feel there are only certain topics that are okay to talk about in here." He looks around the room deliberately, taking in all the reactions. "I guess I don't feel I can completely trust everyone yet."

"What would you be talking about if you could trust everyone?" I ask.

"About being an alcoholic."

"Good! You needed to say that. I'm glad you did."

Gary is surprised by my reaction but remains silent. The

men exchange several nervous glances. Nobody is quite sure what to say.

"If you licked that, you're doing better than my old man did," Mitch says, breaking the silence.

Gary nods and looks at the floor.

Some more time goes by. We are all watching Gary.

"Look, Gary, that's something neither of my parents could do," Ed says suddenly. "I think it's great."

"What's your reaction to Mitch and Ed?" I ask.

"I don't know." He looks over at me suddenly. "I wonder if people just say it's great. I don't know how to react to that."

"Well, I mean it," Mitch says emphatically. "You must be pretty strong if you managed to lick alcoholism . . . and, it's okay if you don't believe me. I have a hard time believing people sometimes, too."

"Are you still drinking, or what?" Paul asks.

"No, I've been dry for five and a half years."

"Hey, that *is* good."

"I'm glad you told us, Gary," Burt says. "I'm glad that you felt you could say it."

Gary acknowledges Burt's comment but lapses into silence again.

Gary's silence indicates he is not yet comfortable discussing his alcoholism. Yet I want to encourage him in some way. "You took a real risk tonight, Gary," I say. "How do you feel about it now?"

He shrugs. "I'm sort of embarrassed really." Finally, he looks up at me. "But I'm glad I got it off my chest."

"I wish you'd got it off your chest earlier!" Paul exclaims. Paul is heating up again. "This is just what I'm talking about. I can't get anything out of you guys!"

"Now wait a minute, Paul." Ed cuts him off. "It sounds to me like you have a few secrets of your own. This is the first time we've heard about you sneaking around on the outside looking for some 'support' group. Is that what you mean by 'sharing'?"

Paul shrugs. "Yeah, okay. Don't get me wrong. I'm *glad* to hear about Gary's story. I just want *more* of that, and less criticism."

Gary is shaking his head. "I don't think so, Paul. I think you want something completely different. You want us to jump up every night and say, 'Go, Paul! Down with Sarah!'"

For once Paul is *completely* speechless.

INTERPRETATION

Sean's unexpected decision to drop out of the group has almost no impact on the men in tonight's session. In my experience it is more common for group members to have a much more powerful, sometimes vehement reaction to the abandonment of the group by an individual they have trusted. Sean's decision did come as a surprise to me, as I anticipated more cooperation from him in discussing any possible separation. It is a rare occurrence, in my experience, for a patient simply to drop out of a group without discussion. It turns out that the reactions of the other men, virtually all of whom expected Sean to simply vanish, were much more on target. This speaks to the value of the group process. Through direct observation of Sean in the group setting, the men had a very accurate sense of how Sean would deal with the confrontation in group and the emotional pain of the separation from Sandi if things got too intense for him to handle. When it came to this, Sean reacted with passive hostility by abandoning the group and refusing to deal any further with his feelings of pain and embarrassment over the breakup.

But Sean's story goes much further. In a turbulent individual session after his return from Phoenix, Sean told me that his father had just been released from the hospital following a near-successful suicide attempt over his failed business. An outraged Sean related how the family business had, just a few weeks before, nearly collapsed after his father had gambled away all the assets of the corporation in a binge that stretched over a year. Not only were these events disastrous for Sean professionally (his future in medical school depended on these funds), they also had a catastrophic effect on his very idealistic view of his father and family. Sean was angry that his father's gambling problem had been hidden from him, he was furious at his father for throwing the entire family into complete chaos, and he felt betrayed by his father's handling of his own medical school trust fund, which evaporated in the gambling binge. Sean had never felt this kind of anger toward anyone, especially in his family. The embarrassment and shame of these events were really overwhelming for Sean, and it was unfortunate that his choice to leave the group came at a time when the group could have helped him cope with these feelings and adapt more successfully. The group would have experienced Sean as a more "real" person—and definitely could have connected easily to his anger at his father.

The simmering anxiety of Sean's departure was amplified by Mitch's nervous tapping tonight. There is definitely a sense of tension in the air. I am gratified that Mitch feels comfortable enough with the group to bring in and openly discuss a dream, and that he was willing to hear the men out on their reactions. Mitch's dream was an anxiety dream. It was about loss; certainly about the loss of his father, but also about the possible loss of Lynda if he can't bring himself to propose in time. The loss of Sean tonight prompted him to talk about it, even though he could not remember the content of the dream. I had learned from Mitch in individual sessions that the funeral was very revealing to him: Mitch saw Lynda during this period as he'd never really seen her before. He appreciated that she took time off from work to drive down to Alabama for the funeral, and she spent many late nights with him grieving and feeling guilty. It was during this trip that he realized he and Lynda were made for each other—that he was deeply in love with her. Much of his anxiety over a proposal of marriage is based on Mitch's fear of failure in a second marriage, not his fear of his choice of Lynda. The former is a reasonable fear, if the problems that caused the collapse of his first marriage have not yet been resolved. This is an issue we have discussed in the group, because the likelihood of similar problems existing is huge unless they're recognized and resolved before a second marriage. Mitch is actively recognizing and resolving the issues of his first marriage, although he continues to deny himself credit for these changes. He has also considered that his proposal may be a response to fill the void of his father's death, an issue Paul brings up this evening. While Mitch's answer to Paul offers no solution ("I really don't know the answer, Paul"), it is much more likely that his father's death has simply been a catalyst for action by Mitch: It has cleared the way for Mitch to examine his relationship with Lynda and given him the opportunity to fully consider whether his relationship with Lynda is a wholesome one.

Paul's advice to Mitch comes in Paul's unique style: direct, forward, almost confrontational. Later in the session, we learn of Paul's dissatisfaction with the group and his search for a support group as a replacement. Paul has been shaky with this group since the third session, and at various times has felt picked on, insulted, or neglected. The fact is, Paul is very confused. Although he has been in and out of therapy for much of his adult life, he still has no idea of what he really wants from therapy or from the group. He quit his last group because it was too confrontational, yet he's mad at this group because they don't share enough with him. The truth is the men do share a great deal with Paul, but it is difficult for Paul to make a connection because he's never felt comfortable with interpersonal relationships of any kind—he has so little experience in this area. Paul also withdraws any time anger is expressed in the group, because it is so frightening to him. His search for a support group is a reflection of this. Traditionally, support groups are much more comfortable and non-threatening to men like Paul because, unlike therapy groups, there is less confrontation, little expectation of absolute honesty and vulnerability, and a great deal of unequivocal support. This support is what Paul seeks and what Gary, at the end of the session, parodies ("You want us to jump up every night and say, 'Go, Paul! Down with Sarah!' ").

It is interesting that Gary, who has been Paul's ally in group so far, chooses to engage in this little parody of Paul's behavior. In fact, Gary is very angry at Paul for thinking (silently) of leaving after he has established this connection to him. Gary is very careful about the connections he makes, and his greatest fear is an attachment to a woman that will make him lose all control. In discussing what he believes is a tendency to become "addicted" to women, Gary closes on the subject of his real addiction to alcohol. Toward the end of the session, Gary decides to make the leap by revealing this addiction to the group. He takes a real risk here—a risk of rejection, judgment, censure—but makes the leap nonetheless, for several reasons. First, he has long expressed a desire to talk about other problems in his life, and the fear of "addiction" is very powerful to him. Second, he has wanted to open up more in general as his connection to Paul and the other men has grown stronger. Third, and most important, Gary feels the group slipping away: Sean has left abruptly, Paul is shopping around, Ed has questions about what he is getting out of group, Burt and Mitch are resolving their relationship problems and therefore may not be around much longer—all of this is very threatening to Gary, who is committed to staying. Tonight Gary opens up as a way of saving the group. He wants to reinforce his connection to the men and guarantee that the group will stay together. The group is very important to him. For the first time in his life, Gary feels he belongs.

SESSION 13

//

THE VALUE OF ANXIETY

" . . . So I want more feedback from all of you. Just tell me what you think. Give me a reaction right away. That's all."

Paul has just finished a tedious, rambling monologue while swinging slowly around in the black leather chair. His eyes have yet to make contact with anyone. He's just floating along.

"Okay!" Mitch says with a sudden rush of energy. He reaches forward and seizes the chair with his hand and stops Paul in mid-turn. "How's this? I was so mad at you last week I could have *killed* you!" His enormous frame is only about nine inches from Paul's limp form, but Paul's face remains impassive. No response at all.

"Well, I'm glad to hear your honesty," Paul says smoothly. "But I don't know why you're so mad at me."

Mitch releases Paul's chair and folds himself back into

the couch. He coughs and slowly crosses his legs. He is waiting to cool down before he answers.

"Mitch, how does it feel for you to hold in anger, hold it in for the whole week since last session?" I ask.

Mitch's eyes shift to me, but he doesn't move. "I don't know."

Silence.

"I think . . . well, he's just been bugging me, you know?" he says finally in exasperation. Mitch is eyeing Paul warily. "He wants us to spill our guts all over the floor, to give him instant feedback, and meanwhile he's out shopping for another group!"

"So what?" Paul shrugs. "I want to keep my options open. At least I'm honest with you guys. I don't like what I'm getting in here."

"Paul, you don't like what you're getting *anywhere*," Ed cracks. Gary catches Ed's eye. Grins flash all around.

Paul frowns. It's the first response he's shown all evening. His black chair slowly spins to face Gary.

"I'm just trying to be more direct in dealing with everybody, okay?"

"Yeah, you look *real* direct Paul," Gary says sarcastically. There is a twinge of anger to his voice. Gary knows something but he won't tip his hand.

"Since we're all being so direct," Ed says. "I'll go next."

Paul's chair creaks one notch to face Ed. Once Ed has Paul's attention, he comes to life.

"Why in the *hell* did you treat Sean like a kid? He's not your son, you know. You can't just abuse him at will. You drove the poor guy right out of the group!"

"No I didn't," Paul responds coolly. "He just couldn't handle it. Nobody drops out just because they don't like me."

"That may be, Paul, but you treated him like *shit!*"

Paul holds Ed in his gaze for a long moment. "Really?"

Ed's face falls. He looks around at the others in mild exasperation. He can't believe Paul is missing this.

"Nothing seems to satisfy you, that's all, Paul," Gary says softly. "Last week I finally got up the nerve to go into this whole thing about my alcoholism and you yelled at me about *that!*"

Paul looks mildly surprised. "I *liked* the last session."

"What did you like about it?" I ask.

Paul has to swing nearly completely around to face me. "It's the first I've heard about his alcohol problem." He sighs. "I was glad to hear that he faced it down. And I was thinking: He must have had an awful time as a teenager, running to booze as an escape."

Paul is trying to build a bridge back to Gary, but Gary is watching him silently over folded arms.

"Well?" Paul asks.

"I'm not going to dig this all up again. I haven't had a drink in six years. That's it."

"Sounds like you're warning us not to expect too much from you," I tell him.

Gary shakes his head. "I just don't want to talk about it every session, that's all. A lot of it's behind me."

Silence.

"I was on the other side of that whole mess," Ed says softly.

He looks at Gary for a moment, then over to me.

"Both my parents drank like fish," he sighs. "My dad was a hotshot city councilman and was falling-down drunk at speeches and conventions all over town. I spent half my life just trying to find something to do to keep myself occupied, and I was only nine years old! I almost never saw my mom in the house—she was off with my dad schmoozing it up and drinking it down." He runs a hand slowly through his thick blond hair. "I remember making up stories to tell my friends just to cover for them; you know, 'They're both on medication,' 'They just get weird sometimes,' 'You know parents,' 'They're stressed out,' that sort of stuff."

Burt leans forward on the couch to face Ed. "Did it ever get any better?"

"After I got away, it got better," Ed replies with a hint of a grin. "College was an incredible relief. I had a lot of catching up to do with people." Suddenly he looks very intense. "You have no idea how lonely that was before college. I was just so mortified I avoided almost everyone!"

"Do you see your avoiding everyone as continuing even now?" I ask.

"Sure. I've never been the type to talk much to people. And I just can't take the leap and get married. I hesitate, analyze, study, reflect, think. I do a thousand things, but I never propose!" He grins at me.

"Some of your hesitancy makes sense, Ed," I say. "Lets face it. Your parents didn't exactly have the kind of marriage where you'd be champing at the bit to jump in yourself."

"But I *do* want to have a family *sometime*. I just don't know if Ellen's the one."

I nod. "That part of your hesitation is related to your perfectionism. Which helps you at one area, your work: You're a scientist, you're very ambitious, you're used to everything lining up, you want Ellen to be predictable before you'll propose to her. And you're afraid to commit to a decision because you're afraid it will be the 'wrong' decision."

"So is there anything *wrong* with knowing what you want?"

"Not at all. It's just a little unreasonable when you're talking about people. The reality is: People aren't perfect. If Ellen were predictable, you'd be bored."

"But I don't have a whole lot of time left. I may have a shot at a job on the West Coast, and Ellen won't go with me this time unless we are *definitely* getting married."

I pause a moment. "Ed, the most important thing for you right now is to know what you really feel. Take your time with Ellen. You've both been doing better without the pressure of a deadline."

Ed seems pleased with this advice. He stretches his legs out under the glass table and smiles.

Mitch nudges Ed in the side. "Come to me for advice if you get cold feet next time."

"Why?"

Mitch smiles. "I proposed to Lynda."

"Whoaa!" Gary exclaims, sitting up straight. Ed is so stunned, he's stone silent.

"Yeah, it was great. She wanted a ring, but I hadn't bought one yet, so I raced upstairs and looked around." He's grinning wildly. "It came down to a choice between my college ring and a cigar ring."

"So what'd you choose?" Burt asks. He's smiling back at Mitch.

"I went with the college ring. She said that would do for now."

"So when's the big day?" Gary asks.

"We're thinking about the end of July. That's a slow period at Lynda's law firm. Plus, we'll be able to get married in the church she's gone to her whole life."

Ed has recovered sufficiently to speak. "So what made you finally go through with it?"

Mitch shrugs. "Maybe some of it was my dad's death, I don't know. All I know for sure is I don't want to lose Lynda. She's too important to me."

Ed nods. Meanwhile Paul is just grinning slyly.

"What's your reaction to all this, Paul? You've seemed so subdued all evening. I haven't seen you energized about anything," I say.

Paul freezes up suddenly as though he's been caught.

"Paul?"

He inhales deeply, then slowly lets it out. His chair has

stopped its slow revolutions. "I really should have told all of you."

"Told us what?" Ed asks suspiciously. Gary is already nodding even though Paul hasn't said a thing yet.

"I've started on medication."

"No kidding," Burt says. "What kind?"

"Xanax, right now. It's great."

Burt frowns and Paul notices his confusion.

"It's an anti-anxiety drug my doctor originally gave me for this bladder trouble I was having a long time ago. I stayed away from it at first, but . . . boy, is it great. I just feel terrific. It's so much easier to handle Sarah and the kids, work, even group."

"Are you having bladder trouble now?" I ask.

"Nope."

"But you're taking Xanax anyway?"

He nods, a little sheepishly.

I frown at Paul, and he immediately jumps to his own defense.

"Look, Sarah made me take it, okay? And I don't regret it a bit. Everything is so much more even in my life now. I'm even going to go negotiate buying a new car right after this session."

"If Xanax makes *that* fun, I want a cut, Paul," Ed cracks.

I feel a slow burn rising inside. "Paul, here's a 'should' from me: You should have talked to me before taking anxiety pills. Why do you want to use a mood-altering drug?"

"It's medicine, okay?" Paul says defensively.

"No, it's not okay. Did your doctor know you are in therapy?"

"It's no big deal."

"It is a big deal. We could have consulted to coordinate your treatment. It's better for you in the long run. But you have to understand something, Paul. You're here to resolve anxiety, to *face* it. You need to learn what's causing the anxiety. Otherwise, it'll keep recurring and all you can do then is pop another pill."

"It's a physiological problem with me," Paul protests. He's actually shrunk a bit in his chair.

"Paul, look. I'm not meaning to chew you out. I do want you to see that anxiety is a natural *feeling*. It's just as valid a cue to us as feeling happy or sad. Anxiety means you're afraid—but it can be positive for you by helping you to pay more attention to your fear and get through the fear easier. It's better not to mask it when you're trying to figure it out."

"Xanax works better. I'm going to be on it for two months," Paul says defiantly.

Before I can respond, Gary jumps in. "I knew you were high on something ever since I came in here," he says with a shake of the head. "I could see it in your eyes. My whole life I've been around people zonked out on something. I can spot it in a second."

"Look, it's a doctor's *prescription*, okay?"

"Right. Paul, you can get a doctor to prescribe *anything*."

"So what? I still like it."

We are almost out of time and I feel it is important to connect to Paul on this issue, at least on some level.

"Paul, will you consider a compromise with me? Will you agree not to take the Xanax on your therapy days?"

Paul looks a little disappointed but sits with this for a moment. He rubs his shoulder slowly and looks off over the heads of the men on the couch. At last he opens his mouth. "Deal."

INTERPRETATION ─────────────

In tonight's session Paul starts out with the truth ("I want more feedback from all of you") but knowingly sits on a lie ("I really should have told all of you"). Gary picks up on Paul's deception almost immediately but doesn't trust his instincts enough to comment out loud. I also notice something about Paul as the evening wears on: he lacks his usual tension and harshness. Ironically, Paul is trying to be present in the group and win the trust of the men. Paul claims a desire for honesty even though he has been dishonest in both of the most recent sessions: in his clandestine search for a "support" group and his hesitancy to admit being on tranquilizers. Gary is both angry and disappointed with Paul. The alliance they've shared in group is being strained by Paul's secretive actions and his decision to use mood-altering drugs—a condition Gary angrily dismisses as being "zonked out."

I, too, was disturbed by Paul's decision to take a tranquilizer. Since Paul knows my position on using any tranquilizers while in therapy, he first hides and then vehemently defends its use ("Sarah made me take it," "Xanax works better"). I take the time to explain to Paul why I believe the drug will only detract from his progress. It is important for him to understand that I can be angry without rejecting him, which is a new experience for Paul. I want him to see that I am concerned that he is standing in the way of his own progress. My therapy focuses on insight, combining *understanding* and *feeling*, and the method is wasted when someone chemically dulls the feeling. Most men have a huge struggle connecting with their feelings in the first place. Dulling them with tranquilizers makes that struggle even harder. Paul's attempt to suppress his feeling of anxiety is a mistake: Anxiety is a normal reaction to something or somebody one fears. The only way for Paul, or anyone, to master the fear is to understand

and face the feared situation or person. At this level, anxiety is a useful cue. It pumps up our adrenaline. It gives us a surge of energy. Anxiety gives us a winning edge in any stressful situation. When the anxiety builds to the point where it interferes with normal day-to-day functioning, then tranquilizers may be prescribed to avoid feeling overwhelmed. But I believe they interfere with a person's ability to gain insight during therapy. Paul and the others are here to face their anxiety, not cover it. That's exactly what the men are doing in here—attempting to gain mastery over their anxiety.

Mitch's proposal to Lynda comes so impulsively that he even finds himself without a ring. Clearly Mitch is moving very fast toward marrying Lynda because she has played a stronger role in his life since his father died. By partially filling the void created by his father's death, Lynda's relative importance to Mitch has grown. He's worried about losing her, too. At this early stage in the grieving process, the urgency of the proposal is related to filling his emotional vacuum. Mitch doesn't announce his engagement at the beginning of the session, because he's worried that the men might disapprove of his sudden decision. However, he is comfortable in making the announcement as a way of supporting Ed. I am encouraged that some of the men are willing to share the news and events of their lives in a way that offers real support.

SESSION 14

///

ANGER, AGGRESSION, AND DEPRESSION

"I would like to start tonight."

Burt looks around the room discreetly after this whispered announcement. He coughs briefly and shuffles on the couch. Burt looks solid and trim tonight in yet another bright new wool sweater. The sun is setting on a cold, brisk Washington day. Maybe Burt feels invigorated by the frigid air. Tonight is the first time he has started group.

"I just don't know what to do about JoAnn."

Silence.

Burt is examining the couch arm as he is picking it. Since Sean left the group, Burt has taken Sean's spot on the far left of the couch. He looks lonely in that corner tonight.

"All I hear about is her career, how she won't marry me until she gets her M.A." Burt pauses and looks right at me. "I

152

just don't know if I want to continue this relationship if she keeps putting me off!"

Ed has been watching Burt carefully this whole time. "Do you want to get married right away?" he asks.

Burt shrugs. "Hell, I don't know. I'm just so damn sick and tired of *waiting*. I waited too long before ending a relationship the last time, and I don't want to get stuck with that again."

Gary leans out to see Burt across Mitch's body. He's frowning. "Been through what . . . ?" he asks.

"Oh. I went through this whole thing with my wife. We put off having children so we could do the career thing, and we really—both of us—got into that. At the time I thought it was a great choice. So when we were finally ready . . ." Burt pauses to look at Gary, then shakes his head sadly. "Well, she had a Dalkon shield and developed one hell of an infection. So that shot having kids at all!"

"Burt, not wanting to repeat a mistake is on target. How might Rosalind and JoAnn be similar?" I ask.

A puzzled expression spreads across Burt's face. "Hmm. Well, I know they both had terrible times with their fathers—that's the first thing that comes to mind. And towards the end . . . Rosalind was depressed and withdrawn so much it damn near drove me crazy, I just had to get out, get away from her." Burt stops to examine his shoe. He looks up at me. "JoAnn can get that way, too, you know."

"Why do you keep going after the same kind of woman, anyway?" Paul demands irritably from across the table.

Burt looks over at Paul and smiles. "Paul, that's actually a good question. I don't really think they are alike in most ways, but they certainly can get depressed. And come to think of it, they can really piss me off when they go into these depressions."

"Yeah, well, I'm on JoAnn's side on this one, that's for

sure," Paul responds, with a shake of the head. "Don't you understand? Kids just fuck up a relationship."

"Paul, I *want* kids, okay? That's not the issue. I would have married JoAnn in a second when she got pregnant, what was it, eighteen months ago? But she wouldn't do it. She insisted on the abortion." Burt's gaze drifts back to me. "And . . . the fact is she said she *would* get pregnant just as soon as we got married." Burt slinks back into the couch. "I never thought *that* would be the problem."

"My God, Burt, you sound just like Ellen!" Ed exclaims.

"Yeah, so what? I'm forty-five years old. I want to be a father before Social Security."

"No. That's okay, I understand." Ed smiles. "It's just when you were talking I suddenly saw *Ellen* sitting there."

"Maybe you two *should* swap girlfriends," I suggest, lightly.

"Haven't we been through this girlfriend-swapping deal once before?" Gary asks with a grin.

"God, that wasn't the session I missed, was it?" Burt says suddenly, laughing before all the words make it out of his mouth.

Ed shakes his head. He's still grinning. "I don't know, Burt, I just think maybe JoAnn needs to hear some of this directly from you. Maybe she doesn't know how important it is for you to have children. You should go to her with some of this."

Burt nods slowly.

"I think Ed has made some good points, Burt," I say. "I wonder if this delay over the M.A. is an excuse for you to break up with JoAnn. If so, you'd better break up with her before she finishes!"

"I'm not thinking like that right now. I *want* to marry her."

"Then why break up with her because of this one delay?"

He shrugs. "You tell me."

"Burt, let's try a role-play. I'll be JoAnn."

"Ready."

"Burt, my career is important to me. You know that. You know how hard I've worked. I don't want to give it up completely right now. Children are so much responsibility, time, energy. If I had to stay home with a baby, I could kiss my career goodbye right now!"

"I'm not asking you to give up your career, JoAnn. I just want children sometime in the near future."

"Well, it seems that's exactly what you're asking. I have goals just like you. Not only that—I want us to live together for a while before we have kids."

Burt frowns. "Now, *that* I don't understand."

"Look, Burt. I just want to feel more secure with you, with our relationship, our marriage, before we have children."

The frown slowly evaporates from Burt's forehead. He breaks the role-play and looks at me. "I can see her saying that."

I decide to let Burt sit and reflect on this, without further comment.

"Well, *I'm* feeling a lot better today, at least," Paul says with a sudden surge of energy. He uncrosses his long legs and sits forward to face Burt directly. "Got a raise, got a new car, had my lawyer write Sarah and insist that *she* pay some child support since I've got all these damn bills and I'm supporting *her* adultery. She's away weekends on my money! Can you believe it? Anyway, I'm pretty glad with where I'm at now. I had a date with a couple of women and I went out Saturday night on a third date with this one. My parents even sent me a five-thousand-dollar check that I didn't expect as a down payment on my new condo."

Gary snickers. He won't look at Paul directly.

"Where are you, Gary?" I ask.

He looks right past Paul and straight at me. "I'm fine."

"I think you should trust your instincts on this. What's going on?"

Gary's look intensifies. At first it appears he isn't going to say a word, then he explodes.

"Man, I'm *just sick of this!* This dude's high as a kite, he's fucking whacked out on Xanax, and we've got to sit here and listen to him drone on like a fucking imbecile!"

Nobody moves. Burt is frozen stiff. Paul is as calm as ever: the Xanax at work. Mitch is eyeing Gary nervously but after a time starts to nod his assent.

"The truth is, I got bored as soon as Paul started, too."

Paul finally catches Gary's eye. "I'm not high," he says.

"Sure you're not. That's why you've got that half-assed smirk on your face two seconds after I yell at you. Nothing's getting through to you, Paul."

"Oh yes it is. This is exactly the kind of feedback I want!"

"Okay, Paul," Ed interjects, "here's my contribution. Why do you keep popping in when another conversation is going and switch the subject to you? I wanted to hear more about Burt and JoAnn."

"So what? Why don't the rest of you jump in, too? Throw an elbow or two and people will pay attention to you, that's what I always say."

"Maybe Sean caught an elbow or two in the stomach," Ed says with a smirk.

"I don't want to hear about Sean, okay? He's already chickened out. I want to hear about the men in this room! Just interrupt me if you want to say something."

"There's no interrupting you," Mitch says angrily.

Paul stops. He's watching Mitch.

"Al has to practically *beg* you to shut up for ten seconds so you can *listen*, so you can hear what is going on in here!"

Paul's eyes have grown wide. In spite of the Xanax, Mitch has gotten to him. The sheer bulk of the man has intimidated

Paul into complete silence. He looks nervously from Mitch to me and back. He won't move at all.

I look at my watch and realize we've just gone over time, but I don't want to come in quite yet. Too much has gotten stirred up and needs to be addressed. There is no stopping the group tonight.

"Look, I don't like where this is going," Paul croaks. He slowly breaks his visual lock on Mitch and looks over at me. "I can still remember what this was like. When I was in seventh grade I got beat up more than once. I don't need this! I don't even want to ride down the elevators with these guys! Can I stay here and ride down with you?"

I nod. "But, Paul, you know the rules: No physical violence against anyone or anything. So I don't think you have to be concerned about something really happening here. And I understand you are the target of some serious anger. What you do have to learn is how you become insensitive and lose those around you, and then find yourself completely alone and boring. This ends up alienating everyone."

"I still want to ride down the elevator with you," Paul says emphatically.

Mitch is still glaring at Paul.

"Mitch," I say, "you've got to let out some of that anger. You're sitting on so much anger I can feel the tension way over here!"

Finally Mitch's glare focuses on me. "You want me to get mad at you?"

"I'm here to help you figure it out, Mitch, including how you might get mad at me. I don't take what goes on in here personally. So yes, get mad at me."

"Oh come on, Al, what the hell is this?" Gary interjects angrily. "We're supposed to yell at you? What the hell are we doing in here?"

"Do just *that!* Get it *out!* Even the talking is letting it out and this is the value—experience it."

"Awww shit, I don't *believe* you."

"I know. You have to try it to learn how to do it."

Gary is shaking his head, but Mitch and Ed are nodding slowly. As the fever in the room cools, the men realize we've gone ten minutes over. There is a slow shuffle for coats as everyone stands and prepares to leave. Paul waits five minutes after everyone else has left and slowly plods out the door.

INTERPRETATION

The intense feelings of anger and confrontation in tonight's session have been valuable catalysts in demonstrating much of the value and purpose of group therapy. It is only in the group environment that interactive behavior can reach such a fevered pitch. The men are faced with runaway feelings and are so confused they need guidance to understand what is appropriate behavior, what they are supposed to do, and what is considered acceptable. This gives me the opportunity in the aftermath not only to show Paul the consequences of his behavior in group, why there is so much anger directed right at him, but also to connect his behavior with Mitch and Gary and to explain the value of these emotions and the importance of facing and experiencing them, as opposed to ignoring them.

The anger starts with Gary, who has felt cheated and excluded from his alliance with Paul by Paul's choice to take the anti-anxiety drug Xanax during therapy. Mitch's anger at Paul resurfaces from last week and focuses on similar issues: Paul's lack of appreciation for others, last week by secretly looking for a substitute group, this week by droning on and on without regard for others. In fact, in both sessions Paul has given a mixed message: he says he wants to hear reactions, but he can't deal with them once they come out. The increasing honesty and expression of feelings from all the men tonight made Paul exceedingly anxious. In his childhood, Paul's way of dealing with such anger was to withdraw, to "go away." As an adult, Paul has made the same choice: Xanax. The Xanax is Paul's way of "going away" tonight—of hiding from his anxiety and trying to bolster himself in group. Paul wants the men to think he is doing well. He goes into a rambling discourse on how much success he is enjoying and how his life is free of stress and anxiety. Gary and Ed react with anger, and Mitch first gets bored and then angry, too. Ironically, while Paul is trying to put the best face on his life, the men's reactions are just the opposite of what he anticipates. They sense he is regressing and missing the whole point of therapy: he's losing touch with them and even with his own life. In short, they feel cheated and annoyed, and their anger is a natural reaction to such behavior.

When Ed blames Paul for forcing Sean from the group, he releases an avalanche of anger on Paul. This avalanche is something Paul cannot deal with—it is a place he cannot be. He is used to tuning out Sarah and ignoring his children, but he *can't* tune out the men. He simply does not know what to do. He is frightened by this experience, and I need to assure him that no physical harm will come to him.

Yet something larger is going on here as well. With words like "beat up" and "fear" being tossed around, the men have to stop and question themselves: Could they go out of control? Could things get physically violent? That's when the men turn to me to reestablish control. I move the discussion away from feelings and toward intellect by assuring the men that verbal sharing of feelings is always acceptable, and that violence will *not* be tolerated. This is designed to reassure the men that I have control, and I will use it. I also demonstrate to Mitch and Gary, both of whom are extremely angry with

Paul, the value of their anger and the importance of sharing it and, if necessary, focusing it on me. Gary, Mitch, and Ed— the three men who confronted Paul tonight—all came from families where the parents could not deal effectively with anger and went completely out of control. It is my goal to demonstrate that the same feelings of anger can be handled differently, and responsibly—*in* control—as adults.

///

THE POWER OF COMBINING THOUGHTS AND FEELINGS

"Why are you in my seat?"

Paul is standing directly over Mitch, who has calmly seated himself in the black leather chair right next to mine. This is the chair Paul long ago claimed for his own.

Mitch slowly looks up at Paul but doesn't say a word. Paul tries again.

"Do you have something you want to talk about this week, or what?"

Mitch smiles. "No. I took it just so you couldn't have it."

Paul shrugs and backs into a seat on the couch. "Not to worry. I'm not going to talk about myself tonight anyway."

Ed and Mitch exchange a glance. Mitch is smiling but Ed just shrugs. Neither looks very convinced by Paul's statement.

There is a silence that stretches into several minutes.

Paul is sitting tight and Mitch is enjoying a few swings in the leather chair. Gary and Burt are both very still. Ed looks distracted; it takes some time before his even voice breaks the stillness.

"You know, there's a very good possibility I'm going to lose Ellen."

The silence returns and Ed sits quietly examining his feet. He's waiting for a question or comment, but nobody says a word.

"Okay," Ed continues, shifting to face Mitch with his back angled in Paul's direction. His face is drawn; he looks tired.

"I just don't know what to do! I finally got Ellen to go with me to the National Gallery last Sunday, after harping at her for God knows how long, and she just moped through the gallery like a petulant little zombie. She absolutely wouldn't say a word to me. I couldn't even get an answer out of her at lunch!" He's shaking his head miserably. "It got so bad I sort of edged my way ahead from her and basically spent almost two hours by myself, wandering around. About four-thirty I figured I better dig her up because they were about to close, and I found her—ten feet away from the main entrance on those lounge chairs, just staring into space."

Ed's head continues its slow shaking from side to side.

There is a grunt from Paul's direction. "So'd you guys have a fight or what?"

"No. We didn't." Ed's back is still to Paul—he hasn't moved.

"She just hates you in general, right?" Paul blurts out.

At this Ed slides back on the couch so he can see Paul on the far left end. He's glaring straight at him.

"She hates to talk in general, Paul. You'd know that if you'd heard a single thing I've ever said in this group." Ed stops abruptly and pulls off his glasses in one deliberate motion. He rubs his eyes slowly and continues.

"There is no talking to Ellen about anything. We'll get three sentences into a conversation about something, I don't know, Van Gogh, and I'll challenge her on some point and boom! that's it, she'll stop cold and give me this vicious stare"—Ed glowers at Mitch, mimicking Ellen—"and go dead silent." The glasses go back on. "If you think you'll get anything out of her, boy are you sadly mistaken. Nothing. Nada. Ice-cold dead silence."

"Yeah, well, marry her anyway," Paul persists. "At least you like her, right?"

"The truth is, I'm really worried about this."

"Would you *look* at me?" Paul demands.

Ed swings around suddenly, his eyes in a crazy exaggerated stare. "Okay?!"

"Jesus, I know where Ellen is on this, you know? I can't believe you're still mad at me from last week! Why the hell won't you let me help you?"

Ed rolls his eyes. "It's not like you've done much for me so far, Paul. God knows how long you'll be around anyway. Find any nifty support groups out there?"

"That's not fair: I'm here, right? I'm trying to connect to you and you're on this intellectual binge going on and on about Van Gogh. Then you're mad at Ellen because she can't argue like you, she's just not fucking good enough, huh?" Paul breaks off and looks away, but then has another thought.

"If I were Ellen I'd close you out, too."

"Yeah, well, lucky me."

"Don't you ever have anything nice to say about her?"

Ed grins wickedly. "Oh sure, Paul, like we've heard the sweetest love stories about Sarah. I've got this vision of her as some monstrous vulture, sucking blood out of you by the gallon."

"So what?" Paul shoots back. "I think of Ellen as this quiet, oafish dolt tagging along after you while you give her failing grades on her answers to your questions. If you got any more intellectual, your head would explode!"

"Jesus Christ, Paul, I've had about enough of this. I didn't come in here for a pissing contest."

"Great! I can't tell you how illuminating this discussion has been. I'm thrilled you let me help you out. It's a pain in the ass trying to deal with you. No wonder Ellen clams up. We're both wasting our time with you." Paul folds his arms and slides back on the couch away from Ed. His bitter stare is locked on the carpet.

Silence.

"Have you two given up on each other?" I ask calmly.

"You bet," Ed mumbles. Paul just glares at me out of the corner of his eye. Eventually, he nods.

I don't want the conversation to end without resolution, so I encourage them.

"This is not exactly the way to go about learning to resolve a conflict."

More silence.

"Look," Ed says suddenly, "I just don't know where to go with this guy!"

I nod. "I understand where you're at, both of you. But there is value in Paul's reaction: He's able to see where Ellen is, and that could be something to learn from."

Ed scowls. Paul finally looks right at me.

"I'm not going to do it. I'm not going to get beaten up by him. That's it!"

I allow some more silence before coming in again.

"I encourage both of you to stick with this. You can learn more from each other by interacting than by smoldering in your corners. You're repeating in here what happens in your relationships outside."

During this entire exchange Burt has grown completely still. Gary has slid so far back in his corner that he's almost hidden by the palm.

I'm about to ask for others' reactions when Ed grunts.

"Look. Here's the deal. I know Paul might be able to help, okay, that's fine. It's just that . . . well, I'm really *scared*. I'm just afraid of losing her."

"What other feelings?" I ask.

Ed has buried himself in the couch now and appears to have actually grown smaller.

"This possibility—it makes me . . . it hurts. It's sad. But if I can learn from Paul, then I'll make myself hang in."

Paul sighs quietly. "You're too demanding of Ellen, and she's afraid she's not going to say the right thing."

"I . . . don't want to lose her." Ed's voice has developed a quiver. "I'm sad to realize that I might be driving her away."

Ed is connecting on a truly emotional level. These are real feelings from Ed and I feel for him.

"I understand that, Ed, I can feel it," I say. "Another thing"—I allow a small smile—"I'm glad you're in touch with 'sad' and 'scared.' It's easier to connect to you when you include feelings in what you say."

Ed scratches the back of his neck and nods back at me slowly. He's growing more relaxed; this has been a burden lifted from his shoulders. Even Paul, who has actually begun to look at the other men again, has sat forward and is listening to my words. As soon as the last phrase is out of my mouth, Paul jumps in.

"Look, I want to ask you guys something. Why is everybody so down on me? I really want to know."

"I think . . ." Burt says, but pauses for a moment to reflect. "Paul, this is the deal. You interrupt quite a bit of the time. You take the conversation to where you want it. Sometimes I think you don't really listen to anyone else!"

"Does that bother you?" Paul asks.

"Well, sure," Burt replies, a little surprised.

"Would you be willing to *tell* me when you get annoyed?"

"I could do that."

"How about you?" Paul asks, looking at Mitch for the first time since the session started.

"Paul, my first reaction to you is negative."

"So tell me when that happens, okay?"

Mitch shakes his head. "Sorry, that's not really part of my personality."

Paul shrugs and moves on to Gary.

"Well?"

"You think I haven't tried? Stopping a freight train is easier than interrupting you, Paul."

Paul nods and grows silent. He has ignored Ed.

Gary is still watching Paul. He looks agitated and coughs nervously.

"Paul, here's an example: I've wanted to talk all evening about something." He looks over at me and shakes his head. "Leigh and I broke up last week." He lets out an almost imperceptible sigh and then seems to remember where he was with Paul.

"Oh . . . so I wanted to talk about this, and as soon as you and Ed have your battle, *you* pick up *again*, and I'm sitting over here wondering how I'm going to be able to edge in."

"Oh. Okay, how do you feel about your breakup?"

Gary smiles weakly. "I feel like a complete failure, that's what. I should've ended it last November, but as usual I just hung in there. Same old pattern. Stick with it no matter what. Now I'm afraid I won't have anything to talk about in here. No woman to complain about."

"We talk about a lot of other things in here. *You* do, too," Burt offers. "I was real interested in that story about your father."

Gary shrugs. "Yeah, but my relationship was the first to go down the tubes, right? Not only that . . . shit, *I'm* the only recovering alcoholic in here." Suddenly Gary looks away from the men and out the window. "I just get the feeling I'm a hell of a lot more fucked up than any of you."

Ed and Burt exchange surprised looks.

"You really think so?" Mitch asks from the leather chair.

Gary nods. "Yeah, and I'm this lowly insurance estimator, just work out of my house. The rest of you are like, what, lawyers and all?"

Burt breaks into a wide grin. "Not on your life. You know I work on Capitol Hill. For the army."

Paul looks at Burt and back at Gary. "I'm the lawyer. Patent attorney, remember?"

Ed raises his hand. "Epidemiologist."

"Okay, I know, so everybody's different, it's just—"

"Gary," I break in, "what's going on?"

Gary frowns at me. "Huh?"

"You're all over the place: down on yourself, down on Leigh, down on the guys—and I'll be next. No one's response can satisfy you. You're very hard to pin down tonight."

Gary stiffens and peers at me for a moment.

"Why are *you* putting me down?"

"I'm describing my sense of you now. No point in anyone putting you down—you're already doing it to yourself! You won't hear any of the support anyone is giving you tonight."

"Yeah, okay." He sighs. "The truth is, I thought I was being more open, more vulnerable, I guess. I just heard it as a put-down."

"You are being more open and vulnerable, but you're stopping there and missing everyone's understanding and acceptance. Their reaction to your openness is support—not a put-down." I pause to watch Gary's reaction. "You're not in your real family right now. We're different."

Gary shrugs. "I never thought of it that way."

"Who in your family would put you down? Who are you expecting me to be like?"

"You want me to say my father?"

"I want you to continue to see the truth and reality."

"Okay. I see what you mean. No matter what I said at

home, he always put me down. I do worry that people are going to put me down, so I shy away from them."

"You're catching on, Gary."

"Well, I've got to give you credit, Al." Gary pauses and smiles at me. "I was a wrestler in high school and I don't like to be pinned down."

INTERPRETATION

The frustration and anger toward Paul from last week continue to fester in tonight's session. In the closing minutes of last week's session, I restated the guidelines of group therapy: any emotional confrontation is encouraged, no physical confrontation of any kind is acceptable. Mitch is more comfortable with the limits and feels free to simply take Paul's chair. Paul immediately discounts the idea that Mitch may be mad at him, which he clearly is ("I just took it so you couldn't have it") and tells himself it's just because Mitch may be "needy" ("Do you have something you want to talk about this week, or what?"). Paul has, in fact, walked straight into the lion's den this evening. The men are basically ignoring him. This does not sit well with Paul at all: He continually tries to edge in with Ed, who is already upset with Paul from last week.

As their confrontation escalates, Paul does make a very good point about Ed's tendency to remain intellectual: it is annoying him and he realizes that his frustration with Ed is similar to *Ellen's* frustration with Ed. Paul understands Ellen: he'd want to walk off, too! When both Ed and Paul clam up and refuse to engage one another, the cycle is complete. Ed and Paul duplicate in group what Ed and Ellen (and Paul and Sarah) have in life: a recurring standoff. Since this is ordinarily the stopping point between Ed and Ellen, I came in to emphasize that both men must go beyond this point in order to make progress. Ed is the first to consider that this suggestion has some validity because he's willing to be pushed, to take a risk because he is genuinely afraid of losing Ellen. Ed is visibly upset. As much as Ed dislikes Paul, he wishes to go the extra mile to keep Ellen. Ed *is* in a hard place. Ellen won't address any of these issues and won't go into therapy. Since Ed is making this effort himself, he stands much to gain from this process, and I only hope Ellen can keep up with him.

Once the situation with Ed is resolved, Paul goes fishing for attention. It is clear to Paul that the men are ignoring him, and he wants to do something about it. Tonight he is trying a new tactic. Whereas last week he chose to be calm and reserved by taking Xanax, tonight he is aggressive and confrontational. He goes around the group asking each member to tell him when they're mad or annoyed at him. Even though this is not really successful, since only Burt agrees to it, it does make sense. Paul wants desperately to make a connection to these men even though he continually alienates them. This is why Paul's most important lesson in the group is to learn his effect on others. It is a difficult lesson for Paul to learn.

Gary, meanwhile, is making another advance. He has taken in a lot of valuable information tonight. Initially he believed a relationship was needed to be "in this special club": he learned tonight that the men are interested in his whole life. He also thought he was more "fucked-up" than the others. Tonight it is clear that this is not the case ("You really think so?" Mitch asks with surprise). Finally, Gary has always felt a nagging inferiority on the professional level. He has always assumed that because the other men were more highly educated that they were also more capable and successful than he was. He doesn't yet know that he actually makes more money than anyone else here. Most men measure their success by the amount of money they earn or by the prestige of

their profession. Gary takes a risk making himself more vulnerable, by admitting feelings of inferiority. In this entire process, Gary is accepted and supported, but he won't accept
this support. On every subject when some encouragement
comes his way, he interrupts and denies that what he does,
what he feels, is worthy of respect. It is difficult for me, or
for any of the men, to figure out what Gary actually wants
here. This is the origin of my "pin-down" comment: He really
is quite slippery, very elusive. I want Gary to hear, to consciously recognize and acknowledge, the support he gets this
evening. Gary's defensive reactions are based on his family
dynamics, which he has continued to use. Now he recognizes
that most of the "real" world is not out to put or pin him down
and that he doesn't need to be so defensive. Gary has made
a valuable and supportive connection to this group and is finding it difficult to allow the group to actually give to him.

DREAMS:
THE INSIDE STORY

Paul has reclaimed his chair. He is sitting absolutely still, peering at Mitch with his jaw thrust forward. Mitch and Burt plop into their seats on the couch and give Paul a quick look. Mitch is grinning slightly.

Paul looks as though he's about to speak, but he waits until Gary and Ed get settled. They've just finished up a long story from the waiting area and are sharing a quiet laugh.

"So here's the deal," Paul begins. His jaw is relaxed now as he glances around at the men. "I've got a new squeeze. She's great, her name is Patti, and I've been out with her twice, and on Saturday, we slept together for the first time." He lets out an almost imperceptible sigh. "Boy, was it nice to sleep with somebody else for a change. Not only that, she suggested, no, insisted, I use a condom."

Gary smiles wryly. "She's afraid you're going to give her something, Paul?"

Paul snorts. "Hell no, *I'm* the one who's glad. From the way she talks I'll bet she's still hung up on her ex, and she's probably sleeping with the guy. But I still like her. She reminds me of Sarah in some ways. And my mom. She's all right."

Paul's gaze has slowly shifted from Gary to Mitch during this exchange. Paul is checking to see if Mitch is listening. He's not. Mitch is instead examining one of my paintings behind Paul's head.

"So is this woman going to be your new girlfriend?" Gary asks, bringing Paul back.

Paul shrugs. "Who knows." He brightens suddenly. "But I'll tell you what, I'd like it. She's got terrific tits, clear out here"—Paul indicates their fullness with his hands. "New implants she got just three weeks ago."

"Do you *like* her, Paul?" Burt asks quietly.

"Oh, sure. We had a real nice talk right when she got out of the hospital. She really opened up to me and told me all about her life. She even went into this horrible story about how her father raped her when she was twelve. *Twelve years old.*" Paul shudders slightly, then falls silent.

The silence continues.

"Paul, what are you feeling as you're telling us this?" I ask.

At first Paul does not respond. His head is tilted down away from me and he does not move when he finally answers.

"A little tense."

"I can understand that," I say, "considering your confrontation in here last week."

Paul looks up abruptly. "So what do you guys think? Let's hear some feedback."

Mitch rolls his eyes, and Paul catches him doing it.

"So?" Paul demands.

"You're boring me Paul. I lost interest already. Lots of facts and nothing about what's going on inside *you.*"

Paul's foot is tapping rapidly but he remains quiet. His eyes are still locked on Mitch.

Now Ed coughs nervously and pauses. Ed looks distracted tonight. He's much more rumpled in appearance, and he looks dejected. Nonetheless, he decides to jump in.

"Well, there's some truth to that, Paul. You're starting to launch into a long story about Patti's tits, about Patti's life, and we're not hearing anything about you. If Al hadn't stopped you to find out what *you're* feeling, we'd probably all be hearing about how her apartment is decorated and why she hates her job. Isn't this exactly what you said you *didn't* want from us?"

"I just want you guys to be honest," Paul shrugs.

"I can do that," Burt says with a slight smile. "My opinion is this. You're moving too fast with this Patti woman. Take it easy. Take it slow."

"Wait a second," Gary interjects. He's got his hand out like he's hailing a cab. "Just stop a second. Give him a *chance*, okay? How can you judge this woman so fast? I don't even know anything about her." Gary looks at Paul momentarily. "I wanted to hear more about you and her." Everyone is silent.

Paul grins. He is surprised, yet pleased, by Gary's sudden vigorous defense.

"Can I go on now?" Paul looks around and then continues without waiting for an answer. "If you want to know how I feel, I feel good to have sex again."

I nod at Paul. "What are your feelings at the moment?"

This time Paul does look at me. "I'm just glad to be in a relationship. That's all. It's tough out there. Really lonely."

Gary is nodding again and I sense the alliance between these two, shaken in recent weeks, gaining some new strength. I want to pull the discussion together.

"I think you both are in a similar place. Neither one of

you has a woman right now." My gaze wanders over to the rest of the couch. "Everyone else is in a committed relationship—Burt, Ed, and Mitch—and you are all sleeping with your women. So this is something we need to recognize." I pause to watch Paul, but he registers no reaction. "I'm concerned, Paul," I continue, "that you threw away the real heart and meat of the reactions from everyone tonight."

This surprises Paul. He looks over at me and frowns.

"The only strong response you had was to Gary, and his response was just empathy—he gave no feedback, no suggestions, no feeling."

"Hey, wait a minute. It was my honest-to-God reaction!" Gary protests.

"I'm aware of that, Gary. But it was the comment Paul had the *least* to learn from. He needs to hear everybody and be aware of the effect he's having on them." I turn directly to Paul. "Gary's empathy is fine; he's on your side on this. But you have to pay attention to the others' reactions, too. They're just as real and important for you."

"I heard them."

"You may have heard them, but you responded as though it was water off a duck's back." I stop to dig up in my mind an image that will appeal to Paul, something that will make a connection to him.

"Paul, look at it this way. It's like the new tits on Patti. They look great—they get your attention. But they're fake. There's nothing there. If you were to suck on them—try to get some nurturance from them—you'd find out they are dry."

Paul just stares at me, then slowly nods. "Okay. So I should focus on *you* as my new test of reality."

"Not just me. *Everyone* in here is a test of reality. You need to hear every one of them. Try not to tune them out. The fact is, Paul, the group is willing to cooperate with you more than you realize."

Paul smiles and taps Gary's knee with the back of his hand.

"You know, the two of us should hit the bar for a drink sometime."

A ripple of laughter runs through the group. Even Gary is amused. He's shaking his head slowly. But Paul's face is totally blank.

"What? What'd I say? You think I'm a queer or something?"

"Oh, for God's sake," Mitch mutters.

"Here's a good example of where you need to pay attention, Paul," Burt observes wryly.

"What?" Paul is beginning to grow restless.

"Paul, remember?" Gary nudges him on the arm. "I'm a recovering alcoholic. I haven't been in a bar in over six years."

"Oh, sure." He shrugs. "Sorry about that."

Gary smiles. "It's okay. I've been pretty hard on you the past few weeks, so I'll let this one go."

Ed has sat in stony silence throughout this light exchange. I know what has him so preoccupied. He avoids my gaze by looking out the windows and then staring at the side of Mitch's head.

"Ed, you can't avoid saying anything," I murmur.

Ed freezes and takes a deep breath. His head swings over in my direction.

"Look, this is pretty hard. My father died last Wednesday night."

Mitch gasps. Gary suddenly sits up and faces Ed. The light tone in the room vanishes.

Silence.

"God, not another one," Paul mutters finally.

Ed eyes Paul. "Yeah, another one." He shakes his head and looks over Paul's shoulder. "I couldn't believe it myself, you know? My sister called me in the middle of the night, and I'm sitting there thinking, *This can't be happening, there must be some kind of mistake. It can't be my father,'* and this goddamned thought kept running round and round in my head." Ed now has his whole head buried in his hands. Everyone is very still.

"So I didn't know what to say! I'm sitting there listening to her and suddenly it dawns on me what's happened, and I start sobbing and shaking so hard I drop the phone, and shit, I just lost it. Thank God Ellen was there to talk to my sister."

Ed stops to cough and runs his fingers slowly through his hair.

Silence.

"You need to say more, Ed," I urge.

He looks up. "I didn't even say this to you, Al, but—" Suddenly Ed breaks off; his voice has grown thick, and his breathing is uneven. His glasses come off and he reaches for the Kleenex to wipe his swollen eyes. We sit quietly with him for a while. After a few moments of silence and slow, deliberate breathing, he's ready to go again.

"I hadn't even talked to him in six years! I didn't even know he was sick."

"Sounds like you're feeling a lot of guilt, Ed," I say. "Say a little more."

Ed sighs and shakes his head. "Oh, hell, I don't know. I hate to say it, but I was *ashamed* of him. I just wrote him off years ago. Maybe I could have helped him out of this"—Ed looks over at Mitch on his left—"like you were trying to do with your father."

Mitch nods. "Did you ever try?"

"Wait," I interject, "let's keep it in here."

"I was just curious," Mitch protests.

"Well, I'm not sure of that Mitch. This is a difficult topic for you, too. I think you'd rather not deal with Ed's intense feelings right now; after all, you just went through the same thing. So let's keep it here for a while."

Mitch shrugs. "Never mind, then."

Ed looks at me in anticipation. His hands are beginning to shake slightly and I notice his breathing is a little irregular again.

"Ed?"

He lets out a deep sigh. "I had this horrible dream Friday night. I still remember it, because it won't go away and I had damn near the same one last night, too."

"Let me hear the dream. Try to say it in the present tense, as though it were happening now."

"In the dream I have this revolver and I'm out at a shooting range in the desert somewhere and I'm firing away at this target off in the distance. I'm not even getting near it. All of a sudden my arm starts shaking and a shot goes pow! and ricochets off this rock and slams straight into the target. The target turns into a man. The man explodes. I woke up yelling." He winces.

"What do you make of the dream?" I ask.

"I think the man must be my father. It means I killed my father. I'm responsible in a roundabout way."

"What I hear is that you are feeling a whole lot of guilt over your father's death."

"That's for damned sure! And I can't figure it out. He lived by himself, off in this remote apartment without a telephone, and he wasn't in touch with any of us. He was drinking all the time. It was his choice! I was so sure he died of booze I forgot to ask. It turned out the coroner said the cause of death was a heart attack. I felt much better to know he didn't drink himself to death."

"Because?"

"A heart attack just sounds better. I guess it's the shame again."

INTERPRETATION

Paul is connecting to a new love interest in a way that is in itself new for Paul: In contrast to his former interactions with women, he is now, for the first time, making an attempt to learn more about a woman (Patti, in this case) by listening to her ("She really opened up to me") and connecting to her more as a person. Because of Paul's crude, rough manner, he is very lonely, and any hint of acceptance is magnified. Patti is especially attractive to Paul because she is familiar and non-threatening, and she reminds him of both Sarah and his mother, women he understands and is familiar with, even though he is very unhappy with both. Once again familiarity and comfort prove irresistible to Paul. The other men sense this and show some real concern. Burt wants Paul to move more slowly to keep from getting hurt and falling into another bad relationship. The men are sensing some superficiality in this relationship, not only because of Paul's detailed description of Patti's new breasts, but because Paul has given only a surface description of Patti (the complaint voiced by both Mitch and Ed), one that excludes Paul's own feelings about her. Paul's only real connection is to Gary's empathy. Certainly misery loves company, but Paul is drawn far too strongly to the sympathy at the expense of listening to the other reactions. The reason for my breast analogy in the session was to emphasize to Paul, in a way that he would understand, that he will get as much nurturance from sympathy as from Patti's artificial breasts. In this way I continue to stress to Paul the importance of hearing the reactions of every man in the group rather than focusing solely on those that are comfortable or "easy" for him to hear. In fact, Paul's wish for a connection to Gary, the "easy" reaction, is so strong that he ends up losing sight of the whole picture: Gary's alcoholism, certainly a strong and present issue in the group, vanishes from Paul's mind.

Ed's revelation of his father's unexpected death was another intense and sad episode in the group. Ed's initial reaction to the news was denial: his old way of dealing with negative feelings. As Ed catches himself in active denial, he moves into the real effect: shock and overwhelming sadness. Ed is another example of a man who has had great difficulty in his relationship with his father. Like most men I work with, Ed has yearned for a deep, close connection to his father, and he has been repeatedly disappointed by his failure to achieve it. Like Mitch, Ed had made enough progress in his own therapy to consider a reconnection. This is the source of Ed's guilt. He felt that it was his responsibility to do more to rescue the relationship, but he felt he had failed. This feeling of responsibility on Ed's part is an overreaction: it was his father's responsibility, as a father, to nurture the relationship. If there was any failure, it was Ed's father's, not Ed's.

In this session we also see Ed's further growth manifested in other ways: he's allowed himself to cry on and off all week, and Ellen has been a strong support for his change. In many ways, Ed's defensive wall is coming down. He's letting himself be more vulnerable with Ellen, and he learns that this only invites her increased love and support. Ed finds this very helpful at an extremely difficult time.

The anxiety and pain of this unexpected death are amplified in recurring dreams for Ed: an indication of the power and presence of the event in his life. Ed's dream reflects his *guilt* and the *shock* of the death. The killing by ricochet is Ed's way of expressing his anger and hostility indirectly toward his father. In real life, instead of discussing his hurt and anger, he simply ignored his father and stopped talking to him altogether. This is a reflection of Ed's old way of expressing his feelings in general: by indirect, oblique, means. Ed's own interpretation of his dream points up his willingness to deal with his feelings more directly. I think Ed will now pay more attention to *his* role in relationships, especially with Ellen.

MEN WANT CHILDREN

"How's it going, Ed?"

Burt is lounging comfortably on the couch, legs crossed and right arm extended in Mitch's direction. His brow is slightly furrowed. Concern over Ed.

Ed shrugs. "It's been tough, but things are getting better." Ed pauses to brush some dust off his trousers and look over at me. "I've been able to unload a lot of shit in individual. Last Thursday I spoke with Jan, my older sister, on the phone, and she told me about what's going on throughout the family . . . all the other reactions." Ed looks over at Burt and smiles. "All the kids are feeling guilty as hell. We don't know what we could have done differently. He's the one who moved away, yanked his telephone out of the wall, and just disappeared."

Burt nods and gradually looks over at Mitch. Mitch's

black leather boot has kept up a rapid nervous tap during Ed's story, even as his eyes have been glued right to him.

"Any other feelings, Ed?" I ask.

Ed's gaze rolls in my direction. He nods slowly.

"Yeah. Sadness. God, I wish I could have had a *real* father."

Silence.

"Do you miss talking to your dad?" Mitch asks, breaking his own trance.

"Oh, sure. But the truth is, we never really connected. Ever. Even as a kid I couldn't get to him . . . he was off drinking with my mom, living the politician's high life. So I finally gave up." He looks up at Mitch, and I notice for the first time Ed's tight, solid jaw. "It only got worse in the last few years. The guy just vanished down the bottle when my mother left him. Asshole."

"You're still pissed at him?" Mitch asks, surprised.

"You bet. The guy could be a selfish slob. Look what he did to my mother."

As Ed finishes this sentence I'm struck by how alone, lonely, he looks sitting at the edge of the couch.

"Your anger is an appropriate feeling for what you've been through, Ed," I say softly.

Ed nods in my direction and looks over at Mitch. All of a sudden I notice Mitch glowering at me.

"What's going on, Mitch?"

"I'm still pissed off at you. I don't know if I should continue with therapy at all."

"What?" Burt exclaims. "What's going on?" Gary nearly bolts out of the leather chair he claimed from Paul. Both are watching Mitch carefully.

Mitch, however, remains quiet and still. His eyes wander past me and fix on a blank spot on the wall.

"You are in a difficult point in your work, Mitch," I say. "We've uncovered a lot of things in here, so there is a lot of emotion, a lot of anger, in you, including anger at me. Your best bet right now is to go intellectual. Take note of how your life is improving."

"I don't know," Gary interjects. "I've been deep into this negative shit, too. It's making me freaky. I don't know where the hell I'm at half the time."

Burt turns straight to him. "What in the world are you talking about?"

"I don't know what to say in here. All this down emotion is pushing me into a corner and I'd rather just bail out. Screw it! I've been going through mental masturbation all my life, and when it comes right down to it, who needs it? Plus this therapy costs a *fortune*."

Now Gary has hunkered down on the couch and folded his arms in a show of defiance.

I let some time pass before coming in.

"Gary, you and Mitch are in similar places. Like I said to Mitch, go with your intellect. Pay attention to how your life has been improving."

"It hasn't been improving."

I try to suppress a smile. "Listen to me, Gary: Your progress has been very impressive. You've taken several risks in here and made some impressive gains."

He shrugs. "I need more goals. I don't know where I'm going or even where I'm headed!"

"I understand this is hard for you, Gary. Both you and Mitch have tended to withdraw from negative emotion, what's going on right here, right now, and not deal with it. It hasn't helped you in life and it won't help you to run from it now. I would encourage both of you to confront this, confront me! And deal with it."

"Oh that's right, we're supposed to yell at you," Gary says with a hint of a smile.

"If necessary."

"So that's 'getting the feelings out'?"

"Partly. Talking about them is one way of 'getting them out.' You don't have to get enraged or act crazy to let them out."

This gets a nod out of Gary, but Mitch still looks a bit skeptical.

The room grows quiet. We all sit and listen to the downtown traffic for a time.

"Can I get enraged for a moment?" Burt asks suddenly with a sly grin.

I return Burt's smile. Before I can speak, Paul sees an opening and jumps in.

"So what's the deal?"

Burt coughs and pulls some lint off his sweater. "Look, I know this should be good news, JoAnn agreed to an engagement on Thursday, but ever since that night her stress has been sky high! She's jittery and jumpy all the time."

Burt is scratching his palms nervously, his eyes are shifting continuously around the room. "I feel like the only thing she really cares about is finishing her degree. So what's it going to be like if we're married? Kids running around, day care, dog vomiting on the floor, shuttling kids to soccer practice. What's it going to be like when she's into lots of things. Am I going to just be invisible?"

"It'll be craziness. Like it is for all of us!" Paul says with a grin.

Burt is less than amused. "You have no idea what it's like to live with a woman who asks your 'reactions' and 'feelings' every thirty seconds."

"*That's* for damn sure. Sarah doesn't speak to me at all!"

"Paul, *I* don't know." Burt examines the palm plant at the end of the couch. "There are days I wonder if it isn't easier to be with a depressed woman like Rosalind than stick around with JoAnn. JoAnn wants to talk incessantly."

Paul shrugs. "Could be worse. She could hate you."

"Burt," I say, "I have this vision of you when you are with

JoAnn. You end up being barraged with words and feel, well, overwhelmed."

Burt nods emphatically. "Absolutely. It can get intimidating. It can get *humiliating*."

Mitch frowns. "Humiliating?"

Burt nods. "I mean at work. Everybody there either has kids or is pregnant. Every last person. This is no joke! And they all know how desperately I want to have kids." Burt is shaking his head. "They keep asking me when I'm getting married. When I'm having kids. *That's* humiliating. It's even coming out in my dreams."

"Can you remember the dreams?" I ask.

Burt's eyes dart nervously to Mitch and Gary before he answers me.

"I can remember this one. It wasn't a dream: it was a nightmare."

I nod at Burt and wait for him to begin.

"I'm in my kitchen. It's late at night, and I walk into the doorway and I can see my reflection . . . and I'm dressed as a woman! So as I'm standing there, some guy comes into the kitchen and starts to cross in front of me. Before he can make it out of my range, I haul off and kick him square in the balls."

Gary winces and looks away with a half-smile. Paul has a blank look of shock on his face.

"Burt, this is just my immediate association," I say, "but it's pretty clear it's a castration-anxiety dream. Since you feel you are being treated like something less than a man by JoAnn, you get kicked in the balls yourself."

Burt nods.

"And what's your feeling in the dream?" I ask.

"I'm mad. But I don't know why."

"Take a guess."

He grins. "I didn't like the dress?"

I return his smile.

"What do you make of the guy crossing you?"

"It's your turn to answer."

"Sounds like you're mad at being 'crossed,' having your plans blocked, by JoAnn."

Burt is sitting square on the couch, looking pained. He nods reluctantly.

"It might also be helpful to see things from JoAnn's viewpoint," I add. "You are asking her to deal with her thesis, think about getting married, visit her parents, and get ready to be pregnant pretty soon, all within a very short period! That's quite a plateful."

"I know it is, and I really do want to appreciate her view. I'm just nervous about running out of time."

"It might be best for both of you to back away a bit. Take it easy. You don't *need* the extreme pressure of this deadline."

Burt shrugs. "Okay. We'll talk."

Silence.

Paul clears his voice and looks over at me. "I think we need to change this group. Change the format. Try something different."

"What do you have in mind, Paul?"

"A thirty-minute period. Somebody talks for thirty minutes, then we have a time check. We stop to see if anybody else has something going on. Look at poor Brad, here"—Paul motions toward Ed—"his dad just died and he's hardly said a word."

Mitch buries his head in his hands. Burt and Gary exchange looks and smile.

"Ed. My name is Ed, you dolt."

"Oh. Whatever. It was just a suggestion." Paul sits back suddenly and I notice his hands are beginning to shake.

"What are you feeling, Paul?"

"I don't know why I'm in this group if everybody is just going to pick on me."

"Paul, you can't even remember my *name*, for God's sake!" Ed exclaims.

"So what. I'm not mean."

During this exchange I have a sudden picture in my mind of Paul as a little boy trying desperately, and unsuccessfully, to get the other kids to play with him. It's very sad.

"I just don't need this kind of abuse," Paul continues. "I can't get Sarah or Patti to even speak to me. Sarah has been having this goddamned affair for six months, and my kids just caught her in bed, can you believe this, with her lover last Sunday. In my house! I've been feeling like shit ever since. *Damn*, I'm tired of hurting over this."

"And Patti?" Ed asks.

"Oh shit, I don't know," Paul mumbles miserably. "Her life's all screwed up. I'm just trying to help her get her life on track again. But she keeps neglecting me just the same."

"Paul, do you see what's going on?"

Paul shrugs. "Yeah. I'm miserable. Women hate me."

"Look. The rejection and isolation you're describing from Sarah and Patti aren't just outside this room, Paul, they're happening right here. *In the room.* You are playing an active role in being rejected and isolated from the other men. You need to learn how you do this, Paul, how you isolate yourself, or you're going to continue to be left out. You can learn to do it right here. And it won't take long."

Paul brightens considerably. A slight smile, even. He takes a deep breath and runs a quick hand through his hair.

"I appreciate that, Al. I'm glad to hear there is *something* I can do. It's just so damn depressing. But I know I'm making some progress. I don't have the same doubts as Gary over here. I *know* I'm getting something out of therapy. I'm not the same person I was six months ago. In fact, I wish the guys would appreciate it more!"

"Yeah, Paul, but it's impossible for me to entirely erase

my impression of you at once," Mitch says with a shake of the head.

"I wish we heard more from *you*, Mitch," Gary says softly.

Mitch shifts his large frame to face Gary on the other end of the couch.

"I'll talk when I'm ready."

Gary frowns. "I think it would be better if you talk when you're *not* ready. It's tougher, but you'll get more out of it."

"I do what I do. I don't like change. You all know that."

Silence.

"Look, Mitch, I'm going to be honest with you," Gary says abruptly. "I'm not happy with this. I don't appreciate your sitting over there in silence glowering at everybody, staring me down." Gary's voice has begun to quaver slightly. He pauses to recover before continuing.

"I'll tell you what. I've been trying to figure you out, and here's what I have so far. You're sitting on this huge fucking barrel of anger and you're ready to explode at any time." The quaver in Gary's voice has reappeared.

"Gary, are you all right?" Burt asks.

"Sure. I was just . . . well, I was sort of apprehensive about actually saying that, but I'm glad I did."

"I'm not going to explode, Gary," Mitch says calmly.

"Yeah, well, I can see it in your eyes. There is a slow burn going on deep inside. You have this placid, calm exterior, always in control. But I know better. I can see inside of you."

INTERPRETATION ──────────

Mitch's anger at me in tonight's session is a holdover from last week. When I stopped Mitch from interrupting Ed's pain and loss surrounding his father's death in that last session, Mitch withdrew momentarily and has been angry at me ever since. In Mitch's mind, I am being like his father, and his response is identical: anger and withdrawal. It is still hard for Mitch to express his anger directly, because he continues to fear retaliation from his dad. While Mitch occasionally will let out some anger (often in response to Paul), he almost always suppresses or hides it. Gary, on the other hand, who also has trouble expressing anger, is able to pick up on Mitch's behavior immediately and identify it for what it is. When Gary initially prods Mitch to say more about his life, Mitch shuts down further, making him increasingly anxious and uncomfortable. In fact, Gary is quite on target with his observations of Mitch tonight. His confrontation with Mitch is his own attempt to be more connected to him.

Burt has also been sitting on a lot of anxiety, and his threshold was just breached this last week. For the last several months Burt has been playing nice guy at home to JoAnn and has been sitting on his own feelings (anxieties, feelings of inferiority, embarrassment) in an effort to provide support and nurturance to her. There is also an element of anger in Burt that has been buried and just recently surfaced: Burt has been angry at JoAnn for putting so many things ahead of him and his desire for marriage and children. Burt's tendency to sit on anger gets him into serious trouble in relationships: it was the central element underlying his early impotence in his relationship with JoAnn and has been responsible for his own feeling of failure and uncertainty in his past relationship. There is a reason Burt does this. He is trying to keep *JoAnn's* stress down by not revealing his own feelings, but inside he wants everything taken care of (he secretly wants JoAnn to embrace the idea of marriage and children over her studies). The dilemma for Burt is that JoAnn is a talker, she verbalizes her stress constantly, while Burt is the silent type: he has been overwhelmed by words ever since childhood, when he was intimidated by his screaming father. Burt also is experiencing much humiliation. At work he feels like an outsider, as his colleagues—all of whom are married and have children—ask when he's getting married and when he's having children, the very area of conflict with JoAnn. In Burt's dream we see a great deal of his anger, something that he has been holding in and just now overflows into his dream. The kick in the balls in this dream reflects both his hostility and his own vulnerability. His clothes (he's dressed as a woman in the dream) show that he doesn't feel like a man. He just doesn't have what all the men at work have: he is an unfulfilled man. The "good-natured" teasing at work is making him more vulnerable. Unfortunately, this is a low blow to Burt.

Once again we witness Paul's isolating behavior in group and some of the hostility it generates. Tonight's session has been a microcosm of what happens in Paul's life: His alienating, abrasive behavior isolates him from people, so he tries in any way he can to win "approval" (in his life, he supports Patti; in the group, he proposes a better group "format"). However, Paul is not getting nurturance from either of these two areas: Patti continues to ignore him and the men in the group reject his idea out of hand. Paul is replaying in his adult life that which he learned as a child. For many years Paul felt entirely unwanted by his mother, so he attempted to compensate by becoming "important": by being supportive, doing work, being responsible. But this has not worked for Paul in his adult life: he is encountering failure with all the women in his life and he continues to struggle with the men in group to establish and maintain a strong bond.

//

THE THERAPIST
AS FATHER

"I've been thinking a lot about what I'm doing to Ellen."

A long silence follows Ed's statement. He pauses to remove his glasses and rub his eyes; Gary watches Ed go through these motions. We are all very quiet.

The glasses finally go back on.

"I know what I'm doing; it's what you've been telling me in here," Ed says simply. "I criticize her a lot. She's always gotten completely silent after this happens. She'll ignore me, mope around, vanish for hours with a book. The thing is, I never saw it as criticism. I just knew what I wanted and she wasn't it!"

Ed looks over and smiles at Gary. He shrugs back.

"Are you still on her case?" Paul asks. He looks confident tonight, comfortable again in his leather chair.

Ed nods slowly. "Sure. But I don't want to go on like this

190

forever. Not only that, Ellen is taking the offensive. She'll bite back now. Before she would just sulk or hide. So we spend a lot of time tearing each other down. The woman is beginning to remind me of my mother." Suddenly Ed's head bobs up and he smiles. "First time *that* ever occurred to me!"

"How are Ellen and your mother alike?" I ask.

Ed's eyebrows are still elevated. He's just heard my question.

"My mom never had much good to say about me, to tell you the truth. She'd pop in half-drunk from some party right before my bedtime and start bitching about my leaving the door open, or the dishes in the sink or the garbage piled up in the dining room."

Burt frowns. "Were you the maid?"

"Yes."

"Oh." Burt shrugs and looks over at me with a bewildered expression.

"So Ellen bitches about everything now, too. 'Why didn't you make the bed?' 'What did you do with my book?' 'Don't you ever wash anything?' That sort of thing. I never know when she'll be on the warpath."

"What do you think's going on with her, Ed?" I ask.

"I don't know. PMS?" He's grinning.

"Ed, my thought is that Ellen's therapy is having an effect. Sounds like she's trying her wings. Seeing how it feels to speak up."

"If that's it, maybe I better think twice before encouraging her to continue if we move." He still has a hint of a smile. As Ed is talking, Paul has begun to fidget, and I realize he is going to take the floor very soon. I want to offer Ed some advice before this happens.

"I think this connection you've made between Ellen and your mother—it's a good insight, Ed," I comment. "But what you're describing is a relationship with a lot of negativity. This has got to be hard." I pause. "You need to find a way to turn this negativity around if things are going to work out for the two of you."

"You're making too many decisions."

Paul has gotten his comment in even before Ed can respond to me.

"What?"

"You're making too many decisions," Paul repeats impatiently.

"What are you talking about?"

"You shouldn't be thinking about making so many decisions right now. You remind me of Mitch! Your father just died, and you're doing the same thing he did. Running off and getting married!"

"I'm not getting married, Paul."

"Are you going to move to California?"

"I'm still thinking about it. There's a very good chance I will." Ed peers at Paul suspiciously. "It's a great opportunity for a dynamite promotion. Why not?"

"You're moving too fast!" Paul shakes his head sadly. Now *Paul* looks like the disappointed professor, Ed's former role.

Ed swings over to look at me.

"Do you think I'm moving too fast?"

"Stay with Paul, Ed."

Ed looks back at Paul. "Do you have a point to make about this, or what?"

Paul shrugs. "I just wouldn't jump into anything too quick, if you get my drift."

Mitch is getting irritated listening to this dialogue. He looks straight at me. "Can you make any sense of this?"

I smile at Mitch and mentally debate whether to allow Ed and Paul to continue. I decide to come in. Paul has swung away from Ed and is looking out the window.

"Mitch, I think Paul is on to something. Neither you nor Ed have really allowed yourselves very much time to grieve. I know you both had very stormy, rocky relationships with your fathers, but there still was the knowledge, the feeling, that you had fathers, and now that's gone. There's a void in your lives now."

"I know," Mitch says nodding. "I just hope I get over it soon."

Ed looks back at me. "How long is it going to take before I start to feel better, anyway?"

I recall Ed's mental schedule about therapy and I'm reluctant to give him any encouragement in these terms.

"There is no time period, Ed. It is a very individual process. It's not unusual for someone to grieve for over a year."

"Well, I'm not grieving over Sarah anymore!" Paul exclaims.

"Wha—" Ed begins, but his mouth clamps shut immediately.

"Yep," Paul says. "Having a fine time with Patti. Sex is just great, she even grabs me! You know how long it's been since I've had *that?*"

"Paul, I thought Patti was *ignoring* you," Gary says with a frown.

"Not anymore!" Paul looks very pleased with himself.

"She given up that other guy?" Burt asks.

Paul deflates immediately. "Oh. Not really. She's sleeping with him, too."

"Jesus, she sounds like a slut," Gary mumbles.

Paul winces. "She is *not!*"

"Well, that's my impression of her from what you've said, Paul."

"Hey, I like her! I'm sort of . . . wounded by that. 'Slut'!" Paul is shaking his head.

"Paul, do you understand where Gary is coming from on this?" I ask.

Paul looks up at me with a glum expression. He shakes his head slowly.

I look straight at him. "This has been an issue for Gary

in the last several weeks, Paul. You know we've been talking about how Gary is, well, down on women in general right now. There is a lot of negativity around women with Gary."

Gary smiles. "Bullshit, Al, it doesn't have anything to do with 'negativity.' I just think she's a slut!"

Mitch and Gary burst out laughing. Paul sits still, seething by himself. Burt is trying to suppress a laugh. Ed is grinning.

A minute or two passes as things settle down.

"Paul, maybe there is something else we can explore here," I say finally. "Earlier, when Ed was talking, did you recognize your sudden intrusion?"

Paul looks up, surprised. "What?"

"Did you sense you were interrupting things? That Ed might have more to say?"

"Well, I was waiting for a good place to start. I was just afraid I wouldn't get a chance to tell my story."

"Ed was right in the middle of talking about something important to him."

"He cut me off on purpose," Ed interjects.

I glanced over at Ed. "Why do you think he cut you off, Ed?"

"He just wants to get me. Hurt me. He was probably bored, too!"

"I was," Paul mumbles. "I just wasn't that interested."

"Paul," I say. "This is what I was talking about. Your sensitivity to others' feelings and others' reactions to you. These are the two most important things for you to learn in group. It's basic to your work in therapy."

"Yeah, bullshit. It's a dog-eat-dog world out there. Every guy for himself."

Burt looks over at me and shrugs.

"A cute cliché, but not really accurate in our society, Paul. It is important for you to realize that this insensitivity is going to keep alienating you from a lot of people."

Paul flashes me a look of anger. "I have friends! Lots of them! I'm only alienated in *here*!" He pauses to examine his shoe. "Maybe it's time for me to quit group."

Silence.

"It's ironic for you to say that in a session you could get so much out of—things you say you want: expression of feelings, feedback, knowing your effect, being heard."

Paul sighs. "I don't know."

"Since I'm probably off to California in a month or so, I'll be out of the picture, Paul," Ed says with a twinge of sarcasm.

"See, Paul, you can't quit now!" Gary exclaims, picking up for Ed. "You'll have more time in here when Ed is gone."

Paul peers at Gary. "I just don't think we bond very well."

"What?"

"I would like us to *do* something together. Something symbolic."

Gary smiles. "You want us to dance around the room or go big-game hunting?"

"I think we should do a group yell."

"A what?"

"A yell. Just scream all together for a few seconds. At the top of our lungs! It's a great release. It lets out energy and you feel lighter." Paul has begun to speak faster—he's looking around the room for support.

There isn't any. The others look very suspicious. Ed has a broad smirk on his face, but Mitch is looking worried.

"I think you should check out who is going to yell with you, Paul," I say.

"I hate screaming. I won't do it," Mitch says suddenly.

Paul quickly looks at Gary.

"You've got to be kidding! Most ridiculous thing I've ever heard," Gary says.

Burt and Ed both shake their heads before Paul even gets to ask them. He plops back in his chair.

"Isn't *anybody* going to yell with me?"

I sense that once again Paul is completely alone in group and desperately in need of an ally.

"I'll yell with you, Paul, if you want," I say, trying to provide a modicum of encouragement.

Paul perks up. He's all grins.

"Okay, this is how it works. On the count of three, we let 'er rip, okay?

I nod.

"One . . . two . . . three . . . AAAAUUUUUUUGGG-HHHHHHH!"

Out of nowhere Mitch bolts up and over the glass table, crashing into the centerpiece and tripping over Gary's out-stretched legs. He jumps back up off the floor and turns to us, face ablaze. *"I'm never coming back here again!"*

He vanishes, slamming the door.

Complete silence. Every man in the room is stunned.

"Everyone stay here, I want to catch Mitch," I say, moving quickly past the toppled table and out the door. My assistant silently points the way for me.

Mitch has retreated to the conference room. As I enter the room, I find he is off in the far corner, nose pinned to the long glass windows watching the slow drizzling rain.

For several moments I don't say a word. I wait until he senses my presence.

"I'm glad you're here," I say softly.

He shrugs.

"Are you okay?"

He nods.

"Will you wait for me? I'll be right back."

"Okay," he croaks.

I back out and return to my office and the other men.

Paul is pacing nervously back and forth in front of my desk. Burt has stood and half-pulled his sweater over his head. He's ready to go. I ask Paul and Burt to have a seat.

"It's all my fault," Paul mumbles. "I don't belong here."

Burt shrugs. "I'll be away for a couple of weeks, anyway. Maybe this is a good time to quit for me, too."

"You're reacting to the yell, Burt," I say. "Everyone is. It has been upsetting to all of us. Stay with your reactions, but recognize them for what they are."

Burt shrugs and coughs nervously.

"I'm still trying to figure out why the hell you screamed," Gary says. He's glaring at me by now.

"Why do you think I did, Gary?"

"To support *him?* You've got to be kidding!"

"How is Mitch?" Ed asks softly.

"He's okay. Let's end here. We've already gone overtime and I want to spend some time with Mitch before he leaves."

There are a lot of enthusiastic nods.

I return to the conference room. Mitch hasn't moved at all. I make my way around the long center table and take up my own spot in front of the windows at the other end of the room.

"Mitch, I'll leave you alone if you want."

He shakes his head. "No, it's okay."

Silence. The rain has grown into a steady downpour. The room is nearly black.

I edge slowly toward his window panel.

"The scream?"

He nods. "I don't know what happened."

I let out a long sigh. "It touched something, Mitch. Something very powerful for you. We can figure it out later. How do you feel now?"

Mitch shrugs. "I don't know. I feel so weird."

"You're not. Why don't you take a few minutes to be by yourself to calm down before getting on your bike. I'll be in my office if you need me."

Mitch sighs, and turns to me, running a slow hand through his hair.

"Sure. Hell, I can't ride in this rain, anyway."

I leave, thinking he's one of my sons. I've got to raise Mitch much more gently this time around.

INTERPRETATION

A very emotional, intense, powerful session. The conflict be-tween Paul and Mitch over the past several weeks bursts into the open tonight. Mitch feels so threatened by the sudden scream that he panics and flees for survival. He is absolutely terrified by the scream, both because he dislikes screaming in general ("I hate screaming. I won't do it") and, once again, he saw me in the role of his father, screaming at him against his will. Mitch's impulsive, childhood response, running away from the yelling, takes over without warning tonight, as he bolts from the room as a means of escape. Once he is out of the room and taking refuge in the conference room, Mitch returns to reality. He feels quite confused and very embar-rassed by his behavior, yet he knows it is essential for us to discuss it at a later date. In many ways, Gary's explanation of my decision to yell with Paul tonight is right on target: I feel Paul is desperately in need of support. He wants to scream, he complies with my request to check out who would scream with him, and he explains the purpose of the yell itself. The complete rejection of Paul's idea by all the men once again isolates Paul, and I feel he needs to know that at least I am on his side. For that reason, I decide to yell with him.

The others' reactions to the yell are no less revealing. Burt is up and ready to go. Not only is he ready to leave this group session, he is ready to walk away altogether. Burt is upset: he sees Mitch's explosion as the end of the group. Like many men, Burt wants endings to happen as fast as possible. He is much more willing to say, "That's it!" and walk off, rather than deal with the prospect of the group's ending. Paul is initially pleased by my agreement to yell with him but is terribly shaken by Mitch's escape. Ironically, Paul's wish to engage in a symbolic act of "bonding" serves to *further* isolate him from group. Paul is feeling like more of an outsider and is even worried he'll be kicked out of group. Gary is the only man who appropriately expresses his anger at me for agreeing to yell with Paul. This shows how much Gary has changed since the early group sessions: In the first few weeks Gary was much more likely to indulge Paul, to give him the benefit of the doubt, at the expense of the others (once referring to the others as "pussy-whipped" and himself and Paul as the only "real" men), while tonight he berates me for siding with Paul. Gary's connection to the other men, unlike Paul's, has grown much stronger, and he is no longer willing to ally himself with Paul at the expense of his link to the others. Ed has the mildest reaction. He is surprised and curious. But Ed has already begun to disengage from the group mentally as he becomes increasingly committed to moving to California, and therefore he is less threatened by Mitch's sudden and dramatic bolt.

In spite of Paul's struggle to connect to these men, many of his comments in this session are very valuable and reveal genuine sensitivity. Paul has also grown and has been a risk-taker in the group. He is concerned that, like Mitch, Ed is moving toward marriage to fill the void of his father's unexpected death. As I pointed out to Ed, the tenuous nature of his relationship with his father is really irrelevant to the grieving process: He has suffered a real loss, because now the hope or desire of reestablishing this connection is lost forever. Both Mitch and Ed hate the pain they are going through, and they are exhausted by the grieving process. Ed even expects a deadline for grieving. This is a common reaction of men to grief: They want a time limit—a schedule—so they can muster their courage and work through it and be done with it. I do not give Ed any time limit at all; I am concerned that if a deadline is set, he will hunker down and try to reach it without confronting the feelings as they occur. The grieving process goes as rapidly as the man is willing to experience the feelings of the loss.

It is also important to at least give Paul credit for *trying* to "bond" in tonight's session. No matter how it appears, Paul has made progress. His "dog-eat-dog" view of the world is based on how he grew up. He learned to be insensitive with others, particularly his mother, as a way of dealing with her insensitivity to him. In his adult life, Paul had neglected Sarah and the kids for many years, yet he has begun to turn this around, particularly with his children. Paul also treats Patti far better than he treated Sarah. In the group, his connection to Gary is his strongest, so he was naturally upset and angry with Gary for labeling Patti a "slut." He took this accusation very seriously; he wants to preserve his relationship with Gary, not have it threatened. Gary's "slut" comment also revealed much about Gary's own life. Gary is the only man in group without a permanent relationship, and the last thing he wants is to lose Paul to a committed relationship: He would then stand entirely alone as the only "single" in the group.

SECRETS, LIES, AND FAMILY PRESSURE

"No more Paul!"

"Gary, what're you talking about?" Mitch asks, sinking into the couch.

"He's gone, out." Gary jerks his thumb toward the door like an umpire calling Paul out.

Mitch glances over at me and back to Gary. He's getting a little testy.

"Did he *tell* you that?"

Gary nods. "Last week, he caught me in the waiting room before I could leave. He shook my hand and said it was nice knowing me, good having me in the group." Gary shrugs. "He's not coming back."

Mitch peers at me. "Is that true?"

"Yes. He told me in his individual session. I encouraged

him to come tonight and discuss it in person, but he was adamant. I don't think he'll be back."

"Did he give a reason?" Burt asks with a frown.

"He's upset and feels like he doesn't belong here. And he's really afraid of you, Mitch."

Mitch rolls his eyes and slides back on the couch. "What a jerk. I already *told* him I've never hit anybody. What's with this guy? He never listens to a damn thing we say."

"Any other reactions to Paul's leaving?" I ask, scanning the room.

Mitch is still collapsed on the couch. Gary and Burt exchange looks. There is a slight smirk on Gary's face. Ed decides it's up to him to start.

"I don't know about the rest of you, but I'd about had it with Paul, anyway. The guy was really beginning to really piss me off."

This phrase hangs in the air.

Ed is staring at the rug and rubbing his mouth slowly. His gaze has not shifted when he speaks again. "The guy wanted all his precious 'feedback,' and when we *gave* it to him, he never heard a word of it." Ed looks over at Mitch with a shrug. "Last week when he interrupted me, I had this sudden urge to reach over and stuff a sock in his mouth!"

Gary blurts out a laugh that startles us all. Ed frowns. He is not amused.

"I'm serious!"

"Yeah, I know," Gary says.

"I'm with you," Mitch says softly, looking over at Ed. "I like group a lot better without Paul."

Gary looks at his watch. "You mean you like the last ten minutes?"

Mitch eyes Gary for a moment, then smiles. "I almost didn't come here tonight at all."

"But you did."

Mitch shrugs. "Sure. I made up my mind at the last min-

ute. I was in the bookstore downstairs wandering around trying to decide."

"Can you say what your thoughts were, Mitch," I suggest,
"what went into your decision?"

Mitch nods slowly and fixes his eyes right on me. "I
didn't know if I could trust you anymore." Pause. "I didn't
know what was best, come in here, stick with it, or just split
and risk screwing things up with Lynda." Mitch exhales slowly.
"I didn't know a lot of things."

Burt is nodding. "I'm glad you decided to come on in."

Mitch acknowledges this with a quick nod over at Burt,
but he's still stiff and awkward.

"What else, Mitch?" I ask.

"I can't understand it. Why in the hell did you scream
your head off with Paul last week when I told you that I hated
yelling?"

"I'll answer your question in a moment, Mitch, but first
tell me what you are feeling toward me."

Mitch is beginning to steam. "I'm getting angry again. I
was angry last week! You really pissed me off with that little
screaming stunt."

I nod and scan the room. "Any other reactions to what
happened in the last session?"

"He's right, Al," Gary says softly. "None of us wanted to
do it. Paul was trying to cram another goofy idea down our
throats and we weren't buying it. Now, look, I *know* you
wanted him to feel he wasn't completely alone, but *he was!*"
Gary slowly looks away. "I think you made a tactical error this
time."

I look over at Burt. "You haven't said much. What was
your reaction to last week?"

"I got scared. I definitely thought our group had collapsed."

"Because?"

"I just couldn't see how it could go on anymore. I thought everyone would be scared away."

Silence.

"Okay," I begin, "I've given that session a great deal of thought. Gary, your description is pretty accurate. I *did* sense Paul's frustration and alienation. I wanted him to have at least one ally. If I could do it over again, I would tell Paul I would join him in a scream *after* group—and anyone who wanted to join, could."

Gary smiles. "You two would've still been all alone."

"Yeah," Mitch cracks, "now Paul's *completely* alone."

"You know, Mitch," Gary says softly, "Paul really was afraid of you. I think your dash out of here last week scared the living hell out of him."

"I tripped over *you*, not *him.*"

Gary smiles. "I know. I have the marks on my legs to prove it. But that's not what I mean. I think your size intimidated him. Hell, it intimidates *me!*"

Mitch frowns.

"Do you recognize people can be scared of you, Mitch?" I ask.

"Yeah, I've heard that, but I don't really see it myself."

"Oh, come on," Gary protests. "How can that be? You look like Robocop in leather, for Chrissake!"

Mitch blinks a blank look at us all.

Ed gestures in Mitch's direction. "I back off a lot with you, too. There are times I want to push you, find out what's eating you, but, well, it's probably safer just to let you steam on low boil all by yourself."

"Look, Ed," Mitch says in exasperation, "I'm sorry I'm so scary. You don't know how frustrating it is to be stuck like this."

"Well, what *is* bothering you?"

"I don't know where to begin; I'm worried. Am I just getting cold feet with Lynda, am I going to fuck up *another* marriage, am I going to end up single, on the street, by myself?"

Gary smiles. "You're in a bind either way by that description, Mitch. If you're with Lynda you're 'fucking up the marriage'; if you're without her, you're single: 'on the street.'" Gary pauses and catches me with a look out of the corner of his eye. "Being single isn't all that bad, you know. I used to think it was, but I kind of like it now."

"I wouldn't. I don't want to lose Lynda."

"Join the club," Ed says glumly.

"Ellen?"

"Yeah, and you know what? I've actually been feeling a lot better about Ellen. I can see where there's some hope for us. But" —he sighs— "all I'm getting from her is anger. She's still really pissed about the way I treat her. So I'm hearing a lot of criticism: 'You're too demanding,' 'Why do you want to control me?' 'Can't you just leave me alone?' Ed looks over at Gary with a wry grin. "But at least she's talking to me!"

"Maybe she's another JoAnn in the making after all," Burt observes with a grin.

Gary snorts. "You guys can have it."

"It's a lot better than staring at the back of her head as she storms out of the room," Ed says with a shrug.

"Are you two sleeping together?" Gary asks suddenly.

"We're in the same bed."

Gary pauses. "Okay. Are you getting laid or not?"

"I haven't touched her in six weeks."

Gary's eyes grow wide with surprise. "I'd say the prognosis is baaaaad for that relationship."

"Would *you* want to have sex with somebody after snipping at her heels for an hour? It's a turn-off."

"So what are you going to do about it?" Gary asks.

Ed shrugs. "Ellen and I were at a party last week up on Connecticut Avenue. There's this woman I know from work, Anna, who was there, and she was giving me the serious eye."

Ed pauses to look straight to Gary. "You know, I could *see* something happening right in that living room under the right circumstances, if she came up to me, said the right things, started flirting. I think I'd like it. Who knows what would happen?"

"*Did* anything happen?"

Ed shakes his head. "It's just a thought."

Silence.

"Speaking of thoughts. I've thought about leaving group lately," Gary says straight to the palm in the corner. "We're coming up on my six-month time limit for therapy."

"Say more about it, Gary."

Gary looks from the palm to me. "It's just I've been feeling better, you know. I've set certain goals. I don't want to be around in group therapy for too long."

I nod. "The time limit, though. That's just another pressure."

"Yeah, and that's just therapist talk," Gary shoots back. "I've got other things to spend my money on."

"Gary, I understand that, but look. It's been my experience that when a patient starts using money as a reason for leaving therapy, particularly one whose business has grown as much as yours, it's usually a smoke screen for something else."

"I'm just setting my priorities." Gary's jaw has grown rock hard.

I'm struck by how quickly Gary has been overtaken by anger. It's time for me to move this discussion from the intellect into feelings.

"What's your anger at me, Gary?"

"You're trying to tell me what to do. I'm not going to let you do it."

"I see."

"Don't try to invalidate me, Al. I don't want you pushing me in some direction I don't want." Gary's deep, intense eyes drift to the door and then find their way back to me. "What do you think about that?" he asks.

"I think you're projecting on me, Gary," I say evenly. "You're reacting to me like somebody else in your life. Who would push you around?"

"I'm not answering you."

"My guess is that you're reacting to me as though I'm your father."

At this Gary grows silent, and looks away. A few minutes pass. I'm conscious of the clock ticking from behind my desk.

"What are you feeling, Gary?"

Gary coughs nervously. "I'm getting embarrassed."

"What is embarrassing you?"

"My father. My family. The whole mess. I'm embarrassed that everybody has to keep hearing about those losers."

"Can you stay with that, Gary?"

Gary shrugs. "I've just spent so much of my life covering for them—lying about the drinking, you know. It's my first reaction. It makes me sick that it still happens. I'm tired of it. Things got so bad in high school, lying so much, that I started drinking *myself.*"

Silence.

"Gary?"

He looks up.

"What's going on inside?"

"I really feel awful. I feel *mortified.*"

"Why mortified?"

"The secret's out."

"Who is mortifying you?"

"You are."

"No, but it seems that way to you . . . I see that . . . It's coming back, Gary. You are feeling what you felt as a teenager. Mortified by your father and his attempts to hold you down—to stop you from growing up. I won't hold you down. I'll help you grow up where you missed."

Gary is absolutely still. There is no sound or motion in the room. The others are watching Gary carefully.

Slowly a calm grin spreads across Gary's face. He looks up at me and I return the smile. Smiles of recognition.

"You know, Al, I figured I'd inch *something* out of this therapy for myself someday, and, well, it looks like we made it."

INTERPRETATION

Paul's decision to abandon the group without discussion or reflection is triggered by his perception that Mitch is totally out of control—he is afraid of a direct physical attack by Mitch. In recent weeks, Paul had become increasingly intimidated by Mitch's quiet, angry undercurrent, and the explosion in last week's session was simply too much for him to bear. The suddenness and finality of Paul's decision (which was, after all, largely made in the waiting room right after group ended) are due to Paul's feelings of fear, rejection, and alienation from the group—his sense that he has not been accepted and is not fitting in. This has always been Paul's supreme struggle both in group and in the outside world: how to get along with people. Unfortunately, Paul is the one who will miss out by this sudden and irrevocable decision to leave group. This action itself is a repeat of his childhood: when upset or confused as a young boy, Paul would automatically escape or withdraw, and therefore never learned how to confront his fears or resolve his conflicts. Nonetheless, Paul *has* grown from being in group. He is now, more than ever, firmly committed to divorce. Also, his relationships with Betty and Abe have literally never been better, and he has had some measure of success with new women, a first in his adult life. Many men accomplish some goals in therapy and then decide to stop. A few do return to build on these initial successes and continue to grow in new areas.

Mitch's outburst, on the other hand, results in a major breakthrough for him. For the first time, he is able to get angry at me directly. Instead of withdrawing (his old behavior), in tonight's session, Mitch squares off against me with some very harsh words ("You really pissed me off with that little screaming stunt"). Mitch's very decision to return tonight indicates that he values the group and recognizes how it is helping him, particularly in his relationship with Lynda. Much of what Mitch is learning right now is integration of the intellectual (which he always had) and the emotional (which he always buried). This learning process can be very difficult sometimes. Mitch admits outright that he is confused: he doesn't know if he can trust me, and he doesn't fully understand what is happening. Yet he's willing to sit with those mixed feelings and risk trusting that I am on his side. Mitch knows I won't abandon him, so he doesn't abandon the group.

Unlike Paul, Gary and Ed have chosen to deal with their feelings and reactions to Mitch. This is how they will get through their fear (unlike Paul, who will remain afraid of Mitch). In the aftermath of Mitch's explosion, Ed is more open and willing to express both fear and anger. Gary has made progress on this front by openly confronting Mitch on his anger two sessions ago, pointing out that he scared Paul to death last week, and then even getting openly angry at me. This represents significant growth for these two men, both of whom are adult children of alcoholics, who are accustomed to abuse and neglect. It has always been hard for either Gary or Ed to take the risk of trusting other men.

Ed's revelation of his struggle with Ellen indicates that this relationship is at a critical crossroads. Although Ellen has begun to open up, much of this dialogue takes the form of criticism, a terribly destructive force in any relationship. It has been my experience that such criticism is always damaging to a relationship. It hinders real communication, reduces the desire for intimacy or sex, and in the area of sex, can lead to impotence. In fact, the situation between Ed and Ellen is ripe for some outside influence. If they were married, it would be an ideal setting for an affair. Ed's fantasy of flirting with another woman at a party is an honest recognition of where he is with Ellen at this point. He yearns for more warmth, acceptance, and physical intimacy.

Gary is the group member who has made the greatest strides in recent weeks. His assessment of Paul's departure, Mitch's terrifying effect on Paul, and even my tactical error are all right on target. These are a good indication of Gary's increasing sensitivity. His willingness to say these things up front in group is evidence of his growing confidence and self-esteem. It is still, however, much harder for Gary to express anger directly. His "safe" way out has always been humor. So his anger at me toward the end of the session is initially expressed through money. In this session, he is very wary of me and is worried I am trying to control him. His natural response is to try to take some of that control back by "denying" me the money. As we see in the session, the real issue is simply that Gary is afraid of me—I represent his controlling, domineering. alcoholic father. I engage Gary directly to show him that I am *not* his father and will not *treat* him as his father did. When Gary finally has this insight, he is relieved; he moves from anger and distrust to relief and humor. He has taken another step toward equal relationships with peers and men in authority.

SESSION 20

//

INDECISION AND PERFECTIONISM

A driving rain is pounding at the windows. It seems it's been raining all afternoon; the office has a certain dark pall to it. Ed and Gary amble in drenched from the knees down; Burt's hair is totally soaked. Mitch hasn't even shown up yet. He's probably caught in the middle of the storm on his motorcycle.

While shaking out his trousers, Gary looks over at me.

"Where's Mitch?"

"I haven't heard from him. He's probably out there," I reply, nodding at the windows.

Gary shrugs and collapses into the couch. Burt and Ed settle in and spread out—there's lots of elbow room with only three men in the group.

Ed coughs and takes a quick glance at the other two. "Well, for what it's worth, I've got a new deadline, but this one's self-imposed, I guess." Ed pauses briefly to examine his shoes, which have blackened from the rain. "Between now and the fifth of next month, I've got to make the decision: marry Ellen or move on."

"So what's the verdict?" Gary asks.

Ed's eyes grow wide as he takes a deep breath. "I don't know. Ellen and I are talking now, of course, and that's great. But there are always those other things . . ."

Ed's eyes shift to the door, which has just swung open to admit the enormous, and sopping wet, Mitch. Mitch smiles and I notice his hands are a bright red. I can imagine how cold it was on the motorcycle.

"Look who's here," Gary cracks, "the Incredible Hulk!"

Mitch glances over at Gary and snorts. He crosses in front of me and parks his gear by my desk and then moves quickly to find a spot between Ed and Burt on the couch.

"So, Mr. Hulk, how can we help you?" Burt asks with a grin.

Mitch frowns. "Did I miss something?"

At first nobody answers.

"Not really, Mitch," I say finally, "but since we're on the topic now, do you have any reaction to it? This is the second week it's come up."

"Reaction to *what?*"

I see Gary smile out of the corner of my eye.

"Your size. You're a big man, Mitch. That motorcycle gear makes you look even more threatening." I look over at Ed and Gary on the couch. "Both of you talked about being afraid of Mitch last week."

"Yeah, you can be pretty intimidating," Ed says calmly, "particularly when you're pissed about something, which has been most of the time lately."

Mitch looks surprised. "I really don't give it much thought, you know. I am what I am."

"Mitch, what I'm saying is this: It's important for you to know the effect your size has on others."

Mitch shrugs. "Okay. It's not that I don't believe you. I just don't realize it most of the time."

Gary smiles. "I remember you scaring the bejesus out of Paul." Gary reflects on this for a moment. "It was pretty funny, actually. He didn't even bother to find out *why* you were so mad!"

"Yeah, well, it took me a while to figure it out *myself*. Look, did I interrupt something?"

"Ed's got another deadline," Gary says with a hint of sarcasm. "The fifth of next month?"

"Yeah, that's right. Marry Ellen or hit the road for California, by myself."

"So which way are we leaning?" Mitch asks.

"We're leaning backwards," Ed says through a grin.

"You know, the way you tiptoe around that woman," Mitch says suddenly, "you'd think there's something seriously wrong with her!"

Ed shrugs. "She's put on a good twenty pounds, and she won't get off her butt to do anything, no gym, no classes, nothing to, I don't know, improve herself, I guess."

"It sounds to me like you're still afraid of making the decision," Gary says in a cool tone.

"Afraid? How's that possible?"

"Consider it for a moment, Ed," I say quickly before he can move on. "Assume Gary is right. There is some fear in you. What are you afraid of?"

Ed sighs. "I'm afraid we won't get along. We won't talk. We'll just have children behind a white picket fence and live this boring miserable quiet life."

"Okay, try the reverse: What's the fear if you decide not to marry her?"

"We'd be alone. We missed an opportunity. I don't want to hurt her."

All of a sudden Mitch looks very concerned. His voice has developed a serious edge.

"Look, Ed, are you really unhappy with Ellen?"

Ed shakes his head slowly. "No, I'm not *unhappy*, I'm just not *happy*."

"She won't change, you know," Gary says from Ed's right elbow. "If you think she's going to change in some major way soon, you're wrong."

Ed looks at Gary with some expectation, as though he anticipates Gary will say more.

"It's sort of like what happens with an alcoholic," Gary continues. "You marry one thinking, 'They'll quit drinking when they're married and have a nice, safe happy home'— and, boy, is *that* a mistake."

"I understand that, Gary, I just know what I want."

"Ed, you want perfection," I say.

"What?"

"You have some perfectionist tendencies, Ed. You're trying to be perfect. You're trying to be the opposite of your parents. I know how hard it is for you to make this decision. What if it's the wrong one? What if it doesn't turn out 'right'? Plus, you expect Ellen to be perfect."

Ed grins back at me. "So?"

"Here's an idea, Ed. Give me your ideal. What would you want, *right now*, if you could have everything your way?"

"Okay, let's see."

Ed grows quiet as he reflects on this. His eyes squint slightly behind his rounded frames. A frown slowly begins to form on his forehead.

"I can't really tell you. I don't know." Ed looks up at me quickly. "But I *will* make a decision by the fifth. Count on it."

"I believe you."

"I do, too," Mitch says softly. "I just hope it's the right one. I know how important Lynda is to me, and I have this feeling Ellen is someone special to you, more important than you might think." Mitch glances at Ed and over at me. "I find

I want to spend a lot of time around Lynda now. I think it will be the same when we're married."

"How's that coming?"

"It's coming," Mitch sighs. "We've done everything on her mother's list: announcements addressed, selections for the church organist, rings done, flowers ordered. But still . . . I get the feeling lately that I'm paddling upstream against this powerful current, like a river of events that are already in motion"—Mitch spreads his hands in a helpless gesture—"and I can't do anything to stop them!"

Burt looks over at me. "Aren't these called 'cold feet'?"

Mitch gives Burt a look pleading for sympathy.

"Sorry. I didn't know you were that upset."

Mitch nods. "That's okay. When I get like this, Lynda just pats my knee and says, 'Calm down: take it easy.' "

"So how's Lynda handling it?" Burt asks, trying again.

"Oh, she's doing better than I am. I think Lynda is ready for this, while I'm sort of just gliding along."

"You know, Mitch, I can feel your tension clear over here," Ed interjects. He looks at Mitch for a long moment, then shrugs. "Maybe it's just because I'm going through the same damn thing."

"Yeah, well a lot of my shit isn't about this marriage, it's about my other marriage. I've noticed since the engagement that all this flurry of activity has me freaking out—and I'm starting to retreat: Go off, be by myself, sometimes for quite a while." Mitch stops and shakes his head sadly. "There is *no way*, no way I'm going to fuck up this marriage like I did the last one."

Silence.

"It was *all* your fault?" Gary asks.

Mitch looks up. "What?"

"The marriage. It busted up just because of you?"

"Hell, I don't know. I just don't want to make the same mistakes twice."

"Mitch, some of this pressure you're feeling about getting married is natural," I say. "But your worry about repeating mistakes is an overreaction. It's an extra burden—something you don't need right now."

"*That's* for sure."

"It's a bit ironic, too. You're much more aware of how a relationship works now than you were in your first marriage. You're opening up more and you're talking to Lynda when you are upset. The old problems won't be big issues anymore."

Mitch's eyebrows shoot up. "I haven't been opening up, I've been running away! I've had to escape from Lynda and the wedding deal twice this week."

"No, I mean in here. You're much more open now than I've seen you at any time since your father died. It's been impressive. And it's okay if you need to be alone for short periods of time."

Mitch smiles in appreciation but remains quiet.

The silence continues. The rain has stopped outside and the traffic noises are filtering up from below. We sit listening to the street sounds of the city.

"Does anybody need their windows cleaned?" Gary asks suddenly.

"*Windows?*" Burt asks, astonished.

"Yeah, windows. I'm dating this Armenian woman, and she cleans houses for a living." Gary stops and looks around, ready to tally up the takers. "Well, *nobody* does windows anymore, right?"

"Is that why you're dating her?" Burt asks with a grin.

"Not quite. But not far off. She does my cooking *and* my windows." Gary smiles back at Burt. "Her name's Marta. She's a little firecracker: Cute, petite, five-foot-one, hot as a flame."

"Okay," Ed says. "Since Paul's not here anymore, I guess I'll ask: "Are you sleeping with her?"

"All the time. That is the reason for the relationship. I'm

real clear about it, and so is she. It's so different from what Leigh was like in bed: She was a large, gangly virgin. This woman . . . well, this woman is European, plus she's small, easy to handle."

"Is this going to go someplace?" Burt asks.

"Oh, who knows? I'm not worried about it at all. Listening to you all," Gary's hand flips over at Mitch and Ed, "I'm not sure I *want* it to." Gary stops and lets some time go by. "I just realized sitting here that I'm not even the slightest bit jealous of you. Listening to all this sort of makes me feel, I don't know . . . less guilty about not being married or in something serious."

"You don't want a relationship?" Burt asks in surprise.

"It's not that, Burt, it's just that it sounds so hard for all of you now. Who needs it? I'm relieved to only be dating for right now. I'm in no hurry to have kids."

"Do you think you'll ever have kids?" Mitch asks.

"I'd imagine so, at some point. Actually, right now I'd like to have the *experience* of having kids without the reality of it, if you know what I mean. It's too bad there isn't a 'Rent-a-Kid' place where you could pick up a little critter for a few days to see what the experience is all about."

INTERPRETATION

As Ed approaches his latest deadline with Ellen, he continues to manifest the most significant characteristics of the classic perfectionist facing a tough choice: indecision and procrastination. Ed and I have discussed at great length the connection between his efforts to attain perfection and his indecisiveness with Ellen. This is not an unusual combination. To Ed, avoiding a decision means avoiding the danger of being disapproved of, rejected, or judged "bad" or any possibility of making the "wrong" decision. Ed continues to carry in his head the "voice" of his overcritical mother. In fact, he has incorporated these attitudes from his family so well that he is now his own biggest critic. A lot of this criticism is dumped on Ellen as well. The hope for Ed lies in his willingness to make changes. His attitude toward Ellen has improved dramatically after his earlier confrontations with Paul. Ed is learning his part in his conflicts with Ellen. In tonight's session, Mitch encourages Ed to consider just how important Ellen is to him. There is a lot of support for Ed in the group tonight, and he continues to make himself more emotionally available.

Meanwhile, Mitch is having a man's normal reaction to a big wedding, especially a second formal wedding. Ironically, Mitch's willingness to face his anxieties, and the fact that he feels more anxious as a result, have led him to believe he is regressing. In fact, a year ago Mitch would have chosen to avoid dealing with any of this. He's always preferred the status quo, so all the changes involved in the engagement and the wedding would have simply scared him away. Mitch continues to make progress so rapidly that he's able to deal with, albeit with some anxiety, Lynda's moving in, redecorating his house, and arranging for the wedding. Lynda revealed, in a very valuable couples session, that she too dislikes change and recognizes that things have been easier since Mitch has been in therapy. Lynda is learning that Mitch will respond more willingly to changes when she presents them as a learning experience.

Gary is much more comfortable in group tonight and is able to enjoy relating the excitement of a new girlfriend. Much of Gary's openness comes from his increasing trust and confidence in me: As Gary realizes that I'm supportive of him, his own self-esteem, both in the group and in general, is strongly enhanced. This is a significant step for Gary, whose feelings of inferiority in the group ("I'm a hell of a lot more fucked up than any of you") have festered for months. Over the last few weeks Gary has gone from feelings of jealousy (over the others' relationships) and inferiority (professionally) to a sense of equality and acceptance ("I'm not even the slightest bit jealous of you"). Gary is pleased with this new sense of himself. He has a new love interest with whom he has an easy time and no self-imposed pressure to call it a "serious" relationship. Gary mentions for the first time tonight the possibility of having a child, another sign of his growth and his broadening perspective. Some of life's other choices are now becoming visible to him.

//

LONELINESS IN A RELATIONSHIP

Burt is beaming. He's sitting back on the couch with his long arms spread wide, taking in the whole scene. He's sharply dressed in uniform tonight. This is the first time Burt has shown up here in his army uniform. Burt cuts a very solid, impressive figure in a full dress uniform.

Ed, Gary, and Mitch filter through the door and shuffle toward their seats. They've barely settled in when Burt nudges forward and looks straight at Mitch.

"It's official!"

Mitch smiles. "What? Are you a general now?"

"JoAnn and I are engaged!"

"I thought you two were *already* engaged," Mitch says through a frown.

"No, no, we just agreed to do it at some time." Burt is all smiles again. "That time is now!"

Ed coughs and starts to rub his palms together nervously. "Tell me, Burt, how'd you actually *do* it? Propose, I mean."

"I didn't. JoAnn proposed to *me!*"

Ed looks taken aback for a moment and swings around to look at Gary, who's shaking his head.

"It was great," Burt says excitedly. "We were just lying there in bed in the hotel—we were out at an army convention in Denver. She looked me straight in the eyes and said, 'I know how much it means to you. I want to marry you. I want to have your children.' "

Ed flashes a grin at Gary, who is also smiling by now.

"What happened to cause all this?" Mitch asks. He's still vaguely confused. "Did her biological clock go off in the middle of the night, or was it the altitude?"

"I don't think that's it," Burt shrugs. "It was just such a nice, calm, quiet time in Denver. We spent almost a week out there at the Armed Forces Convention. You know, away from the hassles of work and commuting. We got involved with each other again, started listening more, started *touching* more." Burt pauses to rub the back of his neck. "The sex was *terrific*."

"So that's it. Now it's all beginning to make some sense," Gary says under his breath.

Burt returns his grin. "I met her parents for the first time, too. We stayed at her folks' place for a few days. I got along famously with her father." Burt pauses and looks past me for a moment. Then he's seized by a sudden thought.

"And she wants to get married before she finishes her degree. Isn't that *something?*"

"Amazing what a little good sex can do," Gary cracks.

Burt shakes his head. "No, I think she's really come around, Gary."

Gary sighs. "I think so, too, Burt. And you know what? I'm really happy for you, because it's what you want." Gary is looking over his crossed legs at Burt. "But . . . JoAnn sounds so *powerful* to me. I don't know, I guess I'm afraid she's going to run your life. I mean just *look* at this woman. She decides to get married, so she proposes!"

Burt shrugs. "She's a powerful woman. She knows what she wants. Right now she wants *me.*"

"How does that make you feel, Burt?" I ask.

The glow returns to Burt's face. "Terrific!"

"You know, it seems so *easy* for you," Ed says in something near a whisper. He's looking down, away from Burt.

"How so?"

Ed coughs again, and looks up, catching Burt's eye. "Burt, you have one good week together, and everything falls into place! JoAnn comes around, *she* proposes to *you*, and you ride happily into the sunset together!"

"That's not really fair, Ed. You know how long I've had to wait for this. How much work it's taken. I've damn near had to plan it step by step!"

Ed nods. "Sure. I'm just bitter. Pissed at myself."

"Why?"

For several moments Ed says nothing at all. Finally he lets out a deep breath and his head falls back onto the couch. He's staring at the ceiling.

"I was out of town last weekend, too. Houston. When I was hanging out at the pool, I thought a lot about Ellen. How I missed her. That weekend I wanted to be married. The feeling was there. So I called her on the phone Saturday night and told her what was going on." Ed's head rises off the couch and he looks over at Gary. "I told her I was *ready.*" Ed's head descends back down. "So on the plane back, wouldn't you know it, the jitters start. I'm thinking, *'What the hell am I doing?'* So that night she met me at the airport. She was really excited, and we rode back into town in complete silence. Ellen didn't know what to think, and after we got to my place, I told her. . . . I said I just wasn't sure about it after all."

Silence.

"What did she say?" Burt asks softly.

"She just broke down crying and ran out of the room. I couldn't talk to her that night at all."

Burt lets out a breath and looks at Mitch. They shrug. Gary is still staring at Ed.

"Did you break up with her?"

Ed's head shakes slowly from side to side. "Not even close." At this Ed sits up and shifts his weight forward on the couch so he can see everybody directly. He looks at me and back at Gary.

"That morning, Sunday, I woke up and she was gone. I freaked out, just lost it. I started crying like a baby. I honest to God thought she had gone looking for an apartment—I figured I'd really blown it and lost her."

"So where was she?"

"Well, she was still around, believe it or not, I just didn't know it. She'd gone out to the backyard to our garden, we planted a flower garden together last month, and she was just sitting out there by herself, toeing the dirt and staring at the scarlet roses."

"What was that like for you, Ed?" I ask.

Ed blinks at me for a moment, then smiles. "I was so relieved she was there. She didn't leave."

I nod back at him and allow some time to go by.

"Ed, when you were riding back on the plane and had your second thoughts, what were your fears about marrying Ellen then?"

Ed shrugs. "Well, you all know these by now. I was afraid we wouldn't be able to talk about anything. Share ideas about plays, movies, art. Comment on life." He looks at me. "I really don't want to be alone in a marriage."

"Can you think back to when you were younger for a moment. How is this a repeat of what went on in your family?"

"I—" Ed cuts himself off before the words leave his

mouth. He sits for a moment to reflect, then looks over at me.

"When I was in fifth and sixth grade—ten or eleven, I guess—I remember padding down the stairs at night to ask my parents for something: help on homework, sometimes water, sometimes just to get them to listen to me. My mom would always take me by the hand and drag me back upstairs and lock me in my room. I could always smell the booze on her breath. I hated being alone in that goddamned bedroom."

The room has grown silent. Gary has been nodding during this story. Burt looks uneasy.

"Ed," I say, "can you see that your fear is of being all alone again? Alone in the marriage like you were in the family. You're afraid Ellen is going to do the same thing your mother did—"

"She *is* like my mother," Ed interjects.

I nod. "Remember, as an adult you have more options than you did as a child. Ellen is not literally your mother. She may have similarities, but there also are some differences—for example, she doesn't drink. You do have some choices with Ellen you didn't have with your mother."

"I know. I'm working on that. We are still talking, which I'm glad about."

"Is it doing any good?" Gary asks.

"Oh, sure. It's a *lot* better than being left alone." Ed eyes me for a moment. "She's not just walking off when she gets mad. Anything's better than the ice treatment."

"How long have you and Ellen been together, anyway?"

"Two years, off and on. One year living together."

Gary waves Ed off. "Awww, you'll stay together. That's a long time. You two are *used* to each other." He's smiling.

"Do you identify with that, Gary?" I ask.

"Not really. I haven't been in that place in years. Right now I'm just enjoying Marta. This woman is one hell of a handful, let me tell you!"

"I thought you said she's a little one, a petite, what, European?" Mitch asks.

"Oh, she is, but she's on fire. Listen to this: She dropped by my house on Saturday and hung around until Sunday afternoon. She came back on Monday while I was trying to get some work done and dragged me into the bedroom and wouldn't let me out!" He's grinning wildly. "She left this morning at six. A.M."

"What? You were fucking the whole time?" Ed asks with a sly grin.

"Yep."

"You're kidding."

"No, I'm weak. And tired, come to think of it. But I'm happy! For the first time I can remember, probably for the first time in my life, I'm enjoying the foreplay as much as the climax. It's sort of, well," Gary grins at me, "anticlimactic."

"Are you falling for this woman at all?" Burt asks.

"I'll tell you this: I think I'm getting infatuated. At first I thought, hey, it's about sex, that's okay. The woman is a sexual dynamo and we don't have to worry at all about birth control: she's had her tubes tied. But we've started talking a lot, and I'm learning about her. She's Armenian but was born in Turkey. She's only in the country temporarily, as a Swiss citizen, believe it or not."

Ed looks mildly surprised. "You don't suppose . . . Gary, this woman's not trying to *marry* you, is she?"

Gary laughs. "No way. I've been real clear about that. She seems to accept it."

Ed flashes a concerned look to Mitch and Burt.

"You know, she could have lied about her tubes as a way of getting pregnant."

"So? I'd just say, 'That's it, you lied. Goodbye.' "

Ed shrugs.

"What's she doing in Washington . . . besides doing everyone's windows?" Burt asks with a smile.

"Right now she lives with her sister and brother-in-law and takes care of their little boy. He'll be five in September. She seems to be happy, but I think she's a little lonely." Gary pauses to brush off his pants leg. "Frankly, I get the impression she's looking to get married so she can settle down. It'll save her from having to go back to Switzerland and start all over—new job, new friends."

"Yeah, it'll also give her permanent residency," Ed cracks.

"Well, that's true, but I'm not going to worry myself sick about it like you all—I'm just not headed towards marriage."

"Gary," I say, "be aware that this kind of thing happens a lot here in town—people marry for green cards, permanent residency, all the time."

"Sure. She could also *love* me and want to marry me."

"That's true. This is just something to keep in mind."

"Maybe I should break it off," Gary says suddenly.

"No, no, that's not what I'm suggesting, Gary. I'm saying just the opposite—enjoy the infatuation. It's a great feeling. Just be aware that there may be something else going on with Marta. I'm most of all . . . I'm in favor of being responsible."

INTERPRETATION

Burt's surprise announcement of his engagement to JoAnn, and the fact that JoAnn did the proposing, demonstrate the extent of Burt's progress in group therapy. Burt's changes and efforts at accommodation have been so apparent to JoAnn that her reservations over marriage have disappeared one by one, culminating in her own proposal to Burt in bed while on vacation. I learned from my work in couples therapy with these two that JoAnn has always felt the need both to retain her identity and to be in charge. Much of this grows out of JoAnn's determination to prove to her parents that she can, on her own, be a successful professional. In many ways, JoAnn has feared she will lose her individuality in marriage, and only recently has she seen that Burt in fact supports her in her career and her independence. This is a subject that Burt has discussed on several occasions with the group. JoAnn has also come to realize, after the stresses and pressures of daily life melted away in Denver, that Burt loves and accepts her as she is. Burt and JoAnn were treated as a couple at this convention, and Burt's acceptance of JoAnn was complete: She knew there was no need to "prove herself" to him. As many of JoAnn's anxieties and reservations about marriage fell away, the idea of becoming a part-time professional to accommodate children began to appeal to her. For the first time JoAnn knew this is what she has wanted. Burt is happy because this is one less conflict: JoAnn will marry him. He also will be able to have children before he gets too "old." Something Burt has wanted for a long time is now just around the corner. It is an exciting time for both Burt and the group.

Meanwhile Ed's powerful anxiety over making the decision to propose to Ellen is very similar to Mitch's "cold feet" experience. It is quite common for men to grow anxious when they have time to reflect on major decisions. Much of Ed's anxiety results from his unconscious fear that Ellen will put him in precisely the same lonely situation that his mother did when he was a young boy. Ed felt he was unimportant to his mother, and he fears he will end up in the same helpless and lonely position with Ellen. One of Ellen's common complaints about Ed before he entered therapy was that he never shared his feelings with her. Yet on Saturday evening when Ed returns, he does what Ellen has asked: he tells her what he feels. Ed expects Ellen to appreciate his openness but instead she is shocked, and ultimately, very hurt. Ed responds by going through what is essentially a test of Ellen. When Ellen responds with hurt and pain, he waits. When Ed wakes up Sunday morning, many of his old feelings of rejection and abandonment from childhood resurface, and his first thought is that she's abandoned him, like his parents did many years before. But Ellen passes this test: As upset as she is, she doesn't flee, but rather retreats to the garden they planted together. This is a "safe place" for her, a symbol of their bond. It is at this point that Ed realizes not only his love for her but also that, despite the similarities, she is not his mother. Ellen is not going to abandon him.

Gary's development is progressing on two fronts. His level of ease and comfort in the group continues to grow, as he's able to be much more direct in sharing his doubts about Burt's wedding ("I guess I'm afraid she's going to run your life") and his assurances to Ed ("Awww, you'll stay together"). Gary is also enjoying a very intense sexual relationship. This is the first time Gary has been this comfortable and relaxed with a woman, and the first time foreplay has been a joy—fun, exciting, sensuous, sexual, rather than an obligation to him. It is ironic that many weeks ago Gary labeled the other men "pussy-whipped" when in the span of a couple of weeks Marta virtually moved in. I feel it is important to point out to Gary that he could be trapped by this woman, not only because she is (by Gary's own admission) looking to get married but also because she is so much easier for Gary to get along with. For many years Gary dated women who were like his mother: demanding and controlling. He lived with this during his entire childhood and became accustomed to it. Still, he never learned over this period how to defend himself from these women and how to deal with them. Marta is nothing at all like the former women in his life. She's cooperative, giving, nonthreatening, and very sexual. This is something new to Gary and touches his softer side. Yet despite the excitement and joy, Gary remains insecure about the relationship. It takes only one comment by me ("People marry for green cards, permanent residency, all the time") for him to reverse position entirely ("Maybe I should break it off"). This is a new area for Gary. He will become more comfortable with it over time.

"WHAT A RELIEF TO BE UNDERSTOOD!"

"Aren't we supposed to *end* this group pretty soon?"

Gary is in a dour mood. He's planted firmly in his corner seat and is looking at me over crossed arms.

"What's going on, Gary?" I ask.

He shakes his head. "I don't know. I'm totally burned out. My work load is terrible, but my business is about to drop in half. I can just feel it."

"What about a vacation?" Ed asks lightly.

Gary eyes him for a moment without a word. "Impossible. I can't leave. I'm the only employee! I wish I could go to California with you."

"With me and Ellen," Ed corrects him.

Silence.

"Does this mean what I think it means?" Burt asks with a hint of a smile.

Ed breaks into a full grin. "Can you believe it?"

Gary sits forward and looks straight at Mitch. His arms are still crossed. "Five dollars says he can't say it," Gary says.

"You're on," Mitch answers.

Ed's face is momentarily blank. He's looking right at Gary, who's nearly touching his right arm. A slow look of recognition spreads across his face.

"Ellen and I are engaged to be married."

"Damn!" Gary mutters.

"You can pay me after group," Mitch advises him.

Gary shrugs and peers out the window.

Mitch turns back to Ed. "Also, congratulations!"

Burt smiles. "From me, too, really, Ed. It's been a long haul, no?"

Ed is all grins.

"So tell us about it!" Burt says impatiently.

"Well, guys, I took the leap last Tuesday," Ed begins, the smile still visible on his face. "I figured after all this tortuous soul-searching I damn well better get the *proposal* right!" Ed pauses to gaze around the group. Burt and Mitch are sitting forward and hanging on his every word. Gary is staring at his shoe.

"So anyway, here's what happened. I decided to set up a real romantic dinner—flowers, limousine, first-class service the whole way." He shrugs. "By now, Ellen deserves it!"

"So you picked her up at work?" Burt asks.

Ed nods. "Yep. I *knew* I was nervous when I couldn't even dial the number of the limousine service on Tuesday afternoon! It took me three tries, but I made it, finally." He rolls his eyes.

"Wait a minute," Mitch interrupts. "I forgot to ask. Was all this a surprise?"

"Sort of. I sent over a dozen red roses to her school in the afternoon. Turns out this huge bouquet of red roses, with a note, was delivered to her classroom when she was in the middle of a class. The delivery guy walked right into the room and put the arrangement in the back of the classroom where she could see it. She was pretty distracted by the roses sitting there during the last half hour. I'll hand it to her though; she continued right through to the end of class."

"When did you find out about all this?"

"Well, right after the class was over she called to thank me. She wanted me to pick her up after work so she wouldn't have to take the flowers on the metro."

Burt smiles. "So she still doesn't know what's in store."

"That's right. But I was relieved to hear from her, actually—it occurred to me after I hung up the phone that I had never told her anything about this, and she would have just gone home at five and I could have missed her in the limo!"

Mitch frowns. "Are you sure you're a scientist?"

"Yeah. It's just that I'm a total miss when I'm nervous. I'm still amazed I made it through at all, to tell you the truth."

"Okay, so what happened next?" Mitch asks, recrossing his long legs in the other direction.

"Next. Right. So the limo picks me up and I get to the school at about ten of five. The limo driver has this tuxedo with long tails down to here"—Ed indicated the length on the back of his calves. "Plus a top hat and white gloves. No cane. So I'm in the limo and the driver hops out and walks into the school to get Ellen. About this time, a crowd is gathering around the limo. This thing is a Rolls-Royce Corniche, and you know how kids are—anything new or unusual and the whole place converges on you. So I'm sitting in the limo staring at these fourth- and fifth-graders making faces at me, and the driver disappears inside the building. Ellen is sitting inside the main doors holding the roses on her lap, and when the driver walks up to her she just stands there staring at him. She doesn't even stand up. She can't see the limo, and has no idea where this guy came from. So finally the driver says, 'Ed is waiting for you.' She *still* doesn't stand up: She thinks this guy in the tux is about to break out into a singing telegram song. At this point she grabs the guy by the arm and takes him into her classroom, because she doesn't want him serenading her in front of thirty or forty kids and teachers. Meanwhile, the guy has no idea of *where* she is taking him or *why*. He stops halfway and explains that he's a chauffeur, and *'Ed is waiting for you outside.'* This is the third time he's said it. She rushes to gather her things and follows him outside, where I'm besieged by half the school population. The chauffeur gets past the kids and opens the back door, pulls out some champagne and two glasses, and pops the cork into the crowd, showering a bunch of screaming little girls in the front with champagne spray. He then pours out two glasses of champagne for us inside the Rolls and I look over and see a whole crowd of Japanese tourists walking along the street. By now they've spied us. Of course, they have no idea who we are, but they do see the Rolls, so one of them starts snapping pictures, figuring it must be *some* important Washingtonians. So then they *all* stop and start taking pictures, and we can't move in the Rolls because they're blocking the exit!"

"Did Ellen say anything during all this?" Burt asks.

Ed is about out of breath. He shakes his head. "Not a word. I think she was still in shock and embarrassed. She just smiled a whole lot and tried to keep the champagne off her dress."

"So then what?"

"We headed off to Old Angler's Inn. The limo dropped us off in front, and the driver parked it so everybody walking in or out had to go past the Rolls. We sat outside in the garden area and had a wonderful leisurely dinner. And after we finished the wine, I did it. I asked her to marry me." Ed pauses. "Oh. She said yes."

"Did you give her a ring?" Mitch asks.

"You bet. I was prepared this time! It was a beautiful stone. Ellen just loves it."

"I guess that makes up for the jewelry box fiasco," Burt says.

"Yeah, well, I'm getting better at this sort of thing, you know."

"Look, Ed, I've got a question," Mitch says. "What did the rings run?"

Ed hesitates for a moment. It's not clear if he's embarrassed to even mention this or has momentarily forgotten.

"Hmmm. Let's see. The wedding ring was three hundred fifty and the engagement ring was about twelve hundred. That seems about right."

Mitch nods. "Lynda's engagement ring was seventeen hundred, but her wedding ring was only seventy. Mine was almost three hundred, though."

"Hers was only seventy?" Ed asks with surprise.

"She wanted a really thin, petite wedding band," Mitch explains. He shows an imaginary thin band on his ring finger.

Ed frowns. "I've never liked that kind of wedding ring. You can't even see it!"

"Oh, you can see Lynda's."

Ed is shaking his head. "Why do people wear those? It's like they don't even want you to know they're married!"

"No," Gary says suddenly, joining the conversation, "then they just take it off."

"But you can never *see* it," Ed protests. "I wonder . . ." Ed stops and leaves this thought hanging in the air.

"Wonder what, Ed?" I ask.

"Do you think people with thin wedding bands cheat more?"

"If that's the case," Mitch replies with a grin, "you'll have to wear one like *this*." Mitch holds up his right hand and indicates his enormous college ring with his thumb.

Ed shakes his head but remains silent.

"Are you two going to have kids?" Gary asks. He's finally making an effort to be in the group tonight.

"Ellen would like to get pregnant right away." He shrugs. "I'd like to wait at least a few months."

"I would encourage both of you to hold off for a while," I say. "You've got a lot of changes coming up in your life: new marriage, new jobs, new house, new *state*, for that matter. You two need time to adjust to being married first. Then you can think about having kids."

"Yeah," Mitch nods. "They're major stress factors, no doubt about it. There's no use getting into something that may cause the whole marriage to fall apart."

Ed looks back at Mitch with a frown. "You really think that could happen? You sound pretty down on Ellen and me tonight."

Mitch sighs almost imperceptibly. "It's not either of you, Ed. I think I'm down on marriage in general, as an institution. I haven't been able to even touch Lynda in over a week, and that's really weird for us. Normally . . . well, usually we hug and play around and get real physical all the time." Mitch's eyes have shifted to the blank wall behind me. "I'd sure like to know what the hell is going on, I'm just not turned on. I hope I'm not impotent."

"Don't worry," Burt says, "Al knows how to fix that one."

"I think I'm going to be practical for a moment, Mitch," I say. "No psychological interpretation."

"*That's* a first," Gary cracks.

I know something is going on with Gary but I want to continue with Mitch first.

"Isn't Lynda sick now?" I ask.

"Sure. She's *still* sick, going on two whole weeks. She's got this virulent case of mono that's knocked her out almost completely."

"I wouldn't think she's feeling very sexual now." I pause to consider another thought. "*Can* you two have sex, Mitch?"

Mitch snorts. "If you can call it that. The doctor says no kissing and no oral sex at all. And if we actually *do* anything . . ."

Suddenly Mitch's voice drops and he mutters, "Although I can't imagine it"—he looks up at me again—"we have to use a condom."

"It seems natural not to feel sexual right now, Mitch," I point out. "You're taking a fun, casual act like sex and making it into a chore, needing to remember things to keep from catching mono yourself. That's a real distraction in sex."

Mitch shrugs.

"Another thing. I'm glad you're bringing it up after only four days. Before it would be weeks, if ever, before you'd talk about something like sexual problems in here. You're much more spontaneous and open in group lately. It's good to see this change in you, Mitch—it's very positive."

Mitch smiles. "I just wish I had more *optimistic* things to be open about."

"Can we talk about ending?" Gary blurts out.

"Ending?"

"Yeah, the group. Aren't we through in two weeks? I'd like to know, because I can't afford this anymore. I'm dumping all this money into therapy just so I have someplace to complain. I don't need it! It's a luxury that's got to go."

"You're using money as an excuse. You're making more than you ever have in your life," I say.

"Weren't you listening? I *told* you I'm afraid my business is going to drop off."

Gary is sitting very still, steaming by himself at the end of the couch. He's staring straight at me but won't say a word.

"What's your feeling about group ending, Gary?"

"I'm ready. I knew it was coming. Don't *you* think I'm ready to end?"

"What's your feeling about it?"

"I don't *have* any *feeling* about it! Do *you* think I'm ready to end?"

"You sound full of feeling, especially anger, at me."

"So you tell me, what's it about?!"

"Gary, no games please. Let's figure it out together."

Gary is sitting immobile, arms crossed, eyeing me carefully.

"You've been progressing all along. I suggest that you not end therapy yet. You can still get a lot more for yourself. So if you do stop after the six-month commitment—pay attention, I'm not rejecting you, I'm not abandoning you, I'm not giving up on you—you'll be the one leaving."

Gary's body visibly relaxes, and he scans the room.

"Am I the only one who's not ready to stop?"

"No. Ed has more work to do when he gets to California. Burt and JoAnn are seeing me as a couple, and Mitch may continue with both group and individual."

"But isn't it time for us to stop, Al?" Mitch asks. "You said six months."

"The six months was to assure you a minimum of learning and changing, not to stop you in the process."

"Makes sense," Burt nods. "But I'm ready to stop group as planned."

"That's fine." I turn back to Gary.

"What else besides business is bothering you, Gary?" I ask.

Gary scratches his face and shrugs.

"I don't know, Al. I've got to visit my parents again next week. My dad's practically an invalid, he's got this rare nerve disease, it's something like Parkinson's Disease. So he just sits there staring at the TV. He can't even talk anymore. I don't think he even knows I'm there! Mom spends all her time wandering around the house bitching about having to take care of *him*, so . . ." His gaze shifts to the windows. "It's all so depressing, let me tell you."

"So the family problems are part of your anger and depression?"

"No," he answers quickly.

"Your answer is so fast, Gary, you're not even considering. It would be helpful to at least think about it. It would explain most of your feelings: Depressed . . . angry . . . tired . . . and burned out."

He sits quietly with this for a while.

"I don't think they are related."

"I think they are."

"So what do you suggest I do?"

"I'm not suggesting you do anything right now, Gary, except say more about your anger."

A flash of hot anger crosses Gary's face.

"Look! I'm paying you all this money and you're not doing a damn thing! I have to pay *all* the money and I have to do *all* the work!"

"Gary, I'm here to work *with* you," I assure him. "It's true you have to work at it—it's your life and you have to live it."

"So just tell me where I should go! What should I talk about?"

"Your mother. We've heard a lot about your father, but you've avoided talking about your mom."

Gary is eyeing me again. I know he doesn't want to say anything negative about her. He gives in. Finally, he looks at the floor and shrugs.

"I'm fed up with her. I wish she would leave me alone. She is always complaining and acting like the victim. She calls me on the phone and whines about how Dad's illness is such a fucking burden on her. She thinks he's doing it to get even with her. Always the victim. *God*, it's *so* depressing. And when we get into an argument, she won't fight back—she used to, all the time. Now she gets this 'poor me' voice and whimpers, 'Why are you mad at me, what did *I* do?' " He gestures in disgust.

"It sounds like the guilt trip all over again," Mitch says simply.

"Huh?"

"If you don't take her burden away, she's going to just

curl up and die—like when she used to threaten suicide if you didn't stay with her.

"Yeah, well, I'm just tired of listening to the bitching. The woman complains more than . . . well, more than *I* do."

I stay out and let Gary sit with this discovery.

"Can you say anything more about your bitching, Gary?" I ask.

He lets out a deep breath. "I'm not proud of that. I know I bitch a lot." He looks over at me. "I'll never, ever be as bitter as she is, though. It'll never happen.

"I agree. Because you made the decision to change, and she didn't. Otherwise, you could have ended up the same. And that's your main anger and fear right now."

"Now, *don't* lose me again. You are saying I'm better off than she is, aren't you?"

"Yes, I am. But their recent problems have stirred up your old fear of ending up like them. You 'divorced' your family when you started your alcohol treatment. You've been moving up ever since. You won't end up like them."

INTERPRETATION

Ed's excitement and lightness in telling the entertaining story of his engagement to Ellen are the direct result of his relief at having finally made a decision. Ed is no longer blocked in by his fear and procrastination: the demands of his perfectionism. In tonight's session, Ed looks and behaves like a "freed" man. It is clearly the most fun he's had in group so far. And the other men become playful, too: Mitch and Gary make a wager over whether Ed will actually say out loud that he was engaged to Ellen. Ed's enthusiasm and relief are infectious, and the mood in the room tonight is initially upbeat. Men's light-hearted humor really raises the energy level of the room.

When Mitch switches the subject to the price of engage-ment and wedding rings, we see some elements of traditional male competition reappear. This competition goes beyond the elements of economics. Mitch and Ed compare the prices of rings for their women in the same way that adolescent boys in the locker room may compare or joke about their penis size. (This is no coincidence. The ring and the penis are both for women.) Ed's momentary hesitation to answer Mitch re-flects his realization that he and Mitch are about to cross from a place of mutual support to one of competition. Once in this mode, Mitch goes further by suggesting Ed will need a broad band, implying he feels Ed is likely to cheat. While the origin of this comment can be traced back to Ed's affair fantasy a few weeks ago, Mitch is still on a competitive footing with Ed from the wedding ring discussion, and this, coupled with his own negativity surrounding the situation with Lynda, prompts him to remain competitive and confrontational. I'm glad he did. He's on target. Mitch feels that Ed and Ellen are not ready for marriage.

In fact, what Mitch is experiencing is regular, ordinary wedding jitters. Like many men, Mitch has surges of anxiety and doubt as the big day approaches. Both Mitch and Lynda find themselves in a situation that is common to engaged cou-ples: the partners enjoy each other less as so much energy, time, and effort goes into planning a formal wedding. In this case, both Lynda and Mitch are experiencing the anxiety and stress, though it manifests itself in different ways: irritability and jitters in Mitch and a physical reaction in Lynda (Lynda's lab tests cast doubt on whether she actually has mononucle-osis). The most significant sign of progress in Mitch's discus-sion is his willingness to bring up the difficult sexual issue of impotence in front of everyone, and not be intimidated. Cer-tainly a long step from the "old" Mitch. This will help him deal with future sexual problems that may arise naturally in the marriage.

From the beginning of the session Gary's mood is out of sync with the atmosphere in the room. Since this is in such sharp contrast to Gary's attitude of last week, I know something had occurred to cause this shift. Gary's attack on me is almost an exact replay of his mother's treatment of his father and comes on the eve of his worrisome visit to his parents. Gary puts me down with the same complaints his mother uses on his father (he's ineffectual, he won't talk, he doesn't help me). Tonight is the first time Gary is able to criticize (and complain about) his mother openly and see similarities in himself, since he had identified with her as a youngster. He has always been extremely reluctant to say anything negative about his mother. While she used guilt to control Gary, she was, nevertheless, his strongest ally in the family. Gary wants to protect himself when he becomes equally depressed and feels he is the victim. So he falls into the old pattern of denial: "I'm not like her." As Gary is able to identify the similarity between himself and his mother, he is able to move beyond his fear that he will be like her. He is adamantly committed to change. Good for Gary.

Gary's anxiety about group ending is a natural response. He has moved into a trusting relationship with the other men and he's going to miss them. At this point, he can't say that directly: it's not the male thing to do.

SESSION 23

//

"SHADOW" MOTHERS AND THEIR SONS

"I'd like to start the group tonight," I say.

Gary glances up at me with a look of mild surprise. Burt and Mitch look puzzled but sit forward. Ed's gaze shifts from the empty black leather chair to me. I wait until I have everyone's attention.

"Since next week is our last session," I begin, "I'd like to extend the time by twenty to thirty minutes. Will that be okay?"

Glances around the room, several nods.

"Will it cost any more?" Gary asks.

I smile. "No, it's on the house."

"One thing, Al," Burt says suddenly. "Let me check with JoAnn and get back to you."

"Don't tell me she's running your life *already,*" Gary says, leaning back in his corner seat.

Burt gives Gary an even look.

"Not quite. JoAnn and I are meeting downstairs at the end of group next week, so I'm not sure how much time we'll have. We want to go someplace and celebrate the end of group." Burt looks from Gary over to me. "It should be okay, though."

I nod. "I'm glad to hear it's going to be a celebration for you, Burt. We haven't heard much out of you recently."

Burt coughs nervously and shrugs. "I know. To tell you the truth I was ready to quit after that scene with Paul. I figured it was about over, anyway. But it just didn't seem right." Burt catches Gary's frown out of the corner of his eye. "The commitment, I mean. I figured I was in for the six months and I was going to stick with it."

This seems to satisfy Gary.

"Anything else going on, Burt?" I ask.

"Oh, there's plenty going on," he says running a hand over his blond hair, "but now that JoAnn and I are in couple therapy with you, the importance, urgency, I guess—a lot of it's gone away." He pauses and looks to his right at Mitch. "I mean, JoAnn and I are engaged, after all."

"So you don't miss talking in here?" Mitch asks. He looks relaxed tonight—sitting far back on the sofa with his arms spread wide.

For a moment Burt is lost in thought and doesn't answer.

"I sort of miss it, actually," he says. He looks around at the men scattered along the couch. "I should take advantage of what we've got left. There is a kind of . . . support I get in here I don't have with JoAnn in couples." He smiles over at Mitch. "I'm glad you brought that up."

Mitch is grinning back. "Sure."

Silence.

"I need to take a little time, guys," Ed says in a weary voice. "I've got some bad news, again. I found out last Wednesday that my mother has a tumor near her right hip, about here," he indicates the spot on his own hip with his palm.

"Cancer?" I ask.

He nods gravely.

More silence.

"So what are the feelings, Ed?"

Once again the glasses come off, and Ed scratches his forehead slowly. His glasses are sitting idly in his lap.

"You know," he says in a labored voice, "I can't feel any sympathy for my mom. Isn't that awful?"

Mitch is peering across the couch at Ed but remains silent.

"Are you pissed off at her?" Gary asks calmly.

Ed shakes his head. "Not really. But when I spoke with her yesterday—I called to check up on her—I could *tell* she was smoking a goddamned cigarette, and *that* pissed me off." Ed's voice has developed a nasty edge.

"What's the prognosis, anyway. Is she going to be all right?" Burt asks with concern.

This brings Ed back. "It's too early to tell." He takes a deep breath. "That's *another* thing." He looks over at Gary with sudden intensity. "Can you believe this woman has no health insurance? I spend ten years on her case, trying to get her to get some coverage." He shakes his head sadly. "It's my *field*, so I should know, right?"

"What did she say," Mitch asks with a frown. "Did she just refuse?"

Ed shakes his head slowly. "Not quite. She just protested she was healthy as a horse. Why did she need insurance? So now she can't get near a policy with anything less than a ten thousand deductible."

A look of disappointment crosses Mitch's face as he looks away.

Ed is watching Mitch and sees his response. He exhales a long, deep breath. "Ellen feels I should help her out."

"Are you going to?" Gary asks over his shoulder.

Ed looks back at Gary to respond, but no words come out of his mouth.

The room is still.

"Ed, is the problem money . . . ?" Burt asks softly.

"No."

"I don't know what the big deal is," Mitch says in a booming voice. Burt is so startled he jumps slightly. "She's your mother! If it were my mom, I'd be right there with the wallet out."

"It's not quite the same thing," Ed says testily.

"How is it different?" Mitch is leaning forward on his right knee.

"Mitch, look," Ed begins, peering straight at Mitch. Their faces are only eighteen inches apart. "My mother is a boozer. Our relationship hasn't been worth two shits since I went to college and escaped from that nut house. I don't feel real charitable towards a woman bent on self-destruction." Ed's face has gone crimson, and he's breathing in short, quick breaths.

"Hey," Mitch says, throwing up his hands, "that's fine. I'm just telling you what *I'd* do, that's all."

Ed wipes his mouth slowly and nods.

"What's your mother like, Mitch?" Burt asks. "We haven't heard much about her."

Mitch grins. "She's okay. She lives by herself in a town house up in Silver Spring." He stops to examine his boot and has another thought. "My mom's in pretty good health, except that she probably drinks a little too much."

Burt smiles back, but Gary and Ed throw each other a troubled look and shake their heads.

"You know, Ed," Gary says in a calm voice, "I know what cancer can be like. Once the diagnosis is made and all the doctors get into the act it can be so incredibly expensive—

and devastating." Gary pauses. "It's like standing in front of this racing freight train about to mow you down."

"Yeah, tell me about it," Ed mumbles.

"Ed, have you spoken with any of your brothers or sisters about this?" I ask.

"Not yet. I suppose that's next."

"It is a family crisis and the whole family should be involved."

"Yeah, I know. I've been avoiding it, to tell you the truth."

"I want you to understand that it's not your sole responsibility, Ed. You have other things to do. Settling in with Ellen and your marriage, for one."

Ed sighs. "There's a lot to do. Oh"—he has another thought and looks at me expectantly—"I think I should announce our wedding agreement."

"That's fine, Ed."

Ed scans the group. "Since I don't have any family members in town for the wedding, Al here"—he glances my way—"is going to come to our wedding." Ed pauses. "I'd invite the rest of you, but you know the rules: no socialization outside of group."

"*That's* a relief," Gary says with a sly grin. "I'd need three new suits to go to all the weddings in *this* group!"

"Any reactions to my going?" I ask.

"I'm glad you have the rule," Mitch says evenly. "It might be hard for us to be together at the wedding."

Ed nods and remains silent for a moment. "How are things with you, Gary?"

"Not great." He shrugs. "I drove straight here from my parents' house, and I'm still edgy. The old man's getting worse, not better, and my mom's being her old charming self."

"Still bitching?" Ed asks.

Gary nods. "That place is depressing. It smells old and damp. My mom wanders around the house mumbling about my dad like he's some rotten sack of potatoes she should throw out." Gary pauses and looks back at Ed. "You know what? She cornered me in the kitchen Friday night and said *her life had been wasted* caring for my dad. Now ain't that some shit?"

"Have you thought about a nursing home?" Mitch asks.

"We're doing that. In fact, that was *another* argument," Gary shakes his head. "They're going to live in a small cottage in this retirement village, and there are good support services for my dad there. And she tells me she *couldn't decide* if she should spend a lousy ten bucks an hour to have some help taking care of him. *That's* what I'm up against here."

"Was your mom always at home when you were a kid, as a homemaker?" Burt asks.

"Yep. The truth is I always thought taking care of everybody was what she *wanted* to do—I thought it gave her life some meaning."

"Aw, hell, maybe it does," Mitch says with a flick of the hand. "She may just be blowing off steam. It can't be easy. That life."

"Yeah, well *being* there certainly wasn't easy. I wasn't looking forward to it. It was the first time I'd seen my older sister, she's forty-four, in about, what, five years? And she was sipping a drink the whole time. Same old story. A slow, painful suicide."

"Gary, is your dad going to make it?" Mitch asks in a low voice.

"Yeah, his mind's about gone, but he's a fighter. He sits in his chair all day, he can hardly get up, he goes like this," and Gary suddenly bends way over in a crouched position and hunches up his back and tries in one long, slow effort to rise up off the couch. He gets about halfway up, and collapses back with a grunt and a heavy sigh. He looks up. "It's so pathetic, I can't stand to watch him—I just walk over and lift him out of the chair."

The room grows quiet again.

"Gary," I say finally, "it looks like there's some separation between you and your family. I'm glad to see you've been able to do it. You need this distance from the craziness to maintain your own individuality and your sanity. I appreciate that this hasn't been easy for you. Your mother, and Ed's, are like shadows—not really a full mother."

"Yeah, well, you're right, there's not a shred of sanity in that house."

Gary notices that I look at the clock, and he quickly turns to Mitch.

"Are you going to continue with me in another group after these two guys run off and get married?"

"I'm getting married, too, you know."

Gary frowns. "I know, Mitch, who do I look like, Paul? I just want to know if you're going to stick with another group."

"Did I miss something?" Burt says suddenly. "I thought group was ending next week."

"Let me clear this up," I say. "Gary and, possibly, Mitch will have more group therapy in another group."

Burt looks at me and nods.

Mitch picks up with Gary again. "I haven't decided whether I'm going to continue or not."

"Are you concerned about the change that represents, Mitch?" I ask.

Mitch leans back so he can see me as well. "I may just want to continue with individual alone."

"How do you feel about group ending?"

"I'm glad it's ending. We've done a lot of stuff in here. I'm going to miss it, though. I don't know what I'll do with this time, I'll have to go right home. It'll be one less boys' night out."

INTERPRETATION ——————

Ed's issue with his mother appears quite simple on the surface, as Ed chooses to present his problem to the group as a straightforward choice: Should he provide financial help to his mother or not? In reality, this problem has much deeper roots and is anchored in Ed's difficult and troublesome relationship with a preoccupied and neglectful mother. Since his alcoholic parents had a codependent relationship that excluded him for much of his early life, Ed was left alone to figure out right from wrong, establish limits, and determine guidelines. Ed had to do his own parenting. One result of this process is a strong perfectionistic tendency: Ed still has trouble with guidelines. Another is his anger at his mother for her exclusive and destructive relationship with his alcoholic father and her absence in his life. Ed has a "shadow" mother. He finds himself in the unfortunate position of being without the kind of strong, supportive mother-son relationship that would make him want to take care of his mother. He lacks a familial bond. Like many men, Ed finds himself in a role reversal at this later stage in his life. Forced to be his own unwilling parent in childhood, Ed is now expected to assume the same responsibility for his own parents in their advancing age. One consequence of extended life expectancy in our society is that men like Ed are finding it necessary to deal once again with parental conflicts that they avoided, dumped, or abandoned long ago.

Gary, too, has a shadow mother who provided woefully inadequate parenting. She focused her love and attention almost entirely on Gary's father, to the exclusion of the children. Once Gary matured into adulthood, the mother engaged in emotional blackmail ("I'll kill myself") to keep Gary around to give meaning to her life. Aside from his resentment at this treatment, Gary has picked up a lot of his mother's negative behavior, some of which surfaced in tonight's session (complaining, bitterness, feeling like a "victim"). One important lesson Gary has learned well is that he has to stay away from his mother and establish and maintain a certain distance in order to maintain his personal integrity and self-esteem.

Mitch, on the other hand, has a close relationship to his mother and feels a strong urge to protect her. So far in group Mitch has steadfastly refused to say anything even vaguely negative about his alcoholic mother ("She probably drinks a little too much"), because he feels she's the only one who's been continually supportive of him. Mitch is his mother's favorite. As such, Mitch is surprised and disturbed by Ed's confusion about what to do about his mother. This would be a simple and direct choice for Mitch.

Burt contributes the least to this discussion, because among these men his relationship with his mother is the easiest. She is in good health and has been left in a comfortable material position following her husband's death. Although Burt is not close to his mother, she is supportive of him and is relatively easygoing.

Virtually all the men I have worked with over the years in therapy have had difficult, disappointing relationships with their fathers and have struggled to maintain decent relationships with their mothers. One result of this feeling of neglect is that these men—Ed, Burt, and Mitch included—desperately want to be loving, available, involved fathers. These men want to provide their children with the support and nurturance that they missed in their early lives. This bodes well for the future generation: men are needed in the family.

FROM FEAR TO CELEBRATION

"Mitch called to say he'd be late."

Gary frowns and looks up at me from tying his shoe. "Haven't we heard *that* before?"

Burt and Ed exchange a look of confusion and shrug at each other. Gary finishes with his shoe, slides back on the couch, and glances over at Burt.

"The first session, guys. Mitch calls ahead, says he's going to be late. So much for changing in therapy." An impish little grin slowly emerges on Gary's face.

Ed is looking at me and misses the smile.

"I don't know—*I've* gotten something out of the group . . . at least Ellen thinks so. She says I'm a lot easier—more fun—to be around, even at parties." Ed looks to Burt on his left and shrugs. "She says people listen to me. They look up to me. They care what I think."

"Is it true?" Burt asks.

"It's true at work. I've got two major research projects to wrap up before we head out to California, and people are dropping in all day to ask my opinion on their work, to gossip, to just hang out. It's driving me a bit crazy, to tell you the truth."

"You don't *like* the way they're responding to you?"

"Well, some of it. I do feel good there."

"Another group therapy success story," Burt says with a flourish.

"I don't know about that," Ed counters quickly. "I didn't say it *all* came about because I'm in here."

"So Ellen, your coworkers, Burt, me, see the results of your therapy, but you 'can't' decide whether your work here has paid off?" I'm grinning at him. "Give yourself some credit, Ed."

Ed sits with this for a while and then returns my grin.

"Are you going to do group therapy out in California?" Gary asks lazily.

"I don't know yet. I think I get more out of individual." Ed eyes me warily for a moment and then glances back at Gary. "The group's been good. Don't get me wrong. And I'm really going to *miss* you guys." Ed pauses with this thought for a moment, as though it's the first time it's occurred to him. "Anyway, I liked being in here a lot. I've never had anything quite like this before." Ed's voice has trailed off to nothing.

Suddenly the door swings open and Mitch rushes in and grabs a spot next to Gary. He unzips his riding suit down to his waist while seated on the couch.

"Sorry I'm late."

"I don't know, Ed," Gary says looking across Mitch. "It's only been good for me in here in the last few weeks. Since Paul bolted. It's given me a lot more time to talk." He looks around at the men and smiles. "I think I like this size a lot more."

"Yeah"—Ed shrugs—"since Paul and Sean left I can actually get my foot into the conversation once in a while."

"Sean, wow, God . . . that seems like *ages* ago," Gary says, with a shake of the head.

I catch Gary's eye and smile. "You're not giving yourself near enough credit, you know. You started opening up, and challenging Paul, several weeks before he left. It goes way back. Same with you, Ed."

Ed gives me a skeptical look.

"Who jumped all over Paul for scaring Sean half to death?"

"Oh. Yeah, that's true."

"It's come out in other ways, too, Ed. You've been much more willing to stand up for yourself in group and in the world outside. You make people listen to you. *You* listen more to Ellen. The two of you got married. Remember why you came to me?"

"I think so." He grins back at me.

Gary leans forward on the couch to see around Mitch.

"He's right, Ed. I've heard more from you lately than from anyone. The only guy who's clammed up completely about himself is Mitch."

Mitch is completely still.

"I talked last week."

"You asked about our *mothers* last week."

Mitch is right next to Gary on the couch, and at this comment he slides back and away so he can look directly at Gary.

"Are you going to start in on me again?"

For a moment Gary is silent.

"I just don't know where you are, Mitch," he says coolly. "You're just not talking and it seems like you're seething with anger."

Silence.

"What are you feeling right now, Mitch?" I ask.

Mitch gives me an icy look, then peers back at Gary. When he answers, he addresses me.

"I'm trying not to get more upset."

"What is it, Mitch?" I ask.

Mitch still has Gary locked in his gaze. This time he speaks to Gary.

"You're attacking me, and I don't like it."

Gary is silent once again. Eventually, he shrugs.

"You're really too sensitive, Mitch. I'm not *attacking* you, I'm telling you what I *think*. You're just being paranoid."

Mitch tenses for a moment and quickly looks away.

Gary glances over at me expectantly but remains quiet. Burt is sitting motionless except for his right foot, which is tapping up and down nervously.

Silence.

"Mitch," I say softly, "can you try letting us know what's going on inside of you?"

" 'Paranoid' is not one of my favorite words," he mumbles. Mitch is slowly and deliberately rubbing his palms together. "And I'm not 'too sensitive.' "

"What are the feelings?"

"I'm embarrassed by this. I'm not 'too sensitive.' " Mitch looks up at Gary. "What the hell does that *mean*, anyway?"

"You're upset because I called you 'too sensitive'?" Gary asks with surprise.

Mitch is silent.

"Gary," I say, "I think it's more your tone and attitude that sound harsh or attacking—not really your words."

"Oh. Well, shit, I didn't mean to be overbearing. If it seems that way. It's just my style."

"What's your reaction to this, Gary?"

Gary lets out a deep breath. He's still watching Mitch warily.

"I'm a little edgy . . . nervous, too. You know, Mitch, I

never know if one of these times you're going to pop up again and *deliberately* smack me."

"So that's the fear?" I ask.

Gary nods. "I was the one that got run over when Mitch charged out of here."

"Look," Mitch sighs, "I told Paul this once before. I've never hit anybody in my life! I'm just angry right now, I don't understand it, and I'm trying to figure it out!"

"Do you want me to apologize, Mitch?"

"No, it's all right."

"I have trouble believing you on that, Mitch," I say.

Mitch looks over at me and laughs nervously. "I wonder why!"

"There are so many times in life when we wish somebody would apologize or say 'I'm sorry' whether the hurt was intentional or not," I point out.

"Look," Gary says suddenly, "don't worry about it. I won't apologize if you don't want me to. The thing is, Mitch, I don't know any other way of getting to you except by being a little cynical. So if I rile you up, at least you say *something*."

Mitch shrugs and looks away.

"You know something, Gary?" Ed asks with a frown. "You *do* seem sort of cynical—I got the feeling you've been mad at Mitch the whole time tonight."

"I'm not mad at *Mitch*. I'm mad at myself. *That's* been going on all night. I got a call from my mom on Friday with some bad news. My grandmother, who's ninety-two years old and in a nursing home, has been going downhill fast. My mom said we might only have a couple of days left, so could I make it up on the weekend? I said there was no way. I was going to the beach this weekend, so that's that." Gary pauses to run a slow hand over the back of his neck. "So my sister called first thing Saturday morning before I left and told me my grandmother had died. I said I was just heading out for the beach and she shrieked, 'For the beach!' and it dawned on me, this awful thing I had done, what the hell's wrong with me? So I called Marta and canceled and went on up for the funeral."

Gary's story just hangs in the air.

"Did you feel guilty at the funeral?" Burt asks finally.

Gary pauses and shakes his head. "Even if I'd left Friday, I wouldn't have made it in time to see her before she died. I'm just glad I came to my senses in time to make the funeral."

Burt nods. "Are you feeling better now?"

"A little. I wasn't that close to my grandmother."

"No, I mean in here."

"What?"

"Both you and Mitch looked upset."

"Burt," I come in quickly, "do you have some feelings about what went on between them?"

"Yeah, I was worried about you two." He glances back and forth between Mitch and Gary. "I don't like having to sit around people who get that steamed up."

"Were you going to charge out of here?" Gary asks.

"Probably not."

"Just give my legs some notice, okay?"

"If it doesn't happen this session, it won't happen at all."

We all sit with this thought for a while.

"What are your plans, Burt?" Gary asks in a concerned tone.

"Oh, JoAnn and I are going to stay in couples therapy. I'm nervous but looking forward to getting married. Things are going well. I'm sorry to see the group end, though." He looks over at me. "I'm really glad I got to be in here."

Gary nods. "I'm not going to California or getting married, so I'm thinking of sticking with it in another group. I just don't want to be in therapy for the rest of my life." He looks over at me. "I'm not sure how long I'm supposed to be in therapy until I'm . . . I don't know, 'finished,' or whatever."

I give Gary a smile. "There is no 'schedule' or set time,

but you already know that. Ordinarily, you stay in as long as you make progress and learn and are happy with that."

"How've I been doing? How about a progress report?"

"Oh, I didn't know you wanted one."

"Yeah. Just a 'report card' and how long I'm going to be at this. Not a date, mind you, just an idea."

Gary is pressing me.

"How do *you* feel you've been progressing?"

Gary rolls his eyes. "You're just answering a question with a question! That's not fair. You're just being a psychologist."

"I'll answer you, Gary, but I want your own view first."

"Why?! Why do I have to answer first?! Why don't *you* answer first?"

"Because I don't want *my* answer to influence *your* answer."

"Bullshit, you're playing games with me. Fine. Drop it."

"Gary, I'm not playing a game. I will answer your question, believe me."

"No. Forget it. I'll get over it. I won't be angry after a while. Go bother Mitch."

"Gary, do you really expect me to pretend to concentrate on Mitch while you're sitting there fuming at me? I'm willing to stick with you. I'm feeling frustrated, too!"

"What are *you* frustrated about?"

"I feel you're asking a question you know I can't really answer, and you're trying to back me into a corner, and right now I feel like I'm in your family!"

"Oh, great psychologist, now you're in the family! So what is this, transference?"

"Yes."

"So is that good?"

"Yes."

"Are you supposed to be my father right now?"

"I don't know *which* parent I am, Gary; both of them were so evasive and frustrating and unavailable to you."

"Well, it must be my goddamned father. The son-of-a-bitch would never answer a question. We'd ask 'why' about things and he'd just say 'because I told you so.' We never knew what was happening next. *God,* he pissed me off!"

I pause for a moment. "I really consider that to be a form of child abuse, too, Gary. Your father had an obligation to answer you, to be there for you, that's how you learn."

Gary stops and looks at me with his powerful, intense eyes and then slowly smiles.

I am smiling, too.

"What are you two smiling about?" Mitch demands.

Gary shrugs. "Just smiling."

"I'm smiling because I feel like a good piece of work just got done," I say. I shift my gaze from Mitch to Gary. "The transference is good, Gary, because it allows you to finish some of the negative feelings you had as a kid . . . you won't need the same level of intensity on such things as not having a question answered." I see Gary is still grinning. "It also means you can establish new relationships, that you are changing."

After a pause, Gary looks to Mitch on his left.

"So did you decide to stick in group with me?"

"I don't want to keep being attacked."

"You mean you're not going to do it, just because of *me?*"

"I'm not blaming anything on you. I just said I don't like you attacking me."

"Well, okay, man, listen, I'm sorry. I didn't mean to upset you like that. And whether you want it or not, I do apologize. Okay?"

"Okay. Thanks. I don't want you to feel bad either. I'll be there. I wouldn't change my mind without notice."

"Look," Ed says, "before we run out of time, I want to ask Al: How did you feel at our wedding?"

Burt, who has been a bit tense through this entire interaction between Gary and me, perks up instantly, and looks over at me.

"Oh yeah, how was that?

"It was wonderful. I'm really glad I could be there."

"It was good to have you there," Ed says. "It felt like I had at least *some* family there for me."

"Was Ellen on his back the whole time?" Gary asks, nudging Ed's foot.

"Gary, Ellen was so warm and pleasant, nothing like I'd seen her when she and Ed were in couples therapy together. We had a nice conversation. She looked radiant and happy."

"Of course she's happy, she got what she wanted!" Gary cracks. The grin returns.

Ed, meanwhile, is puzzled. "I didn't know you had much time to talk to Ellen."

"Oh sure," I say offhandedly. "We figured Dostoyevsky's purpose in writing *Crime and Punishment* and we were right in the middle of analyzing Fellini's *La Dolce Vita* when her father came over to dance with her."

Ed tosses a throw pillow at me.

"What did Ellen look like? Traditional wedding and all?" Mitch asks.

"Well, not formal. But she really looked nice: pink chiffon dress, white bouquet, and her hair up in a way I'd never seen it before. Very pretty."

"Did she look good enough for you, Ed?" Gary asks.

"Yes. She really looked good."

"Ed, you looked good, too. You never took your eyes off her as she walked toward you. I was touched during the ceremony."

"Thanks. It means a lot to me." Ed looks pleased.

"Did you two have your honeymoon already?" Burt asks.

"Yeah, we headed out to Virginia Beach for a sort of 'mini-honeymoon'. We'll have the real one when we get out to California. We had a real nice time, except"—Ed looks over at me and shakes his head—"except for this guy who keeps popping up *everywhere* he's not supposed to be!"

"What are you talking about?" Gary asks with a puzzled look. Ed's got everyone's full attention now.

"Well, Ellen and I just finish this candlelight dinner, and she goes into the bathroom, and I turn on the TV, and who is on the *Dr. Ruth Show*—in the middle of my honeymoon, mind you—but everyone's favorite therapist!" Ed is glowering at me in mock anger.

"What?"

"Yeah, he was taped for some showing of the *Dr. Ruth Show* on cable. So Ellen comes out of the bathroom in this negligee and climbs into bed, and of course I'm still sitting at the foot of the bed listening to this interview. So I turn to Ellen and say, 'Look, Al's on TV!' and she says, 'Come on, turn it off and come over here.' I keep watching. She's going on and on about how we've only got one night at the hotel, but when Dr. Ruth says the words 'penis size' she suddenly clams up and gets real interested." Ed is grinning from ear to ear. "Not a thing happened until the interview was over."

"And then . . . ?" Gary says, leaning forward.

"After two months of celibacy, we both remembered how—it was the best we ever had."

Mitch looks across the table at me. "I don't believe it. You would be on *Dr. Ruth?*"

"Yes. It was educational, and I have a much better opinion of her now than I had."

"But did it really happen on Ed's honeymoon?"

"It's a fact," Ed assures him.

"Well, we do have to end," I say. "Wouldn't want to keep JoAnn waiting for Burt."

At first nobody moves.

"I want you all to know," I say, "that this group has also been a great experience for me. There were some very exciting and moving moments with you."

Silence.

I look across the table at Ed.

"Ed, good luck in your new life. I'd be delighted to hear from you. I'll see the rest of you again. Now we're going to stop."

Ed stands up slowly and walks over to me and gives me a hug. This breaks the ice—Gary turns to Mitch and puts his arm around him and slaps his knee. Mitch stiffens.

"I think we'll get along in group."

"I wonder."

"Hey—they'll all be the 'new kids on the block.' We'll be the 'old-timers.' "

Burt is smiling and stretching, waiting to give Ed a hug.

I move away to watch them.

. . . grinning . . . hugging . . . kidding . . . good wishes.

I'm touched by their warmth toward each other. They've come such a long way in this short time. Good men.

INTERPRETATION

The tremendous progress Ed has made in therapy is difficult to measure in any quantitative way, and Ed therefore has doubts that the changes can be attributed to therapy. The evidence for his development, his ability to deal with change with less anxiety and fear of making a "wrong" decision, is irrefutable. Not only has Ed made a marriage commitment to Ellen, he's started moving up in his career, accepted a promotion, decided to move across the country, and signed a contract on a house, all without his characteristic anxiety or perfectionistic procrastination. Ed is only resisting change in the area of entering group therapy in California. This is a typical response for men who have connected with a therapist as well as Ed has with me. Our group is a symbolic "family" for Ed, so he is wary of establishing and losing yet another group (family) in California.

Burt has the least amount of regret over the end of group. He is the most comfortable with this process; it is very natural and easy for him. Like Ed, Burt has a new marriage and a new life ahead, so the ending of group is a natural transition point. Moreover, Burt is content with his life and is happy with the changes he's made and those he's observing in JoAnn. As Burt's relationship with JoAnn settled down over the last several weeks, Burt's career took off: He's had a number of new and exciting professional challenges that have kept him on Capitol Hill. His recent attendance in group has truly required an extra effort on his part. Both Burt and JoAnn are happy to be in couples therapy with me and are making good progress.

The confrontation between Mitch and Gary and their resolution at the end of the session are representative of their development and their bonding in group. A year ago, Gary would never have apologized for the way he phrased a comment, nor would he have been concerned over how such a comment affected someone else. Gary's desire is to maintain a connection to Mitch, and humor, ribbing, and jabbing are all Gary's usual way. Tonight he examines that usual way and realizes that it could be rejecting and hurtful: Gary honors Mitch's response. In fact, it is so important that he offers to apologize twice to accommodate Mitch, and finally *does* to satisfy them both. So Gary has demonstrated his willingness to change in order to safeguard special relationships, such as the one with Mitch.

Mitch is aware of having been the target of Gary's jabs for several weeks ("Are you going to start in on me again?") but has been holding his anger in, letting it build. This is old behavior for Mitch. Gary's forced confrontation gives Mitch a chance to go beyond his anxiety and express his anger. Mitch then realizes that confronting Gary openly weeks ago before the anger had a chance to grow and develop would have meant less anger inside him. Mitch almost lost his opportunity to continue in group because of anger, but he knows the release of anger, when he ran out of the room, was positive and therapeutic. The realization of his overreaction made it possible for him to return. Gary's apology is a compliment to Mitch, but Mitch dismisses it, since he has always had difficulty with praise and compliments. Mitch must let these affirmations in; they will enhance his ego and self-esteem.

The response to Mitch's changes is very similar to the reactions Ed reported in tonight's session. Lynda, his friends, and his coworkers have all commented on how much more open, confident, and expressive he is. In less than a year, Mitch has gone from doubt to certainty and is left with the normal pre-wedding jitters. He's also making some career changes that will give him more independence and real financial rewards.

My confrontation with Gary tonight is intense. Once again Gary is testing me to reassure himself that I won't abandon him. He wants to make sure he is not continuing in therapy with somebody like his father. This is the purpose of my assurance that I am not abandoning him as his father did. In this intense interchange I feel like I've actually been drawn into his family. I sense the "craziness" that Gary had to deal with anytime he needed or wanted anything. This explains his frustration and rage at his father for not caring about him and for rejecting him. Though Gary thinks I'm playing a psychological game, I am in fact being therapeutic to determine what is motivating the question. As Gary and I get into the struggle, Gary sees me solely in the role of his father, and it is impossible for him to be reasonable with me at that moment. He wants to dismiss me ("Go bother Mitch") in the same way he would like to have dismissed his father, who *would not have hung in* with him anymore. Unlike his father,

I stay with Gary. It does not bother me to stay with Gary through his anger. My refusal to shift attention from Gary as his anger grows is the pivotal point in the exchange. At this juncture, Gary starts hearing *me* and realizes that he *is* treating me like his father and not like Al Baraff. His smile is the result of tremendous relief over this resolution and the insight he gains from this exchange.

Ed initiates the hugging at the end of group, and the men follow through with a warmth and sincerity that is not typical of men and would have been *impossible* for them just a few months ago. The men feel comfortable expressing themselves more warmly than with the traditional male handshake.

Goodbyes are difficult for all men. Ordinarily men want to leave, to say goodbye, as quickly as possible and be done with it. In his previous relationship, Ed just vanished when the woman said she wanted to break it off. Ed never saw the woman again and never knew why she left. Burt stuck with a bad marriage far too long, avoiding the painful and inevitable goodbye. The catalytic event in Mitch's former marriage caused an immediate and complete break: a quick divorce and no goodbye. Gary's difficulty with goodbye was the most severe: He was convinced of being "addicted" to a woman; he believed he was *incapable* of saying goodbye. All the warm goodbyes observed tonight suggest that these men will enjoy much fuller, more meaningful relationships in their lives.

EPILOGUE: MEN AFTER THERAPY

In the two years since the group ended, the lives of these men evolved in many new directions. Some of the immediate benefits of group therapy are evident to the men as they work during the sessions, while others take a much longer period to emerge. In reviewing these men's lives two years later, we see some of the positive, long-term changes in attitude, communication, self-esteem, and confidence that can be traced directly to work initially done in the group.

MITCH

Mitch and Lynda were married at the end of the summer in a small, quiet, yet formal church ceremony. Mitch continued in the new men's group for three months and offered encouraging support for some of that group's timid members. Mitch and Gary began to work well together, although they continued to clash over some issues of insensitivity and fear of change as Gary pushed Mitch to open up further. Mitch stopped racing motorcycles soon after the birth of their son, Mark David, one year later, and took charge of the social planning obligations for the family. Mitch and Lynda worked together remodeling the upstairs of their home to create Mark's room. During this period Mitch grew away from his mother's dominating influence and found himself concentrating more on his own new family and his role as husband and father. Mitch has returned sporadically for individual therapy sessions as specific problems occur.

PAUL

Paul, whose divorce from Sarah became final less than a year after he left group, is still single and lives alone in northwest Washington. He dates occasionally. Although he dropped out of group, Paul made progress by continuing in individual and facing some of the conflicts of the divorce. Eventually, Paul succeeded in placing limits on Sarah's demands during the divorce settlement. Over time, Paul learned to reject his domineering mother's attempts to control him through guilt. At the same time, he began to recognize and resist Sarah's attempts to do the same thing. Soon afterward, Sarah got a job and struck out on her own, with the emotional support of her parents. It was a difficult time for her. Paul himself reestablished a strong, supportive tie to his children, especially Betty, who asked to spend the summer with him. Paul and Abe worked together on Abe's college choices. While Paul learned a great deal from therapy about not being controlled by guilt and even to give up some control himself, he still had an issue with anger. Following a life pattern of withdrawing when faced with someone's anger, much as he did in leaving group itself,

Paul eventually left individual therapy prematurely rather than work through issues dealing with anger.

ED

Ed and Ellen moved to California the week after group ended. I lost contact with Ed after he and Ellen left the Washington area. I regret that I'm not able to report on their life or progress, but contact with former patients is more the exception than the rule.

BURT

Burt and JoAnn got married two months after the end of group in her parents' church in Denver. They returned to Washington and made a home of the small rambler they had been redecorating the past year. JoAnn soon received her M.A., and was pregnant two months later. She chose to postpone a career prior to the birth of the baby, Jamie Lee, named in honor of Burt's father, James. JoAnn had a very difficult adjustment period after the birth, and Burt was able to come in as the engaged, involved father by taking time off from a very demanding work schedule to be available for feeding, bathing, and private time with the baby. In fact, Burt was the one who got up in the morning so he could be with Jamie. During this period, Burt also became more confident and assertive in his career, one benefit of which was a special one-year posting to Japan for the whole family.

SEAN

Sean completed medical school and has started a residency in pediatrics at Arizona State University in Tempe. The relationship with Sandi never got going again, and he eventually lost contact with her. Some time later he found out from a college friend that she was involved with somebody else. Eventually, Sean was able to get over the breakup. During a vacation break visiting his parents in Phoenix, he met Debbie, a junior at Arizona State who is the daughter of family friends. Sean's family did pull together, but Sean was forced to take out student loans to get through medical school. The father's extensive personal problems left Sean feeling angry at his father and guilty over feeling this anger. Eventually, this experience had a leveling effect on Sean. He matured rapidly during a fairly brief period of individual therapy.

GARY

Gary continued therapy in the new men's group and immediately took command. Even though the other men were older and more experienced in life, they came to look to Gary for leadership and guidance in group. He was the "pro." During this period his business grew and he finally decided to move his business outside the home. He also purchased a new condo near the State Department. His new office is just two blocks away. His relationship with Marta continued for a few months, but she eventually decided to return home. This separation was different for Gary: the old feelings of abandonment and addiction were less severe and much more manageable. He's now involved with a divorcée who has a six-year-old son. While Gary did get his "Rent-a-Kid," the son's problems became an issue for him. Fortunately, he was able to resolve this in some short-term individual therapy, since his involvement with the new group had ended.

IN CLOSING . . .

The progress and growth we've witnessed in these men during therapy and in their subsequent lives highlight the profound value of therapy as a learning process and emotional education.

A commonly held belief is that therapy is first and foremost an intellectual process focusing on childhood, with no practical connection to the real world or everyday life. Nothing could be further from the truth. In fact, regardless of the orientation or approach of the therapist, therapy is a powerful, lively learning experience. The learning is immediately applicable in day-to-day living once the patient is willing to try it. It is "fast-forward" learning. As such, it's intense, with many exciting moments and surprises—not all pain and melodrama. Moreover, what is learned is not some abstract concept like algebra or external discipline like German, but rather specific and internal: it is about you. The focus on childhood, adolescence, and dreams is to learn how they connect to present-day behavior. Cause and effect is the key to seeing that it all makes sense. Once this occurs, it is very liberating.

Here's how I see my role: I guide the patient through the process, in essence serving as the teacher or mentor. I feel fortunate to have had so many highly motivated students. We became partners in the journey. We've been on some great trips.

1. Duncan Prince
2. Rand B.
3. Raymond Wright van Every
4. Russ — L?
5. Pitkin (?)
6.

L. [scribble]
2.

Couples:

how not to be overcome by
the negative aspects of
yourself (spouse)

appreciate — not change
the diff.

Too unequal —
unbalanced —